A

The Secret Lives of Fortunate Wives

Also by Sarah Strohmeyer

Bubbles Unbound

Bubbles in Trouble

Bubbles Ablaze

Bubbles A Broad

Bubbles Betrothed

The Secret Lives of Fortunate Wives

a novel

Sarah Strohmeyer

DUTTON

DUTTON
Published by New American Library, a division of
Penguin Group (USA) Inc., 375 Hudson Street, New York, New York 10014, USA
Penguin Group (Canada), 90 Eglinton Avenue East, Suite 700, Toronto, Ontario, Canada M4P 2Y3 (a division of Pearson Penguin Canada Inc.)
Penguin Books Ltd., 80 Strand, London WC2R 0RL, England
Penguin Ireland, 25 St. Stephen's Green, Dublin 2,
Ireland (a division of Penguin Books Ltd.)
Penguin Group (Australia), 250 Camberwell Road, Camberwell, Victoria 3124,
Australia (a division of Pearson Australia Group Pty. Ltd.)
Penguin Books India Pvt. Ltd., 11 Community Centre, Panchsheel Park,
New Delhi - 110 017, India
Penguin Group (NZ), cnr Airborne and Rosedale Roads, Albany,
Auckland 1310, New Zealand (a division of Pearson New Zealand Ltd.)
Penguin Books (South Africa) (Pty.) Ltd., 24 Sturdee Avenue,
Rosebank, Johannesburg 2196, South Africa

Penguin Books Ltd., Registered Offices: 80 Strand, London WC2R 0RL, England

First Printing, September 2005
10 9 8 7 6 5 4 3 2 1

LIBRARY OF CONGRESS CATALOGING-IN-PUBLICATION DATA HAS BEEN APPLIED FOR.

Printed in the United States of America
Set in Granjon

For Jen, Patty and Julie—my sisters by heart and my exceptions to the rules.

ACKNOWLEDGMENTS

Though there is no such place as Hunting Hills, Ohio, per se, there are many isolated, upscale suburbs like it from Connecticut to California. Over two years, women from these communities, some of whom I'd met in the course of writing and promoting my Bubbles books, told me about the minor scandals that had rocked their enclaves. This book was inspired by their tales, which were both humorous and startling. Understandably, they've asked that their names be left out of the acknowledgments. But they know who they are and I thank them heartily.

I must also thank retired FBI special agent Gary Hall, who patiently walked me through a white-collar-crime investigation, an extremely complicated and laborious process. In addition, Ted Wendling at the Cleveland *Plain Dealer* was a big help as was John Caniglia and Steve Luttner. My brother-in-law Art Merriman was kind enough to provide color about how a stock brokerage works, though if I've made any mistakes in my depiction, it is definitely my fault.

Finally, I am grateful beyond belief for my agent Heather Schroder at ICM and Dutton publisher Brian Tart who, once again, championed my cause and supported this book through its many starts and stops. With clear, calm guidance Brian kept me on the right path and provided superb editorial insight. I only hope my writing has done his editing justice.

The Top Ten Rules for Hunting Hills Wives

1. Be busy even if you aren't. Act busy. Look busy. Above all, *complain* about being busy. Don't even think of answering your home phone during the day. Why should you? Anyone important enough to talk to will have your cell, of course.

2. Eat voraciously on social occasions. Leave everyone wondering how you keep your teenage figure when little do they know that you'll be living on green tea, celery and alkaline water for days afterward.

3. Always Proclaim Everything Terrific! Remember that any disappointment can be turned into a fabulous windfall with the perfect spin. Did a hurricane rage during your Fiji vacation? How wonderful that you and your husband had an opportunity to rekindle your romance between the sheets. And don't forget that the 1100 score your son received in the SATs is further proof that he's more physical than intellectual, a much more desirable state indeed.

4. Redecorate with regularity, not necessity. If your Christmas card shows your loved ones gathered on the same Ethan Allen upholstery

three years in a row, then shame on you! A true Hunting Hills wife knows that in the end outward appearance really is all that matters, whether it's erasing the tiny lines on her upper lip or switching the living room couches from chintz to leather.

5. Remember that the more you buy, the more your husband values you. However, a smart wife knows better than to walk through the door at dinnertime laden with packages. That's just courting trouble.

6. Please make it a habit to wash a few dishes before your housekeeper arrives to avoid the impression that you are slovenly. A simple coffee cup and spoon rinsed and set aside prominently can do wonders in overshadowing the mounds of laundry or the string of emptied wine glasses and ground-in crackers left over from a party the night before.

7. Speak of your children in the best possible light, even if they are lazy, slutty or destined for federal incarceration. A savvy Hunting Hills mother is well aware that a teen in trouble today is the CEO of tomorrow.

8. Serious books are to be banned in book group. Book group is the one chance a Hunting Hills wife has to break the rules by drinking, smoking and venting about life's hardships. It certainly is not the appropriate time for a postmodern deconstruction of *Gravity's Rainbow*. WARNING: Though a wife may ridicule her husband's adorable foibles—such as not being able to survive without her—she must not, repeat must not, ever reveal that he has been cruel, neglectful, verbally abusive or something other than the absolute ideal mate.

9. Do try and keep your options open in the family income department. If your husband appears headed for a demotion, if he is an alcoholic, drug addict or, worse, lacking in capitalistic enthusiasm, it is acceptable to search for other breadwinners. In fact, it's expected.

10. Remember: Rules are meant to be broken.

The Secret Lives of Fortunate Wives

Chapter One

As the perfect Hunting Hills wife, Marti Denton was too busy at first to notice that her husband, Denton, was slowly, gradually slipping from her life.

She'd been consumed with far more pressing issues at the time. Like making sure that Denton's Brooks Brothers ties were updated and color coordinated with his Brooks Brothers shirts, that his clients were sent silver monogrammed golf ball sets on their birthdays, that she always, always had a supply of his beloved Skittles in the house.

She didn't stop to ask herself why her husband no longer came home for dinner or begged for sex, like the good old days. No bells went off when their communications were reduced to the "to-do" lists he'd started leaving on yellow Post-its by the Krups.

Marti rationalized that Denton's growing inattention was merely a middle-aged man's natural response to the tragic fact that she was now over forty. It was tacitly understood in Hunting Hills that husbands were within their rights to drop an aging spouse who had let herself go, who had become fat and lumpy and—perish the thought!—tarnished by cellulite. Fat and lumpy wives were bad for business and what was bad for business was bad for Hunting Hills.

Except Marti wasn't fat or lumpy. She was quite the opposite.

Like most Hunting Hills wives, she had performed every miracle possible to attain the illusion of being twenty-two. This included a daily application of funky smelling, outrageously expensive anti-wrinkle cream, the secret ingredient of which happened to be cloned baby foreskin. The foreskin element bothered Marti more than the price ($150 per jar) and she would never have touched the stuff except that it really, really worked. She and her friends agreed: sometimes you just have to make sacrifices.

Thanks to the cloned baby foreskin cream and a strict no-alcohol, no-red-meat, no-carb diet, not to mention hours of Pilates and several trips to the plastic surgeon, Marti Denton looked not much older than her teenage daughters, Ava and Lois, even though she was well into her forty-third year. The Loro Piana cashmere sweaters she preferred exposed her iron-flat midriff and her favorite Seven jeans were so skinny that their size was always available on the rack at Saks. Her straight blond hair, highlighted to cover errant strands of new gray, hung in graceful sheets, which she coquettishly tucked behind her ear.

Denton should have doted on her—forget that, *worshiped* her. Instead, Marti began to realize, he was taking her for granted. Yet it was more than the fact that he never took her out for dates or sent her roses or even thanked her for picking up his shirts at the dry cleaner. In this regard he was no different from 99.9 percent of the husbands in America. No, what he was doing was much more weird.

He was spending all his weekends at the office or on the links, often not coming home until Marti was asleep. And there were fewer clothes in his closet. A missing suit here. A pair of pants there. Several ties. His tennis racket and mint-flavored dental floss gone. An old watchband he'd been meaning to have repaired. It was bizarre, Marti thought, the way he was disappearing from her life, right under her surgically minimized nose.

She ran this by Lisa, her best friend, who listened intently and then delivered her diagnosis.

ADD—attention deficit disorder. It was all the rage among the Hunting Hills wives and Marti, who considered ADD a bunch of hooey, was, in Lisa's opinion, dangerously in denial of her own condition.

"You need to focus," Lisa stressed. "He's there. You just don't see him. That's what speed is for. So you don't miss these things."

"What things?"

"Husbands. See? You're already off track."

Marti detested speed, even if it was a fantastic appetite suppressant, so she passed on the pills. She did, however, try to concentrate more, staying awake at night waiting for Denton to come home until she inevitably zonked out on the couch, only to rise in the morning and find yet another Post-it by the Krups.

EARLY DAYTON MTG. C. U. 2 NITE. XXOOO D.
P.S. SWITCH COFFEE. FR. RST. SKS.

That was the last she'd heard of him, this morning. But this afternoon was Lois's Holly School field hockey game, Marti's best chance of confronting her husband as he made it a practice never to miss one of his daughter's athletic events.

Denton was ga-ga for Lois, called her "Muffincakes" and spoiled her with a brand new Toyota Highlander and her very own Visa, Exxon and Abercrombie & Fitch credit cards. Thought nothing of paying the bills blissfully each month, as though every seventeen-year-old girl racked up thousands of dollars in woven minis and hounds-tooth thongs.

At the beginning of the game Marti felt hopeful, buoyed by the brisk, refreshing weather and the possibility of meeting Denton in the flesh. The October sky was a bright cloudless blue and giant oaks blessed the girls' teams with showers of raining golden leaves. The whole scene—the clear sky, the autumn foliage, the flying green-plaid skirts—was enough to make a parent feel good about annually forking out twenty grand for Holly's exclusive single-sex education.

When the game broke for halftime and Denton still hadn't appeared, Marti's optimism slipped several notches, finally reaching such a low point that she decided to call him. It was a risky move that entailed violating several of the innumerable Hunting Hills wives' rules, including that husbands must never, ever be bothered at work unless in that most unlikely of emergencies—a wife needed him to come home for lunch. (And by that, she didn't mean sharing a light salad.)

Marti flipped open her cell phone and scrolled through her speed dials.

1. Ava (her oldest daughter, a freshman at Michigan—State, not the university—who was coming out this Christmas).
2. Lois (her other daughter who was on the field a few feet away).
3. Lisa.
4. Hoffet (for blowouts).
5. Damon (in New York City, for color, because you just couldn't get the right blond in Cleveland).
6. Fred (cosmetic dermatologist, for whatever).
8. Chris (for brows, absolutely).

And

9. Barry.

Ahh, Barry. It was simply impossible to describe what Barry did. The wonders a round gay man with a brick office over Starbucks could perform. Barry was an *experience*. Barry was the reason she felt ready for what he liked to call "the overdue joy" that surely was coming her way if she just told herself she was worth it.

Fat chance of that. She couldn't even keep a husband, much less pursue "overdue joy." She sighed and scrolled past Karen, the Garfield Club reservation desk and Boots until she pressed 12. Denton.

"Denton here."

She was so stunned to hear his real live voice that she was momentarily struck dumb. "Denton? Is that you?" Maybe it was a machine. You never knew with technology these days.

"Yeah. Who's this?"

"Marti." And then, to make sure, she added, "Your wife."

"Hey, Marti. What's up? Something wrong? You got car trouble?"

"No, I . . ." Marti searched for an answer.

Hunting Hills Wife #1 rule was to be busy even if you weren't. Act busy, look busy and, above all, *complain* about being busy. Always let the answering machine pick up messages, never return messages until a sacred twenty-four hours have passed, get off the phone with a sudden exclamation of, "Oh, my god! I've got to go." And never, ever tell your husband that you were freezing your ass on the school bleachers fretting about him.

"No, it's that I haven't been home all day. It's insane how stretched I've been. I thought maybe you called and I missed you."

"That's sweet. Nope."

"So where are you?"

"I'm here."

"Where?"

"Holly. For Lois's game." He made it sound like she was an idiot for not knowing.

"I'm here too," she said, scanning the spectators for a glimpse of him.

"I got here late. How's she been playing?"

"Absolutely terrific!" Though, in reality, Lois was cracking her gum and listlessly whacking the ball when it came her way, showing absolutely no gumption whatsoever. "Where are you exactly? Wait for me and I'll . . ."

"Woops. Got another call." And he was off.

Marti checked the screen on her phone. CALL WAS LOST!

Curses. She hated it when Denton scored the first hang-up. He was always the hangerupper—thereby constantly, constantly making her the hangupee. She tried him back but the phone was busy. Was that whacked or what? How could Denton's cell phone with call waiting be busy?

But at least he was here. Somewhere.

Feeling hopeful again, Marti shut her phone and surveyed the field of cheering mothers and fathers in their field coats and Barbours, hollering "Bank it!" and "Drive it in!" She felt sorry for them. The specters of college admissions directors scrutinizing their daughter's applications and sports achievements were constantly, constantly foremost in their thoughts. There was no relief.

Her gaze finally rested on a woman in the butt-ugliest pair of rip-off Ugg boots, standing on the sidelines, waving to her madly. Karen Goss, Hunting Hills resident Vegetarian Fashionista, the only person Marti knew who actually had her long black hair professionally streaked with gray, beckoned Marti to join her. Aside from the plastic Ugg rip-offs, she was to the nines in a Michael Kors satin jacket. Karen was the kind of wife who had oodles of money and zero sense.

Last spring, she had special ordered a boxy Mercedes G Class 500 with cloth seats because leather was standard on the $78,000 SUV, even though the dealer pointed out she could have gotten cloth for no extra charge on the M class. Karen argued that she was issuing a protest statement to the higher-ups at Mercedes—make cloth an option on *all* cars.

"What are you doing here?" Marti asked, since Karen did not have a daughter on the Holly team.

"Keeping my eye on Birch." Karen nodded toward her wild-haired son who was standing with a group of boys from Tate, the neighboring all-male prep school down the road. "He's supposed to be grounded. He went to a party at Susan Crossman's house Saturday night and ended up pulling in around two, half of the Crossmans' azaleas on his front bumper."

Indeed, when it came to teenage drunken driving in Hunting Hills, potential destruction to expensive landscaping was as much of a concern as the danger to life and limb. Every weekend night, teenagers with several beers in them could be found weaving around the neighborhood in deadly huge SUVs, jumping curbs and destroying bushes, mailboxes, reflectors, small trees—anything foolishly stationed too close to the road.

At least Hunting Hills parents did not have to worry about their children facing DUI charges because they had Roy Phelps on retainer. Roy Phelps was a former county attorney who was now in private practice. All it took was one phone call from Roy Phelps to the right people and any legal snafu would disappear. Including once, legend had it, murder.

"Have you seen Denton?" Marti asked. "He's around here somewhere."

"Not missing again, is he?"

"I don't know. I'm never quite sure."

Birch flipped his mother the bird. Karen flipped him back. "Has it ever occurred to you that maybe Denton's not trying to run away from you? That, maybe, he's running away from Hunting Hills?"

This clearly was crazy vegetarian nonsense since there was no better place on Earth than Hunting Hills. It was like the Garden of Eden for privileged people, only better as the Garden of Eden hadn't come with an eighteen-hole championship golf course or private security—what Marti considered to be divine oversights.

It was hard to find anything negative to say about Hunting Hills. The homes were solid and stately, set well back from the road. The neighbors, some of whom were notorious businessmen or famous athletic team owners, were respectful and educated. There was zero crime, thanks to a small, polite police force and a big white picket fence that separated Hunting Hills from the riffraff. Even the dogs, and there were many, knew better than to soil its meticulous curbs or bark to excess.

If there was one teeny, tiny drawback to Hunting Hills it was this: Hunting Hills was a suburb of Cleveland, a perfectly fine city if you didn't mind gray, industrial places perpetually on the verge of imaginary rebounds. Despite the Rock and Roll Hall of Fame, the Cleveland Clinic and Jacobs Field, the only attractions that ever really caught fire in Cleveland were the Cuyahoga River and Mayor Ralph Perk's hair. It was sad.

One other flaw—there was a defect about Hunting Hills that lent itself to scandal. Inbreeding. Not inbreeding as in a two-tooth, my granddaddy's my daddy, hillbilly way. Rather, inbreeding of a more country club nature. White-gloved, blue-blood inbreeding.

Marti and Denton, for example, had shared the sandbox as children in Christ Church's Episcopal nursery school. But so had Karen and her husband, Bob Goss, and John Harding and his first wife, Boots, and Ty Renfrew and his first wife, Sandra (a piece of work, that one). Their parents had played together, too, and not just on the tennis courts, as they were fond of reminiscing while sipping gimlets on their Gem Island retirement estates.

Some of Hunting Hills' progeny had found its incestuous world terrifying and fled west to California or Seattle or to the mountains of Montana in search of new ideas and interesting topography. But for Marti, Denton, Karen, Bob, Ty, Boots and John—having dispersed to unfriendly New England colleges where snooty kids from New Jersey frequently snickered at their flat Midwestern accents—the inbred atmosphere of Hunting Hills offered familiar security and easy high-end real estate. And so, as soon as they married and bore their first children, they migrated back.

There they constructed humongous homes with twelve-foot ceilings, to which the wives dedicated themselves to beautifying while the men pursued careers in the thrill-a-minute world of corporate finance. Ty went into commercial real estate. John resurrected his father's venture capital company and Denton, the former goofy frat boy, turned out to be a surprisingly successful stockbroker.

It all was going according to plan and everyone was thin and tan and exceedingly happy. The children were off to perfectly adequate colleges, though rarely Ivy League; the men were at the peak of their earning curves and the wives planted bulbs from Smith & Hawken. So the idea that Denton would be running away from Hunting Hills, and not her, was, to Marti, just plain silly.

"It's not Hunting Hills he's tired of," Marti said, "it's me. The only thing I can think is that he's having an affair."

"Really? Who with?" Karen squinted at the other wives, looking for candidates. Hunting Hills husbands and wives slept around on each other and with each other, naturally, but never with outsiders. Though they may not have been loyal to their marriage vows, with the rare exception they were fiercely loyal to Hunting Hills.

"Maybe Boots," Karen suggested, eyeing their friend, who was screaming madly on the sidelines. "She hasn't had a man in ages."

Karen and Marti sized up Boots, whose perky blond head bobbed up and down as she clutched the leashes of her Pembroke Welsh corgis, cheering for her star daughter Ingrid to, "TAKE IT DOWN THE FIELD!"

Marti didn't know how to break it to Karen that Boots engaged in more anonymous sex than Pamela Anderson on a cocaine bender, only discreetly so as not to embarrass Ingrid. She was particularly fond of the service industry: accountants, a chauffeur, plumbers without cracks. This was the beauty of being independently, fabulously wealthy. There was a whole treasure trove of hired men to pick from.

At their last book group meeting—*Love in the Time of Cholera,* though no one had finished it because it had been sooo boring—Boots announced that she had found new love—Jesus. Not *the* Jesus. He pronounced it "Hey Zeus." A half Puerto Rican, half Greek interior designer and the most sought after man in Hunting Hills, hands down.

Boots had shared these juicy tidbits with their book group, to which Karen, unfortunately, had yet to be admitted. The book group was very dear and no one wanted it to become unwieldy. That was the official line.

The unofficial line only the book group knew. It had to do with a secret that must never, ever be aired. This, the Hunting Hills wives understood, was their most sacred duty. Along with writing timely thank-you notes.

Boots, catching the women's stares, brought the corgis over to join them.

"Hi, guys!" Boots was pink cheeked and bright eyed. All her life she'd been pink cheeked and bright eyed. Even Bedo and Alys, her professionally brushed Pembroke Welsh corgis, were pink cheeked and bright eyed. "What are you doing here, Karen?"

"Monitoring Birch," Karen said. "He's supposed to be grounded for driving home loaded the other night."

"Oh, them. Boys. They're such knuckleheads." Boots punched Marti lightly on the shoulder. "Hey, did you see Lois, Marti? She actually got a hit."

Marti felt bad. She was always missing Lois's hits and, considering Lois's hit average, that said loads about her success as a mother. She was sure Denton would criticize her for it later. Now that he was doing his disappearing act, his rare moments of communication centered on critiquing her parenting skills. His favorite jabs were that Marti nagged Lois too much and didn't crack down on her enough, the classic Catch-22 of Motherhood.

Lately, Denton had taken to leaving lists on Post-its affixed to the mirror in the master bath (and, therefore out of Lois's view), instructing Marti on the finer points of raising a teenage daughter.

GET OFF L'S CASE.
IS L TAKING AP LATIN?
YOU'VE GOT TO DO SOMETHING ABOUT THAT F'ING BOYFRIEND.
WHY IS L'S FACE BREAKING OUT?

It had been the same with their oldest daughter. When Ava had announced in the all-important fall of her senior year that she was flunking chemistry, Denton's first reaction had been to turn on Marti. "Mothering. Your one job and you fucked it up!" Then he had stormed out of the room, leaving a shaken Marti to work out with Ava how they were going to get that F to a B, which, thanks to stressful nightly math homework sessions and a one-hundred-dollar-an-hour tutor, they finally did.

"It's Ingrid who looks great out there," Marti said politely. "Really on top of her game."

"That's because of John." Boots walked with her back to the field, the dogs leading the way. Karen followed, shooting reproving glances back at her son. "She's out to impress him because he's bringing around his new wife today." Boots tugged on the leashes. "Claire."

Marti's feet wouldn't move. She was frozen. Stuck in place. Stuck in time. Denton and all worries about him vaporized and in their place was only John Harding.

Did she say wife?

"John is married?" Marti's voice cracked.

"Haven't you heard?" Boots peered at her curiously, the corgis snuffling through the leaves around them. "He eloped with some woman he met in Prague. A journalist. Knew her all of a month, if that. I thought everyone knew."

"Guess not." Marti's mouth was so dry she could barely form the words. She could barely think, the images of their last night together before John went to Europe playing over and over in her mind.

He couldn't be married. He loves me!

"Personally, I liked that public relations twinkie he was dating," Karen said, sounding silly and shallow to Marti's freshly pained ears. "She made great kiwi smoothies. Not too sweet."

"Yes, well, you'll have to find another twinkie, Karen. Miss Smoothie is officially history." Boots scrutinized Ingrid through a pair of mini Eddie Bauer binoculars. "John claims this is the one. His soul mate. *L'aime a la folie*. Never felt this way before, even with me. Blah, blah, blah. I don't care. Why should I? I have my babies to love."

She bent down and kissed Bedo on the snout. It was gross.

The news of John's marriage had a strange effect on Marti. Over the many, many years they'd been friends, she'd written off John Harding as nothing more than a stable and intelligent acquaintance who, frankly, was a tad too bookish for her tastes. Fairly good-looking, but not nearly as ambitious and ruthless as Denton. Now, though, in light of this new twist of events, the image of John with another woman stirred a gnawing, almost desperate, craving deep within her.

It was as though a veil had been lifted and she realized that John Harding was much more than fairly good-looking. He was an Adonis. A hunk. With his wavy dirty-blond hair, his warm hazel eyes and the modest, half-smile thing he had going, why, he was practically Colin Firth! Except that John was also a financial whiz, but with the morality of Gandhi. And so romantic and sexy too.

Why hadn't she seen it before?

"WHACK IT IN!" Boots shouted.

Ingrid raced by, panting. Karen clapped loudly and Marti, belatedly remembering her manners, joined in. At the opposite end of the field, Lois twirled her stick and regarded her mother bitterly. For a minute Marti felt like dirt.

"I suspect she married him for his money," said Boots, getting right back on track. "Why else?"

"Why else?" echoed Karen.

"That's why John's been avoiding me. He knows I'll start asking questions about prenups and the will and how much money she's sucking from him. Can you blame me?"

Boots didn't wait for them to answer. "Of course not. I've got my daughter's financial future to think of. I can't believe how irresponsible he's being, hooking up with a woman he hardly knows, putting Ingrid's financial future at risk."

It was an odd statement considering that John, while once Boots's husband, was not the father of her daughter. But that was what made John so amazing, Marti thought, sighing. He'd taken Ingrid into his arms as a baby and treated her as his daughter from the day her real father left the country swearing never to return. Eventually everyone came to think of him as Ingrid's dad, even Boots, who expected him to do the standard daddy things, like escort her daughter when she came out at the Assembly Ball and set up a million-dollar trust fund should she freak out in college and marry a boy with dreadlocks.

"Probably it won't last," Karen said. "Probably it's a phase. A fling taken too far."

"I've thought of that. I've thought maybe this new wife might be a trophy to bring back from Prague, like that Z3 he bought last year in Stuttgart or the shrunken head he was given in New Guinea."

Marti could tell Boots was pleased by this, how she'd been no shrunken head.

"Besides, John is such a romantic, you know it can't last. The thing with John is that he hasn't yet learned there is no such thing as the perfect woman."

Marti felt dizzy. That was *exactly* the phrase he had used to describe her on that fateful night at Lisa Renfrew's pool party last summer.

"All my life I've been searching for the perfect woman," he'd confessed to her in the shadows of the pool cabana, *"and, looking at you tonight, Marti, how beautiful and sweet and goddamn sexy you are, I realize she's been here in front of me all along."*

And what had she done? Had she turned her face up to him and let him kiss her? Had she thrown herself at him and told him she was his? No! She'd sipped her lemon water and stared at Denton and Lisa in the pool, confused as to why Lisa kept flashing Denton her new fake boobs.

Oh, she'd been so stupid. She'd squandered the one man of any value in Hunting Hills. She'd blown her only chance at "overdue joy."

Then it struck her. She needed to see him and set the record straight before it was too late. She'd get John alone and confess that she hadn't realized before how great he was and that she was madly, passionately in love with him. And once he saw how it was with her, how much she loved him, she was confident that he would take her in his arms and swear off this Claire forever. Absolutely.

She was Marti Denton, after all, the most in shape, in vogue and in demand wife in Hunting Hills.

Feeling much more relieved, Marti applauded heartily as Lois guarded the goal. She didn't even mind that the game was almost over and that Denton, still, was nowhere to be seen.

Chapter Two

Once upon a time a fortune-teller had read Claire Stark's thirteen-year-old palm at the Webster County Fair and predicted that the red-haired, freckled girl would meet a magical man in a foreign country, marry after a whirlwind courtship and settle down to raise three children. Claire, cynical even then, figured that was what the fortune-teller told all the adolescent girls, since falling in love, getting married and buying a nice house in the burbs was the best you could hope for growing up in the heart of Appalachia.

All the girls except Claire.

Claire's most vivid childhood dream had been to become a gorgeous, daring newspaper reporter, a mishmash of odd role models: Mary Tyler Moore. Brenda Starr. Nelly Bly and Polly Purebred. She saw herself in a belted mackintosh over which would spill her long red hair as she reported undercover, exposing abuses in insane asylums or perhaps nobly going to jail to protect her sources. Danger would be at her heels.

Husband. Family. A house to clean. Somehow, these paled in comparison to tracking down international assassins while interviewing snitches and smoking Gauloises with a member of the Parisian underground.

So how was it that one morning she awakened not as Brenda Starr or even Polly Purebred, but as Mrs. John Houghton Harding III of Hunting Hills, Ohio? How could the hillbilly fortune-teller have been so intuitive? She opened her hands and stared at the palms, amazed that simple wrinkles could be such accurate prognosticators of destiny.

Even more amazing, however, was Claire's discovery that she actually enjoyed being a wife. It made her happy to think of building a home with John, of planting a vegetable garden and hoping, praying for the miracle of children. Though, Hunting Hills . . . That was another story.

When John had pitched his home to her as a "quiet rural Ohio community," she'd pictured rolling cornfields, farmhouses with wraparound porches and wash on the line. Like wash lines would be legal in a place like this. Geesh.

She stared out the window, fascinated, as John steered his—their?—Z3 through the posh neighborhood of sprawling mansions and gates, of ponds and willow trees. Swimming pools. Driveways that meandered forever.

He hadn't let on that she'd be moving to a community where the median income surpassed Rhode Island's state budget, where a four-bedroom house was considered a "starter home" and where anything below 400 in the Mercedes line teetered on slumming it.

She felt like Elly May Clampett in Beverly Hills only there was no Pa or Granny or Jethro. Just her, Claire "Elly May" Stark, a genius with roadkill and a can of Campbell's Cream of Mushroom soup. (This was true—her grandmother's recipe for Possum Casserole was legendary. The trick was to fetch your possum at dawn, before the sun beat on it.)

But it wasn't just her impoverished childhood, during which she'd been raised by a narrow-minded, uneducated father and alcoholic mother, that made Claire slightly ill at ease in this world of perfection and privilege. It was her own style. Or, rather, lack of it.

Thanks to her strict Christian upbringing and, later, her Bohemian life overseas, Claire was a fervent believer in substance over materialism. She was just fine wearing an old pair of Lee jeans and comfortable no-name shirts. She couldn't tell a Manolo Blahnik from an Emilio Pucci and, moreover, she didn't care. Fashion wasn't her thing. Ditto for her friends who didn't give a hoot that her hair was often cut unevenly by a charismatic Russian barber at the bottom of her street, but, rather, admired her for her easygoing attitude and determination to make the best out of bad situations.

At least, that was the way life used to be—until she moved to Hunting Hills.

What she had to do was take a deep breath. *In. Out. In. Out.* What she had to do was remember why she was here.

She looked over to John, relaxed against his leather seat as he shifted into third. His sexy, down-turned eyes smiled at her, the crow's-feet creasing in a way she found irresistible, reminding her, again, why indeed she was there.

John Harding was the kind of man most women have given up for extinction. He bore no resemblance to Claire's previous boyfriends, the swaggering and self-centered go-getters. Or the smug intellectuals with excellent jazz collections and numerous post-college degrees and textbook sexual prowess which they used to compensate for their deep and abiding fear of anything resembling commitment.

By the time John came into her life, Claire was convinced that her old-fashioned notion of a quiet, meaningful love did not comport with the twenty-first-century habits of instant gratification and disposable inconveniences. She never expected to find romance with a venture capitalist, a businessman from Cleveland no less, whose background was diametrically opposite to hers.

She never expected to find a man who understood her so well.

"Daydreaming?" he asked.

"Jet-lagged." Claire stifled a yawn. She'd give anything for a nap.

"Glad you married me?"

"Not if you keep asking me stupid questions like that," she joked.

He ran his hand over her leg, which was a bit larger than most of the legs over which he had run his hand in recent years. Claire was not a small woman. She was a hair under six feet with the kind of Scottish bone structure that was suited to hauling firewood or digging coal. Back in Mudville, West Virginia, there were dozens of people who looked like her—reddish auburn hair, green eyes, wide pale forehead and thin lips. All known for their fiercely independent dispositions. Like her.

John told her often that she was the most beautiful woman he'd ever met and though beauty was in the eye of the beholder, Claire couldn't figure out where he was getting his information.

"OK. What's wrong?" he said, after several minutes passed and she had said nothing. (That in itself was alarming.) "You're too quiet. Makes me worried that you're up to something."

She took a deep breath. "Everyone's going to say we got married too fast."

"Fuck 'em." He shifted into fifth. "They don't know anything about us. It's none of their business, anyway."

"But we got married after knowing each other all of twenty-eight days."

"A full lunar cycle," he exclaimed, as though this was somehow assuring. "Don't tell me you're having second thoughts?"

Was she having second thoughts? "Not about you. I guess, maybe"—she caught sight of imposing stone gates marking entrance to the Holly School—"about me."

"You? You can handle anything, Claire. Christ. You worked in a Bosnian refugee camp. You nearly got beaten to a pulp covering a labor strike. I wouldn't expect you to be quaking in front of a bunch of insipid housewives."

"Don't be so sure. To me, socialites are scarier than dockworkers."

John would know what she was talking about, Claire thought, if he were a woman. (Which, thankfully, he wasn't.)

He pulled the Z3 to the side of the Holly School driveway and killed the engine. Turning to her, he said, "Skip it. Let's go somewhere else. You don't have to suffer through this."

"Suffer what? A school field hockey game? I wouldn't exactly call that suffering."

"It's not the game. It's meeting all these people all at once. It's too much. Besides, I'm not thinking of you. I'm thinking of me." His finger traced the edge of her jaw as he leaned over and kissed her, his lips softly caressing hers. "I'm not ready to share you quite yet. If Boots hadn't summoned me home to deal with Ingrid, we'd still be back in Santorini, you know."

Kissing him, Claire could almost smell the Greek island's clean salt air. "I feel like I left part of me there."

"They say it takes three days for the soul to catch up to an overseas flight."

Three days before, they'd been in their own little world, in a private villa hidden amidst a grove of rustling olive and cypress trees. If she closed her eyes, she could still see the delicate blossoms of the white and scarlet bougainvillea entwined around their deck overlooking the bright blue Aegean Sea. Feel the crisp linen sheets against her bare skin as she lay next to her ardent husband, the grenadine-pink Mediterranean sun sinking out their open French doors. It had been a spectacular honeymoon.

John tucked a strand of hair behind her ear. "Do you remember that night I got you tanked on ouzo and talked you into swimming under the full moon?"

"Oh, god. You'll never let me forget that, will you?" It made her blush to remember how, heady with love and Greek brandy, they'd boldly stripped off their clothes and made love in the surf. It was so unlike her—Claire Stark, daughter of hellfire-and-brimstone Caleb Stark, so modest that she still found it difficult to undress in front of her husband. Never in a million years would she have predicted that some day she'd skinny dip on a public beach.

But it wasn't her fault—it was John's. He had the ability to coax out sultry, sexy sides of her that she never knew existed. And he didn't show any signs of halting his campaign to tear down each last inhibition the Mudville Southern Baptist Church had so diligently instilled.

"We'll just have to make our own Santorini here," John said, squinting through the windshield as if the Mediterranean were a few feet away. "Though, somehow, I don't think it'll be the same, getting drunk on Budweiser and making love under the lawn sprinklers."

She had to laugh, even though his frequent references to their honeymoon occasionally did more to raise doubts than allay them. Sometimes she wondered if John Harding was the kind of guy who was easily infatuated, which, Claire decided in darker moments, would explain his hasty proposal and their quick marriage.

If that were so, then what would happen when the infatuation wore off?

"You know, John, it's much easier to be madly in love when you're vacationing in sunny Greece. Now we're back to reality. You'll have to go to work. I'll have to go to work. There'll be bills and stupid fights like who left the milk out and you'll start noticing quirks of mine that'll be annoying. I'm not sure I can live up to the perfection of Santorini."

"You were perfect in Santorini?"

"You know what I mean."

"I do." He closed his eyes, summoning a few choice lines from his vast knowledge of Shakespeare.

Let me not to the marriage of true minds
Admit impediment. Love is not love
Which alters when it alteration finds,
Or bends with the remover to remove.

Claire finished the sonnet for him.

Love alters not with his brief hours and weeks,
But bears it out even to the edge of doom.
If this be error and upon me prov'd,
I never writ, nor no man ever lov'd.

John smiled. "Okay, Miss Perfect-in-Santorini. But can you name the sonnet?"

"116. Hah."

"You sure it's not 130?"

And in some perfumes is there more delight
Than in the breath that from my mistress reeks?

"Thanks a lot."

"It's still one of my favorites, next to 'Oh, Celia, Celia, Celia shits!' He stroked his chin. "Funny that I should bring up Jonathan Swift, now that I'm about to turn you over to the Lilliputians."

"Don't forget that your daughter's among them too."

"I haven't forgotten. Why do you think we're back in Hunting Hills? I want to save her, but I have no idea how."

Ingrid was keeping John awake at night. She was bombing all her classes at Holly and didn't seem interested in any subjects more taxing than boys and clothes and field hockey. Claire's advice would have been to cut off all the kid's credit cards and force her to work, preferably in Cleveland's inner city so she could get a taste of real hardship. But Claire had no intention of making that suggestion. She was wise enough to know stepmothers should be nothing more than gracious hostesses.

"I wish you could have met her when she was ten," John said. "She was such a great kid. Liked to play in the woods behind Boots's house and come home all muddy with twigs in her hair and frogs in her pocket.

Used to give me a big hug and get dirt all over my suit, but I didn't care. I thought she was great. Boots, however, had other opinions."

And Boots's opinions had won out. When Claire met Ingrid at the airport, the girl with the ironed-flat, highlighted hair, significant diamond studs and brazen jeans could barely look her in the eye. She seemed bored by the tediousness of having to meet the only father she knew and his new wife. Kept asking when they were leaving and whining that she was missing out on some party.

"Maybe you could take her aside," he suggested suddenly. "You know, spark her interest with stories about interviewing terrorists. Get her to imagine a world beyond Hunting Hills."

"Yipes. I wouldn't dare. Don't you remember what it was like to be seventeen? All you wanted was for your parents to disappear and leave behind the house, the car, the cash and a stocked refrigerator. The last thing I'd have wanted was for my father's new wife to give me a boring lecture about dysentery."

"You're right. Still, I wish she had a better role model then the women around her."

Claire patted his hand supportively. "Come on. Let's go. If we don't hurry, we'll miss the entire second half."

"Really? You don't mind?"

"I think I can handle a few Lilliputians."

"You know how to handle the Lilliputians, don't you?" he asked, starting up the BMW.

"How?"

"All you have to do is cut the ropes."

"Next time," she said, "I'll remember to bring a knife."

Chapter Three

Marti could not stop staring at Claire Stark. She was soooo not John's type. John's types were cool ice maidens like Boots, whose first new car had been a pristine white Mercedes diesel station wagon presented to her the day she graduated from Middlebury. Or Busty Galore, whatever her real name was, the PR twinkie and smoothie fanatic.

Or herself.

Not this . . . this red-headed Amazon in faded jeans. Marti exchanged glances with Karen who too was transfixed. John's wife must have been a head taller than all the women and her eyes were a startling green. Mesmerizing. Was she wearing colored contacts? If yes, then that was so déclassé!

"Now what are you going to do?" they heard Boots ask Claire, after Ingrid joined Lois and her boyfriend, Gunther, in the field.

"She's going to take a well-deserved vacation," John said, throwing a stick that Bedo and Alys strained to get, but could not fetch since Holly School rules would not permit them off their leashes. "I keep telling her to take some time off, to relax and be a wife. You know, spend her days shopping and getting pedicures. Whatever it is you women do."

Marti prickled at this. Hunting Hills husbands liked to crack that their wives led lives of leisure but, honestly, nothing could have been further from the truth. "You might think we do nothing all day, John, but for your information I work my butt off. Do you know how many committees I'm on?"

"Hold your breath, Marti. It's not worth it," Boots said. "He's just trying to get your goat."

"You know the idea of doing nothing all day has really been bugging me," the Amazon piped up, insulting them right off the bat. "I've been working straight since I was sixteen. I can't imagine not getting a paycheck or having to live off someone else."

Something caught in Marti's throat. A little wad of shock. She coughed and, remembering her vow to Barry to be more tolerant, resolved to let that one slide.

"If you have any ideas, I'm all ears."

"The Assembly Ball is coming up," Boots suggested, knowing perfectly well that the exclusive Assembly committee had no intention of letting some outsider with absolutely no Cleveland connections tamper with its plans. "That's a major undertaking right there."

"The Assembly Ball?" asked Claire, looking to John for a cue, though he only started laughing.

"Or the Humane Society," Karen said. "You wouldn't have to hose down dog poop or anything. More on the fund-raising side."

"Actually, I was thinking about newspaper reporting. It seems like it's the only thing I do well."

"Besides choosing excellent men as husbands." Ignoring a frown from a Holly School administrator nearby, John unclipped Bedo's leash so the frustrated dog could catch a stick.

"You can't work in Prague anymore," said Boots, biting her lip as though Claire's professional future was a vexing concern. "So exactly which newspaper *will* you work for?"

Marti and Karen tensed. Boots had been a troublemaker for as long as Marti could remember, going back to first grade when she convinced Marti to bake Barbie in the oven to make her "Malibu." Not that much had changed since then and Boots had been known to toss sticks in the wheels of several significant relationships. For fun.

"That's true," Claire said. "I can't work in Prague. Though that doesn't mean I can't still freelance."

John put his arm around her. "She's got terrific contacts at *Newsweek. Time. USA Today*. Those editors love Claire and why shouldn't they? There aren't many writers with her talent. She'll have no problem freelancing for them, if that's what she wants."

"Those were international editors," Claire corrected. "Now that I'm in, uhm, Cleveland it's a whole new bag."

"Yes," Boots said. "I could see where that would be a problem. Well, then, there's only one solution."

"I think I see Denton," Karen whispered in Marti's ear, pointing to where Lois was in the field. "Haven't you been trying to get hold of him?"

"Shhh!" There was no way Marti was going to budge from this spot, not with Boots baring her fangs for the kill.

"It's too bad that there's only one newspaper in town, but at least it's a good one." Boots began circling like a barracuda.

John, perhaps seeing where the conversation was going, hurled another stick into the woods, causing poor Alys to practically strangle herself on the leash.

"The *Cleveland Citizen*. I've thought of that," Claire said innocently.

Uh-oh, thought Marti. *She fell for it.*

"Really?" Boots seemed impressed. "Do you think they'd hire you? I imagine getting a job there would be *extremely* competitive."

"C'mon, Boots. Claire doesn't want to work there," John said.

"Actually, I know the editor. Eric Schmaltz. As soon as I told him I was moving to Ohio, he offered me a job working on the magazine. He and I go way back."

"As in old boss back . . . or more?" Boots prodded.

"As a matter of fact, he does happen to be a former boyfriend of mine."

Claire was so painfully naive she was giving Marti fits! *Stop!* Marti wanted to scream. *Boots is leading you to the edge of the plank. Don't take another step. Sharks circling below.*

John testily unsnapped Alys from the leash. The dog dashed to the woods to fight Bedo for the sticks.

"John!" Boots scolded. "What are you doing? You know the rules."

"Fuck the rules. Can't we talk about something else? Claire knows how I feel about *The Citizen*. She knows I'd never let her work there."

Marti winced. Wrong choice of words.

"*Let,* eh." At this Boots cocked an eyebrow, delighted.

"I don't mean *let*. I mean, she knows I'd be very disappointed."

Claire stiffened awkwardly while John clearly was using every ounce of restraint he had to keep from popping his cork. There was more than a hint of anger in his voice as he brusquely called the dogs back.

Marti decided she had to intervene. Someone needed to step in as peacemaker. "I understand where you're coming from, John. After what you've been through with *The Citizen,* after the pain that paper's caused you and your family, who could blame you for not wanting your new wife to work there. Claire probably just doesn't realize how big a deal that was."

John smiled at Marti gratefully. For the first time since their moment by the pool last summer, they locked gazes and she knew then that he was still madly, deeply in love with her. She would put the poor boy at ease by taking him aside and revealing her true passion, definitely, but now was not the time. There was too much mayhem going on. Their love would have to wait.

She winked at him as he clipped the dogs back on their leashes. "Marti's right, Claire. You probably don't completely understand how I feel."

"Actually, that's not true. When I told Eric I wasn't interested, I said it was because of the way the paper had treated your father, John. I mean, from everything you've told me, those reporters didn't check their facts before accusing him of offering bribes, when all along it had been his partner who'd been greasing the palms of city officials."

The women slipped into stricken silence. In Hunting Hills it was considered very rude to bring up messy scandals—certainly not in such brutal detail. Bribes? Greasing the palms? Only a boorish, ignorant person would use such filthy language in public.

Boots knelt to feed cookies to Bedo and Alys who, being sensitive little Welshmen, were so upset by the atmospheric tension that they let the cookies drop pathetically to the ground. "All I know is that if *I'd* been an international correspondent used to jet-setting all over the world, I would go insane if someone had plunked me in Hunting Hills and expected me to be content with the gardening club. I mean, sooner or later, John, you're going to have to get over this grudge you have against the paper. If not for you, then for your new wife here. That's what people in love do . . . that is, if they're really in love."

That was it. That was the final straw.

John shoved his fists in his pocket and changed the subject. "How's Ingrid doing?"

"Impossible. I've had it up to here with her. She does whatever she wants. Wait until you see her cell phone bills." (Though Hunting Hills wives always portrayed their children in the most glowing light, it was acceptable—if not encouraged—for mothers to proudly gripe about how spoiled their teenage daughters had become.)

"I have a great idea." Claire clapped her hands. "John, I'm sure you're eager to have some time alone with Ingrid. It looks like she's leaving the field. Why don't you see if you can get her to drive you home?"

John composed himself. "And how will you get back?"

"I'll take your car. I think I know the way."

Which was when Marti saw her opportunity. "Claire can follow me, John. She'll be fine."

"You hurry up and catch up to Ingrid," Karen added.

John pecked Claire on the cheek and jogged off. Marti watched as his fine form, still handsome and in shape in its mid-forties, crossed the field.

Someday soon you'll be mine, she thought, relishing the anticipation.

Boots stood. "Looks as though you two have some issues to work out, Claire. I suppose that's what happens when you marry someone you hardly know. Personally, I've found that pre-wedding counseling is invaluable when it comes to sorting out these differences."

Oddly enough, Marti found herself feeling defensive toward John's wife, especially when Claire looked as though she was about to cry. "How about you follow me back to my house, Claire? It's just around the corner from John's and you can stop off and have a glass of wine. I'm sure you could use one after today." She frowned at Boots.

"Thanks. You're right. John told me this adjustment might be difficult, but I didn't realize how much."

"Don't worry about Boots," Marti said, as she led Claire back to the parking lot. "Her second marriage lasted less than a year, which is probably why she made that quip about pre-marital counseling. The only pre-marital counseling Boots ever got was to make sure she registered her linens with Libeco-Lagae ."

Claire laughed and Marti realized that she'd have no problem finding out from this unfortunately dressed woman how John had come to be temporarily infatuated with her. In fact, Marti was now so obsessed with planning the best way to pump Claire for information that she didn't notice Denton waving good-bye from across the field, his arms flailing back and forth like an air traffic controller directing a 747.

Chapter Four

Hunting Hills wives were not famous sticklers for the truth. The truth, they'd found, could be so inconvenient, especially when it came to age and children, both of which the wives tended to fudge. What was the point of revealing your true age when you had just paid for the plastic surgeon's second home?

As for children—who inevitably experienced their teenage fuck-ups—it was all a matter of spin. That your daughter was off to an unranked college in Belize was "super news" because "she adores the Caribbean and craves the beach." Even a son's scrapes with the law could be twisted and transformed into evidence that he was a "bit of a risk taker," which everyone knew was code for future business success.

Claire Stark Harding, it appeared, had not been apprised of these rules.

"Maybe it's because I just turned forty, but I don't seem to go with the flow as easily as I used to," she told Marti as she accepted a second glass—a second glass!—of Pinot Grigio, the Hunting Hills white wine of choice due to its lower calorie content and reduced hangover potential. Perhaps Claire hadn't noticed that while it had been Marti's idea to open a bottle, she had taken three delicate butterfly sips while Claire had polished hers off with gusto.

"Still, it's not like I moved from Prague to a wasteland. Hunting Hills is beautiful." Claire pushed back her auburn hair, revealing flushed cheeks. "It's probably the most . . . landscaped . . . place I've ever lived. I can see why John likes it, though I think I could have persuaded him to stay in Prague if it hadn't been for Ingrid."

They were sitting in the glass atrium off the kitchen, a light-filled room with heated slate floors and a sisal rug and views toward the east and the west where the October sun was sinking fast.

"Ingrid?" Marti crossed her ankles, expecting Claire to deliver the standard speech about how much John admired the girl and how he didn't want to miss a moment of her action-packed senior year in high school.

"Drugs is what he's worried about," Claire said bluntly, "though, having met Ingrid, I don't think she's the type. John is worried that she's lost all drive, all thirst for knowledge. He says she used to be a budding biologist, that she used to love collecting water samples in the creek behind her house and testing their pH. Now she freaks if there's dirt on her shoes. Have you seen that too?"

Marti couldn't say that she had. Whatever transformation Ingrid had gone through, it had been, in Marti's opinion, totally positive. Ingrid had been a geeky girl with braids and blotchy skin who used to play for hours in the woods, frankly worrying her mother to death. Now she was a fully formed young woman, her teeth straightened by braces, her skin cleared by dermatology, her hair thickened and shaped by Mario in Chagrin Falls.

What was John complaining about?

The green blinking light on the portable phone caught Marti's eye. Someone was leaving a message. She didn't know who and she wouldn't check until Claire had left. Marti usually turned off her home phone during the day. The constant ringing drove her nuts and if anyone important needed to call her, why they always had her cell number.

"It bothers me though," Claire continued. "I mean, from everything John's told me it seems like he returns to Hunting Hills not for himself, but for other people. Ingrid. His father."

"Hmmm." Marti didn't like to think of icky stuff like Hugh Harding's financial failure, so she changed the subject. Putting down her glass and leaning close to Claire, she asked with a glimmer in her eyes, "Tell me how you and John met. And don't spare a single detail. I want to hear it all."

Claire told Marti she hadn't been looking for love. She'd been looking for a story, particularly a story about John Harding and his project to connect transplanted Czechoslovakians in Cleveland who wanted to invest in their native country with entrepreneurs eager to rebuild Prague.

It bore all the hallmarks of a national magazine feature—touching vignettes of immigrants who had fled Communist oppression only to work hard and make it in America, the reunion of families torn apart by war, plans for a more brilliant future in a capitalistic market. Claire had several editors interested, including a friend of hers at *Newsweek*.

Just one problem. John Harding refused to be interviewed for attribution. Something about having had a bad experience with a newspaper back in Cleveland.

She took him out for lunch and showed him the secret places in Prague the tourists never visited, Kafka's favorite café, an underground tunnel where Jews hid themselves from invading Nazis, a quaint chapel with hand-painted ceilings. All along the way they talked, at first about Prague and Cleveland and then about Shakespeare and, finally, about themselves.

He'd graduated from Williams and had been a Rhodes Scholar finalist. He told her he was divorced from a Cleveland socialite named

Boots, that he served as guardian to Boots's seventeen-year-old daughter Ingrid (whose SATs were pathetic) and that he once played tennis against Jimmy Connors and won. That if he hadn't been forced into his father's business, his ideal career would have been teaching English literature at a small college.

She, in turn, told him about her life—about her dictatorial father who drove her mother to alcoholism, about struggling like a demon to get away from them, finally earning a full scholarship to West Virginia State and landing a post at the *Wheeling Register*. She told him everything except how she had fallen uncontrollably in love.

With him.

This did not usually happen to Claire, falling in love on the job, though she knew plenty of reporters who thought nothing of sleeping with their subjects, whether they were cops or politicians, actors or bureaucrats. It was highly unethical, in Claire's opinion, and so she restrained herself as best as she could from letting John know her true feelings.

Claire's landlady, Mrs. Krozan, who had no ethics, was furious at her for not making a pass at him before he left for America.

"You don't let men like that walk out of your life," Mrs. Krozan had screeched, after John, looking drop-dead gorgeous in a Savile Row tux, dropped Claire off at her apartment and said a polite but platonic farewell. "You throw yourself at them. You grab them by the ankles and bite hard and never let them go."

(Mrs. Krozan, Claire explained to Marti, had dyed flaming orange hair, wore nothing but silk Chinese robes and smoked Camels unfiltered. She was somewhat "odd."

Marti said she couldn't imagine.)

Anyway, that night Claire was in the bath sipping tomato soup and reading a Scottish romance novel in an effort to get John out of her mind when Mrs. Krozan and her yipping, bug eyed, hyperactive long-haired Chihuahua, Bobo, appeared at her door.

"Open up, Claire. He's downstairs. For you!"

Having been lost on the Scottish Highlands with Sir Edmund Frist, the feisty, frisky outlaw nobleman with a manly lust that could not be quenched, Claire had to take a second to comprehend Mrs. Krozan's message.

"Who?" she'd called from her deep claw-footed bath. Men did not usually show up at her doorstep on a Thursday night after nine—or anytime, if one were to split hairs.

"Es that cutie pie. Come quick."

There was only one possibility and that was John Harding.

She was so shaken that at first she spilled the soup in the water and then nearly dropped the paperback before summoning the presence of mind to slowly get out without breaking her neck on the slippery tile floor. She grabbed her white terrycloth bathrobe (which bore a couple of black mascara smudges, but what the hey) and remembered to tie it (that was key) before answering her front door.

Mrs. Krozan reeked of wine and cigarettes. Her face was lit with excitement, almost as bright as her hair, and as animated as Bobo who was in danger of yipping himself into hyperventilation.

"He's come back for you. The American."

"What does he want?"

"Who cares? He wants you!" Mrs. Krozan held up a finger. "Hey. You want I take his pants?"

"What?"

"Pants. I get Bobo to do it." She held up Bobo, sending off another round of mad barking. "Without he have no pants, he can't go."

Mrs. Krozan was definitely from the Old Country, even if she had just moved back to Prague after living four decades in South River, New Jersey.

"Let me handle this." Claire scooted in front on the off chance that Bobo might make a dash and do something awful to John's Savile Row.

She caught him with his hand on the front door. "John?" she called from the top of the stairs.

"I'm sorry to bother you so late at home. Is this, uhm, a bad time?"

He made no effort to hide the fact that he was taking her in, from her bare (and, she was proud to say, for once newly shaven) legs to the V of her robe.

"No bother," Claire said casually. "I was just reading."

"She always read. She has no one!" declared Mrs. Krozan. "She forty-year-old single spinster."

"You speak very good English," John said, flashing a grin that caused Mrs. Krozan to reach for her pack of Camels.

"That's 'cause I'm from New Jersey. South River, you know it?" Mrs. Krozan lit up and closed one eye in the smoke. "I used to run bar in Perth Amboy. Very fine establishment."

(Topless joint, Claire clarified for Marti.)

Claire summed up the situation and decided there were two options. Either she could invite John in or watch Mrs. Krozan jump his bones first.

"So you live alone?" John asked, stepping into Claire's lavender apartment.

"Doesn't it scream it?" She picked up a coffee cup with tea still in it and carried a plate with half-eaten cookies into her small kitchen which really wasn't a kitchen at all but a "kitchen area."

She dumped the plate in the sink and turned around to find him staring at her crucifix light switches. Would the mortification never cease?

"Is this what I think it is?" He flicked down the cross and turned off the kitchen light.

"It's my mother's doing. She gave them to me years ago and I didn't install them until she died because after she died my lights kept going off and I knew it was her and she wouldn't be satisfied until I put up her Christs on a stick." Claire was almost breathless in her rush to get the embarrassing explanation over with. "You know, let there be light and all that."

"Interesting." He flicked the switch up. "I'm sorry that you've lost your mother."

"She's better off where she is." Claire hated to think about her mother's death. It had been a long and painful progress, burdened by eternal regrets. "And you?"

"I don't have Christ on a stick. Yet, miraculously, my lights stay on."

"I mean your mother. We never covered her in our discussions."

"Ahh, she still lingers, haunting me from Palm Beach. Do you mind if I use your john? I kind of ran over here on the spur of the moment."

The bathroom! Claire suddenly remembered the bathroom. Bra on the floor. Panties on top of the hamper. Tampons out for display.

"Be right back. Have to let the bathwater out."

"I don't want a bath. I just want to take a whiz."

But she pretended not to hear him as she slammed the door and bustled about retrieving the bra, letting out the water, dumping the underwear in the hamper, hiding the tampons under the sink and wiping off stray hairs from around the faucet. And finally, in a stroke of brilliance, remembering to flush the toilet.

She emerged to find him studying her bookshelf.

"Lots of Stephen King. You never mentioned that you were a fan."

"Mmmm. *Was.* Most of those are from a friend. I'm holding them for her. Lately I've been into more cerebral stuff. Jonathan Franzen." This, of course, was a complete lie.

"Oh absolutely." He was back to grinning. Claire felt like she was sinking in the sea of credulity.

Seconds later John came out from her bathroom holding a very worn, and slightly damp copy of *The Hussy of the Highlands.*

"Funny. I didn't know Franzen wrote about, what was it?" He flipped over the book and read the back flap. " 'A Highlander whose throbbing and royal loins ache for . . .' "

Claire snatched it from his hand. "Can I get you a drink or something?"

"Sure. Got any scotch? Suddenly I'm in the mood."

She decided that alcohol would be a very, very dangerous addition, considering the situation.

"No scotch, but I have some tea or coffee."

He frowned. "Tea, coffee, romance novels. To tell you the truth, I'd had you pegged much differently."

"The romance novels are for show. You know how men hate brainy women."

"I don't." He moved closer. "I've always been a sucker for a well-turned mind."

He smiled slyly and Claire felt her chest clench. She was unsure if he had shown up to be interviewed or . . . more. Whatever it was, he made her feel incredibly uncomfortable.

There was a loud rap at the door, punctuated by long-haired Chihuahua barking.

John stepped back. "That'll be the merry widow Mrs. Krozan, I expect. And her Velcro pet."

Claire threw open the door and Bobo leaped out of Mrs. Krozan's arms, making a beeline for John's ankle.

"Jump," Claire ordered him. "Get on the couch."

"What? Why?"

"You don't want to know."

"Ach, I'm so sorry," Mrs. Krozan yelled, launching into an emotional tirade of Czechoslovakian.

Bobo bobbed at John's ankle and Claire couldn't decide which would be worse, Bobo committing his famous sin or John kicking Bobo into the goal post. Thankfully, he took Claire's advice just as Bobo lifted his leg and urinated over the spot where John's foot had been only seconds before.

"Bad Bobo. Naughty dog." Mrs. Krozan rushed in and grabbed the blasé Chihuahua. "You know better. We pee on tree, not on man's foot." Bobo licked his paw proudly, having done exactly as Claire was certain his mistress had instructed.

"We get pants other way," she mumbled to Claire before heading out the door.

"Lot of excitement for a single woman on a Thursday night." John stepped over the puddle. "Want me to clean it up?"

"Not in that tux."

She unrolled some paper towel, pulled out a spray bottle she kept for Bobo emergencies and began dabbing at the spot. "So, I assume you came here to finally go on the record. Should I get my tape recorder?"

"Not so fast. There's a compromise I'd like to discuss." John sat on the couch near her and she was aware he had a very good view down her front. "Who's this?"

He held up her picture of a young boy with a dirty white shirt and chipped-tooth smile.

"That's Muhamed Ameti. He was one of the kids I got to know when I was working at Stankovic, the Bosnian refugee camp in Macedonia."

"Bosnian refugee camp," John repeated. "You never told me that. How long did you work there?"

"About a year. I couldn't stand it." She ripped off a new towel. "I mean, in general most of the people were wonderful but the conditions were depressing. We had to beg for medicine and food, dig latrines and haul water. Tons of people cramped together. I can still smell the smell."

"Maybe that's Bobo."

She smiled. "I don't think so. Bobo is a petunia in comparison."

"Pretty tough, huh?"

"Horrific."

"How did you happen to go?"

"A friend of mine, Josie, talked me into it after an, uhh, incident at the paper where I was working in West Virginia." She prayed that was vague enough not to spark interest. "She called it her refugee road trip. She's pregnant and married, now, to a doctor."

"Lucky her."

Claire went to the kitchen area and put on a kettle of water for tea. "And by that you mean . . . ?"

"Skip it. It was sexist and stupid." John took off his coat and tossed it on a chair.

The tux had a paralyzing effect. Claire busied herself rummaging through her tea bags, anything to keep her mind off him, or at least him in *that* way.

"Saint Claire I should call you." He was next to her, his body so close that she could sense his heat, smell the elixir of restaurant smoke, the damp outdoor air and wine. "Savior to Bosnian refugees and helpless widows and who else, I wonder. Maybe a soulless capitalist, if he's lucky."

She found two bags of Earl Grey, closed her eyes and reminded herself that a savvy businessman like John Harding was not above seducing her for a more favorable story. Probably he had sized up the lavender apartment, her soup for one, the romance novels and crocheted tea cozy and concluded she was an easy target. A pining spinster yearning for a man to introduce her to the mysteries of womanhood.

Well, she had more news for him. Single living was a choice, not a curse. So he could save his sexy eyes and expensive British tux and . . .

"Let's talk about this compromise." He sat on the kitchen stool. "I'll do an interview if I can read over my quotes. You don't have to let me read the whole article. I know how you journalists flip out about that kind of thing. I just want see my own words in print before I read them in *Newsweek*."

She turned off the stove. "Really?" Was he bluffing? She couldn't tell. He seemed sincere, but she was skeptical. "Why? What changed your mind?"

"Do you have to ask?"

Claire swallowed. "I'm curious."

"*You* changed my mind. During dinner tonight, despite the laughs and the food and all the friends who had shown up to say good-bye, there was only one person I wanted to be with." John got up and walked toward her, a longing look in his eyes. "Do you know what I realized? I realized that you and I could talk forever. When we're together, I'm alive. Engaged. I feel as though we're of one mind." He was getting closer. "I love listening to you, Claire. Being with you. Looking at you." He paused. "Touching you."

Claire backed up against the door. Nothing in her Investigative Reporter's Handbook had prepared her for a moment like this. John put one hand against the doorjamb and leaned down to kiss her.

A sudden commotion erupted in the hallway. "Hey, Claire! Open up. I have gift."

Claire snapped back into reality and slipped under his raised arm.

"My, my. She certainly is determined, this widow Krozan," John said, clearing his throat and opening the door.

Mrs. Krozan tromped in displaying a bottle of deceptively clear liquid. "Look what I have as make-up for Bobo."

"Gasoline?" Claire asked, feeling dizzy and confused.

"No! Brandy. I brew myself."

"Now we're talking." John patted Claire's shoulder as if to assure her his mission tonight was not finished. "Thank you, dear woman, you just saved me from a cup of tea."

"I know. Her with the tea." She plunked the bottle on the kitchen counter. "Let's have a toast. To Bobo."

"To Bobo," John agreed, helping himself to Claire's cupboard. "What? No shot glasses? Whatever will we do?"

"Teacups. She has plenty of those."

"Hold on." Claire intervened as Mrs. Krozan happily uncorked the booze. "I think this is a really bad idea. Mrs. Krozan, it's very nice of you to bring your homemade"—turpentine, she was tempted to say—"brandy. But John and I are working."

"Bah, work." Mrs. Krozan poured out three healthy doses into the glasses John brought out. "Es almost weekend. No work. What you do, John, for a living?"

Claire slumped against the counter, feeling spent and wobbly. How could John be so composed?

"I'm hooking up Cleveland investors with some entrepreneurs in Prague."

"He's a venture capitalist," Claire added.

"Whoo!" Mrs. Krozan lifted her glass. "Can't let this one get away, Claire."

Claire hid her face in her hands.

"To Bobo and Cleveland," Mrs. Krozan declared. "*Salut*!"

"*Salut*!" John repeated, nudging Claire. "Come on. Don't be a party pooper."

"Yah. No poopers." Mrs. Krozan downed her shot in one gulp, punctuating it with a smack of her lips. "Is good, no?"

"Hmm." John held his glass to the light. "Tastes like gin. If you squint."

"Is the juniper berries. I pick them myself. Come on, Claire."

"Yes. Take your vitamins." John was enjoying her nervousness way too much.

Both of them were staring at her, Mrs. Krozan looking particularly hurt and John looking particularly devilish. To show them up, Claire emptied her glass in one fell swoop. The brandy burned going down and seemed to heat up her whole body, right to her toes.

"Thatta girl." John patted her on the back and left his hand there. It felt warm like the rest of her.

"Another," Mrs. Krozan demanded.

"No!" Claire shouted.

"Yes!" John contradicted, pouring the shots himself.

"Then I go." Mrs. Krozan eyed the booze eagerly. "I promise."

John lifted his glass. "To Claire, the patron saint of refugees, widows and aimless businessmen."

"Whatever." Mrs. Krozan knocked back the brandy and stood up from the stool, teetering a bit. "Bedtime for me, I think."

"I think so too." Claire snatched the bottle and walked her to the door.

"No. You keep that." Mrs. Krozan pushed away the brandy. "Save for your wedding."

Oh, please shut up. Claire fumbled with the knob, the one shot of brandy so incapacitating her that she couldn't even operate her own door.

"Es destiny, you know." Mrs. Krozan pointed between the two of them. "I predict you two will be married before the next full moon." She tapped her temple. "I can tell these things."

"Good night, Mrs. Krozan." Claire practically heaved the old lady into the hallway. "Be careful on the stairs."

Mrs. Krozan lifted her finger to add one more observation but Claire slammed the door. When she turned around, John had his coat on, getting ready to go.

Was this good-bye forever?

"Call you tomorrow?" he asked, shoving his hands in his pockets.

"What about the interview?"

"Sure." He extended his hand.

She shook it. "Sorry it was so nuts."

"Don't be silly." He gave her hand a quick squeeze and opened the door, hesitating. "One other thing I forgot."

"Yes?"

Suddenly his lips were on hers. The move was so quick that Claire didn't have a chance to form a decent protest. But as soon as she felt him kissing her, she acknowledged that the dream had become reality and Claire gave up any notion of remaining impartial, unbiased or professional. Instead she closed her eyes and let him move in deeper. When they broke apart he kissed her again, John taking her by the shoulders and holding her tightly.

It had been so long since she'd been pressed against a man's chest or felt a pair of strong arms around her. So long since she'd inhaled the scent that was more intoxicating than Mrs. Krozan's homemade brew. It made her positively delirious—and laden with guilt.

"I thought so," he said, looking down at her.

She was unable to meet his gaze, certain with mortification that he was about to crow how he'd suspected all along she'd had a crush on him. Was he laughing? Laughing at her pathetic unprofessionalism? "Thought what?"

"I thought you'd kiss like that. You didn't mind, did you?"

Had she minded? Was he daft? "No." She shook her head.

"Then you don't mind if I . . ."

She didn't wait for him to finish. Throwing her arms around his neck, she planted her lips on his, practically wrapping her body around him. John responded ardently, though he ended up having to peel her off him.

"What happened?" she asked, fearing she'd been too forward. "Did I do something wrong?"

"Hardly. And if I hadn't just downed two shots of lighter fluid and a half a bottle of wine over dinner, I would have carried you into your bedroom with all the flourish I could fake. Trust me. But I've got my sights set on the long term."

Claire said nothing. She didn't know what he was talking about. "What long term?"

"How soon you forget the wise and sober Mrs. Krozan." He tapped his temple. "She knows these things. See you tomorrow, love."

And with that parting zinger he was out the door, leaving Claire to wonder if she had been the victim of a cruel prank or under the spell of Mrs. Krozan's homemade Czechoslovakian love potion.

She got her answer one week later—with a marriage proposal.

"That was it?" Marti was incredulous. John and Boots had dated for years—years!—before Boots got fed up and started dropping hints that he marry her or else.

"That was it." Claire sat back. "We both just . . . knew. We clicked."

The solarium was almost dark, aside from the candles Marti had lit. In their glow she gleaned for the first time what John saw in this Amazon, this tall, mysterious beauty. It was not a quality found in a dermatologist's cream or on a plastic surgeon's table. It was an aura of intangible mystery, a sly sense of humor, a possible insatiable sexual appetite—none of which could be purchased and, for that reason, all of which Marti found utterly perplexing.

"Wow, it's late." Claire jumped up. "I better get home. I think I can find the way. That is if I can drive that BMW without crashing into something."

"Two streets down and take your first left," Marti murmured, too preoccupied with the story of John and Claire's courtship to pay much attention.

Marti had never been to Prague, but she imagined that it was romantic, lined with cobblestone streets and mist. *Amadeus* had been filmed there, she once read, and she could see how diehard romantic John Harding, with his love of European literature and travel, might have been swept up in its gothic atmosphere.

If so, the mist would wear off soon in Hunting Hills and then he would come to his senses and realize that this "Claire thingy" had been nothing more than a daring European flirtation, like that date she'd had with Francois, a somewhat dark and greasy guy she'd met in the Louvre during her junior year abroad.

After Claire backed the BMW out of the driveway, Marti pressed a button on the answering machine. There were twelve messages. She scrolled through them all until she came to the last one, the one she'd been expecting.

"Hey, babe, sorry I missed you at the game. Lois played great. I don't know why you keep putting her down. Listen, I'm headed back to the office. All hell's broken loose and I'm up to my ass in work. Don't wait up. Tell Lois to crack down on that calculus. An 82 on a quiz is not acceptable. Love ya."

Denton. They wouldn't meet again until the next morning's Post-it by the Krups.

Chapter Five

"Your mother?" Claire nearly fell out of bed as John put down the phone and gave her the eye-opening news. "I thought she was in Palm Beach."

"She was. That's Fran for you. Impulsive doesn't even come close. When she decides she wants something, she does it. And what she wants is to meet her new daughter-in-law, so she hopped a plane this morning to meet you. She'll be here . . ." He checked his watch. "In an hour."

Claire fell back against the cream colored sheets, her long auburn hair splaying against the pillows. "But we were having such a great morning."

They'd spent it making plans for when Ingrid graduated from Holly and they were finally free to leave Hunting Hills. John proposed taking two years off and backpacking around the East. India. The beaches of Thailand. The mountains of Nepal.

But Claire, who had a fondness for hot baths, clean clothes and real beds, voted instead for a thatched roof cottage in Scotland with a few sheep and a garden. Preferably near Inverness. Or maybe Loch Ness. The monster offered so many possibilities.

"I could start a whole new career in tabloids," she said.

To settle their disagreement, they compromised on a slow and graceful session of lovemaking that ended abruptly with the blaring of their bedside phone. John's mother on ESP overload, assuring her son there was no need for him to pick her up at Cleveland Hopkins. She'd already made plans with her favorite driver to shuttle her around. And since the traffic wasn't too bad, she'd be in Hunting Hills earlier than anticipated.

After he hung up, he said, "We don't have to get going. Not just yet." He caressed her bare shoulder. "You have the most beautiful skin. Do you know that?"

"The human body's largest organ."

"Don't tempt me, Claire." He slid off the strap of her nightgown, his lips following the curves of her neck.

"What happens if she asks me about grandchildren?"

John stopped his kissing. "Does it bother you that much?"

"Truthfully? It's pretty much ruined my life." She turned her head away so he wouldn't see the annoying tears that inevitably sprung forth whenever she thought about her *condition* as Mrs. Krozan used to call it. What had happened to her back in the refugee camp was bad enough—but being pitied for it was far worse.

"You know that it doesn't matter one damn thing to me, right?" John said softly, earnestly. "I married you for you, Claire. And that's all I married you for."

She cautiously looked at him. "You're not just saying that."

"I'm not just saying that. And if my mother asks, which she won't, you can tell her that kids are not something we're thinking about right now. We're having too much fun, the two of us." And he proceeded to do things to her that caused Claire to be incapable of all rational thought.

Afterward, while John showered, Claire tried to recall everything he'd mentioned about Fran Harding Pryce.

Pryce was the name of Fran's second husband Gordon Pryce, a retired Republic Steel executive who'd known John's mother since forever. He'd been close friends with John's father, in fact, and had swooped to the rescue when the man "ran ashore"—Hunting Hills's euphemism for being caught in a scandal.

Fran and Gordon had waited the appropriate year from the day of Hugh Harding's death to announce that they were getting married, which they did in the small chapel in Christ Church. Eventually, Fran sold the Hunting Hills house and joined Gordon in his luxurious winter home in Palm Beach. From all accounts, Fran fit in perfectly. She was rich, white, Anglo Saxon and more purebred than Boots's Pembroke Welsh corgis.

Claire made a mental note to keep a check on her own politics. She wasn't positive, but she had an inkling that Fran was overjoyed by the current White House. Obviously, this was not the time for Claire to rant and rave about a pointless overseas war and discriminatory tax policies. This was the time to smile, discuss the mums, and cross her ankles. In other words, to take her cues from Marti Denton.

Marti Denton. Would they ever be friends? *Could* they ever be friends? Claire didn't think so. Not that she wasn't looking. If there was anything she needed in this insular community of oversized Lexuses and bright swimming pools and couples who'd known each other since they were in diapers, it was an ally. But she doubted Marti, who kept herself composed and reserved while Claire nervously downed two glasses of wine, would be her best buddy. Their meeting the other day had taken on the tense tone of a police inquisition as Marti grilled Claire skeptically about John's marriage proposal. Once Marti had sucked out all Claire had to offer, she would drop her and move on, Claire suspected. It made sense. She had had no fashion sense, no wealth, no connections, had nothing to offer this group of women except John—and now he was off the market, thanks to her.

When John was dressed and downstairs, Claire slipped out of the bed and made her way to the master bath. She turned on the water in the limestone steam shower and searched for a razor in John's medicine cabinet, which could have been straight out of an ad for men's Clinique. Glass shelves held discreet teal tubes of expensive unscented male grooming products. Hair wax. A yellow bottle of moisturizer. Cologne. A tiny blue vial of oil. A steel container specially designed to hold Q-Tips. No razor.

Silly her. She was so behind the times. John probably had his beard professionally removed, waxed, cauterized or whatever it was the Hunting Hills wives she'd met the other day had done to themselves so there wasn't so much as an errant lash on their cheeks.

She ran her hands along her chin and felt the slightest stubble of two tiny whiskers, distressing signs of age. That would never pass muster with Fran Harding Pryce. Possibly in light of Hunting Hills' aesthetic ordinances, it might be illegal.

Steam filled the room as Claire attacked a drawer near the sink. Soap, aftershave and, through the mist, victory: a pink plastic Daisy disposable razor. Another ex-girlfriend memento.

Claire had been finding them all around the house. A pair of ruby earrings in the nightstand, a midnight blue silk lace bra hanging on the door to the walk-in closet and a matching pair of panties (size 2!) wedged between the mattress and box spring. A *Silver Palate* cookbook sat on a shelf by the stove, the recipe for *turbot en bourride* bookmarked.

She was willing to bet that the only turbot in John's repertoire was the one charging the engine of his BMW.

Grabbing the razor, Claire entered the shower and gathered up enough slips of soap to make a full lather. The shampoo bottle was empty, of course, as men are genetically incapable of determining when the shampoo is out and when a sliver of soap is no longer soap, but scum with attitude.

Claire wasn't totally naive. She was well aware that Fran would consider her a freak compared to John's previous girlfriends—thin, stylish ingenues who in grade school had been much more adept at manipulating the male gender than she'd ever be. My Lord, look at the wives. They could have been classified under a separate species. *Femme Perfectus.*

As she dragged the razor along her muscular calf, Claire thought about them and how John had reacted to Boots's needling at the Holly School field hockey game. Though John had been within his rights to be pissed off about the *Cleveland Citizen* and about Boots, Claire couldn't help but notice he seemed somewhat put off by her as well. Their friction was soon forgotten—or, rather, transformed into the cold dawn's heated lovemaking. But what would happen when the passion faded?

What if, seeing how mismatched she was to Hunting Hills, John started questioning their marriage?

Maybe, Claire thought, she was like the funky furniture you fall in love with in the showroom, but send back after the thirty-day, no-questions-asked guarantee when you see it clashes with the paint and carpet at home.

Remember Sonnet 116, she told herself.

Love's not Time's fool, though rosy lips and cheeks
Within his bending sickle's compass come;
Love alters not with his brief hours and weeks,
But bears it out even to the edge of doom.

Yes, that was better.

She turned off the shower, wrapped a thick white cotton towel around her and eyed John's digital scale. Did she dare? She didn't trust digital. There was no wiggle room. She liked the kind in her bathroom back in Prague, the one with the slightly rusted needle that would veer five pounds one way or five pounds the other depending on the humidity (or whether you had one hand against the bathroom wall).

Squeezing shut her eyes, Claire dropped the towel and stepped onto the scale. There were a couple of beeps and then a piercing, judgmental one. She ventured a look, her brain taking a few minutes to comprehend the answer.

She hopped off. Wow, was that thing broken. It could give a person a heart attack, a scale like that. It was dangerous. A killer. She would tell John to take it back or get it fixed, if he could.

Then, on second thought, she decided to say nothing at all. Though she wished she hadn't tried out the scale shortly before introducing herself to Fran Harding Pryce, she of the inconceivable size 0.

Chapter Six

"Aren't you adorable!"

Fran Harding Pryce held out her wispy arms. She was a china doll of a woman with the hammerhead noggin of Nancy Reagan perched on a miniature frame of dried bones and tanned flesh. Her white hair had been cut at a sharp angle, therefore emphasizing her light blue eyes and delicately plucked, expertly penciled brows. Despite her casual red sweater and tailored gray slacks, and her age of eighty years, Fran came off as the kind of woman men would still call cute as a button.

"Oh!" Fran gasped as Claire's hearty embrace caused a "whoof" from her mother-in-law's chest. "Just a peck on the cheek will do fine, dear."

She hadn't meant to put the old bird in full traction. "Right." Claire mentally slapped herself for not remembering the Hunting Hills statutory greeting. First an air kiss to the right and then the left and then step back fast as you can. She executed it perfectly, if belatedly.

Fran's hands took Claire's as she scrutinized her new daughter-in-law, a rather hulking girl of lowland Scottish origin with dull auburn hair styled in an uninspired fashion and perhaps a few chin hairs. This new daughter-in-law of hers was old, Fran decided. Close to forty and she did not have the body of an athlete. Not the long legs of a tennis player or the firm thighs of a horsewoman. Nor, judging from Claire's nondescript jeans and white man's shirt, did she have élan. It was a mystery that John had taken a second look at her, let alone married the poor creature.

Fran could not see this one blending in with Hunting Hills and that would mean social trouble for John, especially in business. This made her mother's heart sad in the same way as if she'd just discovered that her son had been suddenly brain damaged in a skiing accident. A Hunting Hills' wife's number one job was to help her husband in business, even in the twenty-first century. Fran had understood that. So did Marti Swan Denton. What Fran could never figure out was why John hadn't appreciated that about Marti too.

"You must be something special if my son brought you all the way home from Prague," Fran managed to exclaim. "She's beautiful, John."

"No argument there," said John who, Claire noticed, was awfully close to the door in his gray cashmere coat and Burberry scarf.

"Going somewhere?" she asked.

"It is after nine. Unless you've forgotten that I actually have to work for a living."

"Let him go." Fran clutched her hand. "Surely you can stand to be apart from him for a full day. Or are you two still at the stage where you can't go five minutes without sex?"

Claire gasped and went crimson. Fran winked.

"On that note," John said, flashing her a salute. "I'm out of here. Watch yourself, Mother. Claire is under the misimpression you're a sweet old lady."

"Don't know how she would have gotten that idea. Now run along.

I don't want Mr. Big Stuff keeping everyone waiting. Even if he was up all night performing his husbandly duties."

Claire wished for a trap door in the floor.

"I'm sorry," said Fran, leading Claire to the sunny breakfast room that looked out onto a garden patio. "Sometimes I go too far. I love teasing him. Don't you?"

Fran didn't wait for her to answer. "Now tell me everything you've been doing since the honeymoon. Greece was it? I hope it wasn't Mykonos. It's such a Club Med scene there. My, look at that ring!" She whipped out a pair of half glasses and inspected Claire's left hand.

It was, as a matter of fact, the most beautiful ring ever created. A fiery round opal surrounded by brilliant diamonds in a platinum setting. It was an unusual ring, an antique from an Austrian estate, and not particularly expensive. John had showed her diamonds and emeralds and sapphires. But Claire had had her heart set on the opal because it was exactly like the ring one of her favorite romance heroines had received, though she wouldn't tell John that in a million, zillion years.

Fran held her hand to the light. "Opals are bad luck, you know. And so fragile. They crack for seemingly no reason."

"It's lasted a century," Claire said. "I'm sure it will last one more."

They ate a breakfast of grapefruit and fresh fruit—cut melons, grapes, strawberries and kiwi—prepared by John's cook, Elena. Elena was a marvelous invention because she was never around. She dropped by when John was at work. While he was at the office, she itemized his refrigerator, restocked it with prepared fruit, salads and foil-covered gourmet entrées, along with the staples—bread, milk, eggs and, for the pantry, Glenlivet. She also happened to be gorgeous, a six-foot black woman with high cheekbones and full breasts, causing Claire to ponder if John had ever itemized her.

Once Claire had recovered from her initial awkwardness, she found that it was really very pleasant sitting in John's cozy breakfast nook drinking coffee with Fran as the fog burned off the garden behind them and John's beloved Waldo, a brooding Saint Bernard, slept in a patch of morning sun.

Either by etiquette, genetics or, perhaps, general curiosity, Fran seemed completely enraptured by every vignette Claire shared about Prague. Fran was even fascinated by Claire's description of her hometown, Mudville, and all its quirky characters.

In fact Fran listened so well that Claire, always the investigative journalist, started to get suspicious. Maybe Fran was waiting for her to trip up or commit a verbal faux pas that would result in immediate annulment by none other than the Pope, who probably vacationed with Fran on some island off Crete.

John's housekeeper, a lackadaisical woman named Dawn, sauntered into the breakfast room with a pot of fresh coffee. Five days a week Dawn traveled forty miles round trip from the row homes of Parma to take out his trash, unload and load his dishwasher, load and unload his washing machine and be there when the UPS man arrived. She wore an iPod, turquoise tank top and jeans and her blond hair in a ponytail—all of which Fran clearly disapproved.

"Do you have any decaf?" Fran asked as Dawn poured out their cups without so much as a good morning. "My heart's about to fly out of my chest."

Dawn popped the iPod pod out of her right ear. "It's Starbucks. French Roast."

"Decaf?" asked Fran.

"In this house? No way." And Dawn split.

"There's your second project," Fran said, looking doubtfully at the caffeinated coffee. "Get a new housekeeper. Preferably one who owns a bra."

Claire scanned the table to see what had become of that sugar bowl. "And my first project?"

"The kitchen, of course." Fran nodded to the room beyond the breakfast nook.

It was a fine enough kitchen as far as Claire could tell, a hell of a lot better than her cut-out closet in Prague. It had a Viking range, a side-by-side refrigerator faced with the same blond oak of which the custom cabinets were made and a large butcher-block counter in its center. The white Corian counters and pale, pale, lemon yellow walls made it feel light and airy.

"What's wrong with it?"

"It's hideous. Yellow walls and blond oak. Please. I've seen better in Florida and, trust me, that's saying something. You can't possibly live with that kitchen. Especially with the holidays coming up."

"Gee, Fran, I kind of like it. In the gray Cleveland winter it might be kind of nice."

"Pardon?" Fran furrowed her brows. "What gray Cleveland winter? Cleveland doesn't have gray winters. Its winters are blue sky and fluffy snows. Did you know that Cleveland has more sunny days per year than San Francisco?"

"Oh," said Claire, who wouldn't realize until about a week later, while lying in bed and recalling this conversation, the total absurdity of that statement.

"But what I'm saying is that the kitchen isn't really yours. It's . . ." And Fran dropped her voice so low that Claire strained to hear.

"What?"

"It's Boots's," Fran whispered, a knowing eyebrow arching on her forehead.

"So?"

"So this was exactly how she left it when she and John split."

"And he redid the rest of the house?"

"No. But for a woman a kitchen is her domain. It is where her family gathers, where children cut out their snowflakes and paste them on the refrigerator. The kitchen is where a woman creates her oeuvre."

"Ahhh." Claire sat back and caught Dawn frowning as though if anyone was creating any oeuvres in that kitchen it was she.

"Think of all the dinners she cooked for him there. The times he came home from work and found her at the stove."

"They were married briefly, Fran. They never had any children to cut out snowflakes. And, from the look of Boots, I doubt she's ever lifted so much as a spoon."

"OK." Fran plunked down her coffee. "Then think of all the times he came home from work, bent her over that antique butcher block and became Mr. Big Stuff."

Claire thought about it. "You have me there."

Fran patted her knee. "Good. Then let's go look at some designs. I've already made the appointments."

Chapter Seven

Looking at kitchen designs was not nearly as horrific as Claire had anticipated, though by the end of three hours of debating slate vs. soapstone vs. marble vs. Corian and maple vs. walnut vs. oak, she had become dizzy and didn't give a damn about wood grain or durability or trends. This irked Fran, who could argue for a double oven with the same passion Joan of Arc might have used to summon the troops at Orleans.

"It is impossible to live without a double oven," Fran declared. "Think of Thanksgiving. How could you ever cook a turkey and bake an oyster stew? It's impossible!"

Claire did not know Fran well enough to say that she hated oysters and had no intention of serving them alongside a turkey. That green bean casserole made with mushroom soup and French fried onions could easily be microwaved.

"I just think it's excessive," Claire said. "I'm not that much of a cook."

"You don't have to be. I don't cook and I've always had a double oven. I couldn't live without it. Though I suppose you could do what every one in Palm Beach does and order Thanksgiving dinner from Nieman Marcus. Their crab dip artichokes are divine."

"What?" said Claire, who thought Nieman Marcus was a department store.

"I give up." Fran threw up her hands. "Let's call in Jesus."

"Yes," agreed a kitchen designer at Le Cuisinart, the last boutique they had visited. "Jesus has all the answers."

Claire found this statement mind-bending, considering the complete lack of any religious yearnings in Hunting Hills, until she was informed that Jesus was actually Jesus Spanadopolous, a half Puerto Rican, half Greek interior designer who was incredibly in demand.

"Boots will call him for us," said Fran, flipping open her cell phone and pushing one number. "Jesus would do anything for Boots."

Claire tried to not let it bother her that her mother-in-law had John's ex-wife on speed dial.

The next stop in their day—not that Claire had anything to say about it—was the Garfield Country Club for lunch. Claire abhorred country clubs, an aversion born out her childhood. Though most people might pass off West Virginia as a poor, coal mining state, it actually possessed pockets of breathtaking wealth, including the Spring Valley Country Club near Webster Springs.

Claire hadn't been so fortunate as to have been a member of the club. Instead, she'd been a waitress relegated to only certain areas and the more shabby locker rooms. She'd spent two summers catering to the spoiled and neglected rich children who lounged around the pool ordering chocolate soda after chocolate soda, finishing only half of each, and tossing spitballs at her when she came by to retrieve the empties. It gave her the shivers to think about it.

"I don't know. I kind of have a thing about country clubs."

"You'll have to get over that, Claire. The Garfield is crucial to John's business and you'll be expected to do your fair share of entertaining there, like the other Hunting Hills wives."

The familiar feeling of dread swept over her as the driver careened the car into the long, circuitous driveway, past the club gates. As if by magic, Claire's hair instantly seemed all wrong and her outfit off. She was too dowdy for the Garfield, where the fall leaves were brighter orange, the sky was bluer and, yes, as clichéd as it sounded, the grass was greener.

Golf carts carrying men in sweaters and plaid pants zipped past them. Fran waved at one, which was bizarre, as she must have realized that their windows were tinted and no one could see inside.

"That's Harry Harleston," she said eagerly. "I haven't seen him in two years. He's dropped a lot of weight. Must be his new wife, Dorie. She's a tyrant."

"How often do you come back to Hunting Hills?" Claire had been dying to know, but had been too afraid to ask in case the answer was, "every other week."

"About three times a year. I miss it. I miss my friends, though Gordon could care less. That's why we don't keep a place here. Fortunately, John has lots of space."

"Yes," said Claire. "Fortunately."

The driver let them off at the entrance where young men in navy blazers and khakis, who looked like they should have been matriculating from Phillips Andover instead of opening car doors, greeted Fran enthusiastically. Fran nodded at them stiffly and proceeded up the stairs under the yellow and white Garfield Club awning, stopping in shock when she turned into the restaurant.

"Do you see that?" Fran said.

Claire squinted, not knowing exactly what she was looking for. A rude waiter? An irate luncheoner? A crazed hijacker stealing ice water and white rolls?

"Poor Patty Cox." Fran clucked at the sight of a laughing middle-aged woman in a long black skirt and white silk blouse, chatting up a man at the hostess stand. "That's so sad."

"What's so sad?"

"What do you mean?" Fran's hammerhead shark eyes were wide. "She's a *hostess*."

This must have been a tragic misfortune because as soon as Patty spied Fran she went rigid, lifted her chin nobly and held out her hand in determined greeting. "Fran. You look terrific."

Fran murmured sympathy as though Patty, poor Patty was dying from something dreadful, malaria or rabies. "What happened?"

Patty shrugged. "He left me. Simple as that. Ran off with his nurse to get married in Fiji. Isn't that just so trite?"

"Unbelievable."

"High and dry too. Not a penny in the till."

"No!" Fran put her hand to her chest. "He couldn't have. But how?"

"Ask his stockbroker. I suppose if I wanted to hire Roy Phelps for five hundred dollars an hour I could get some of it back, but funny enough, *he* got first dibs on Phelps too."

Claire stood politely by, resisting the urge to ask who was Roy Phelps and how a stockbroker could keep Patty from her rightful alimony.

"Patty, this is Claire. John's new wife." Fran pulled Claire to them. "They eloped in Prague. Isn't that romantic?"

The terms *new wife* and *elope* were not what Claire would have chosen considering the circumstances. It caused Claire to wince and Patty to grimace and gush stiff formalities as she led them to a table overlooking the tennis courts.

"Doesn't that beat all," Fran said as soon as they were seated at the white-linen-covered table. "Patty Cox. A hostess."

Claire suspected that this news bulletin, as well as similar bulletins, was what brought Fran to the club in the first place. Though she hadn't expected quite a windfall.

"I mean, I knew they were having problems. Ben Cox always was a dog, like most heart surgeons. Egomaniacs every one of them. Has to do with the sacrifices they make to get through training, not to mention the competition and then that everyone treats them like gods once they do their first simple transplant. At New Year's parties he was the worst. Patty caught him in the closet with Mira Dorset and Grace Greene all the time."

"Hmmm." Claire looked out the window at the women with sinewy shoulders lobbing tennis balls. For the record, it was Tuesday at noon and Claire doubted very much either of them was on a work lunch break.

"You know where they live, don't you? The Coxes," Fran asked.

"Not exactly. I've only been here a week."

"The Anderson estate on Essex Hill. It's on the register." Fran bit one of her neatly manicured nails dreamily. "I wonder who's going to take that over now. I can't imagine Patty just letting him have it without a fight. And what about the boys? Four of them. Two in college."

"I met them the other day." Claire nodded to two tennis players in the far court, both fabulously in shape and powerful hitters.

"That's Marti Swan and Karen Highsmith. My two favorite girls, next to Boots." Fran waved at them furiously. "John could have gotten together with any one of them and I'd been over the moon."

Claire let that go too. "I thought Marti's last name was Denton."

"It is." Fran motioned for a waitress. "Marti married Jim Denton, a total cipher if you ask me. And of course Karen is married to Bob Goss. He took over Goss Outdoor Outfitters and has skyrocketed it to places his father never imagined. Saved it from tanking, in fact." Fran scratched off a quick note and handed it to the waitress. "You don't mind if I invite them to join us, do you?"

"Not at all."

As luck would have it, Fran had excused herself to go to the bathroom when Marti and Karen, breathless and red faced, fit and perspiring, arrived still in their tennis whites, bottled waters aloft. "Where's Fran?" asked Marti, tendrils of golden hair pasted to her forehead.

"In the loo," Claire said. Turning to the other one, the earthy one, she said, "You're Karen, right?"

"Hmmhmm," Karen was too busy downing water to stop and say, "Yes."

It surprised Claire that, despite their prep school backgrounds and society coaching, Hunting Hills women like Karen managed to be so rude as to not introduce themselves. She suspected that this was more of put-down than an oversight.

"Isn't Fran a gas?" Marti pulled out a cane chair. "I absolutely adore her."

"You'd never know she's eighty," added Karen, done with her water. "That's the value of keeping fit."

"You must work out, don't you?" Marti asked Claire, though her tone of voice implied doubt.

Claire repositioned her butter knife which bore alarming signs of actual use. "Not much. I didn't have a car so I walked everywhere in Prague. And in the refugee camps, of course, you worked out by doing so much manual labor."

Karen gripped Claire's arm earnestly. "Boots told me you did that. How was it? It sounds so fulfilling."

Fulfilling? Was it fulfilling to see children die the quiet, desperate death of dehydration? To see men with soulless eyes roam the fields of mud and filth as babies cried from hunger and cold while their mothers, too weak to offer nourishment, futilely rocked them back and forth? To see prostitution take over as an underground economy and bartering replace charity?

"It pretty much sucked. I still have nightmares."

"Really?" said Karen. "That's odd. I wonder why?"

"You should see Barry," Marti suggested. "I used to have nightmares that I was a giant sea turtle constantly laying eggs and he took care of that."

"Was it dirty?" Karen was trying her best. You had to give her that.

"Awful. And there was rampant diarrhea and no water."

"Did you see people die?"

"Too many." Claire was glad to tell the story in her never ending hope to raise awareness about the camp, which still existed, though you wouldn't know that from reading the newspapers. "Once there was the most loving little boy. He was about three . . ."

"What are you girls buzzing about?" Fran was back, a fresh coat of apple red on her lips.

"The refugee camp where Claire volunteered," Karen said. "Have you heard about what that was like, Fran? Claire saw people die."

"No!" Fran said, sitting down. "Hold on. Have you heard about Patty Cox?"

"I *know,*" hissed Marti, bending close to Fran. "He just dumped her for a twenty-eight-year-old nurse."

"I didn't think doctors did that any more," Karen said. "I thought they behaved themselves. All those ethics courses in med school."

"And he left her broke." Fran shook her head. "Now she's working as a hostess."

"I'd die if Denton ever did that to me," Marti said. "To have to work as a hostess."

"Denton wouldn't do that. He's not the type," Karen said.

"That's what we used to say about Ben Cox," Fran pointed out. "He might fool around, but he wouldn't leave. And her with two children going through college. It is the worst story I've ever heard."

"Yes," agreed Karen and Marti mutually. "Did you hear about Julie and Chris?"

And as the women moved from Patty the hostess to Julie's decision to leave Chris for some lawyer at a firm with five names, as they eagerly gossiped about a bunch of other people Claire didn't know—and never would since no one bothered to introduce her—the worst story they ever heard slipped from their thoughts. Which was just fine by them.

Chapter Eight

It was decided that after lunch Marti would take Claire to the Board and Basket for kitchen quick fixes and that the following day Karen would take her to the Holly School's famous fall bulb and kitchen herb sale fund-raiser.

These were Fran's orders, not offers, and Claire, who felt like she had been strapped to a roller-coaster, gave up and went with the flow.

On the way to Board and Basket in Marti's Audi Quattro, Marti bombarded Claire with a list of "dos" and "don'ts." There were so many that Claire had to fight her instinctive urge to write them down.

> DO: Get your hair done at Salon, Salon in Haywire Falls, but not color. "Reservations":—not appointments—should be made weeks in advance with Bill, a New York–trained stylist with a deceptively simple name—and you should aim to be added to his Palm Pilot schedule. (His "secretary" Sherry would do it, if she approved.)

DO NOT: Miss a "reservation" with Bill since that could put you on his shit list and he would end up snubbing you for the entire holiday season, Thanksgiving through New Year's.

DO: Get on one of the "choice committees and charities": so that you can contribute to society. Most of the good ones—the art museum, the children's museum, don't even ask about the Cleveland Clinic—have been closed out. However, people are always making faux pas—not inviting so and so to join them on vacation, leaving them off the list of a particularly fun party, not including their kid in a camping trip—so opportunities to worm your way in do arise periodically.

DO NOT: Miss Betsy and Doug Klein's annual "pajama party," which used to be a kick when everyone was in their twenties and seeing Scott Clellan in his boxers was a thrill, but now, with everyone hitting mid-forties, was a total drag. Failure to show up could result in Claire suffering an almost irrecoverable social setback.

DO: Get a personal trainer. Joriko—half Japanese, half Swedish—was the one Karen recommended though, alone in the Quattro, Marti confessed that he gave her the willies when he slipped his hands down her yoga tights.

DO NOT: Go to lunch with Alex Danes because Alex Danes is part of Hunting Hills "horsey set" and, besides whinnying instead of laughing, will bore you to death with equestrian minutia that will have you ordering triple Bloody Marys before noon.

DO: Beware of the Hunting Hills Triathlon—a manicure appointment, yoga class and therapy session scheduled back to back. Not recommended for the inexperienced. Marti, who was experienced, executed the Hunting Hills Triathlon every Wednesday and even she had barely enough energy to make dinner reservations by evening.

DO NOT: Get yourself alone in a room with Kit Vickers's husband Val of the Unpronounceable Ethnic Last Name as he is a lecherous drunk who, when not getting his wife knocked up, is trying to lay anything else with two breasts and two legs and even on those details he's willing to compromise.

DO: Hire preeminent attorney—and former county prosecutor—Roy Phelps should you or any of your loved ones run afoul of the law. Roy could clear up any legal mess—from traffic tickets to drunken driving and more—with one phone call.

"Does this happen often?" Claire asked, glad to know at last who this Roy Phelps was. "That people in Hunting Hills get arrested."

"Oh, we don't get arrested. That's the whole point behind Roy," Marti answered.

Claire was about to pursue this when they stopped in the quaintest neighborhood she'd ever seen outside a Norman Rockwell print. Gingerbread shops lined a cobblestone street decorated with wrought iron benches and planters bursting with yellow and maroon mums and purple sage. Trim mothers just like Marti and Karen, a few pushing NASA-engineered baby strollers, exuded healthy maternity. It was the kind of world that you suddenly, desperately wanted to be part of. That is if you could come up to snuff, which of course you couldn't so why did you even ask?

"Where are we?" Claire asked.

"Haywire Falls." Marti got out of the Quattro. "And, yes, that's the real name of the town, if you can believe it. It's named after Randolph Haywire, its founder. See, there are the falls."

Sure enough, as if the town couldn't be any more charming, churning waterfalls cascaded over boulders and into a crystal clear river that ran straight under a bridge in the middle of this fairy-tale town. Flowing willows shed their tiny, browning leaves into the water as the hanging flower baskets on the bridge looked on. Wood smoke tinged the autumn air, adding to the feel of a cozy New England village though they were smack in middle of Ohio.

This was a place where people listened to classical music and NPR and took their dimple-cheeked children to formal dance school, Claire thought. They had fireplaces in their paneled home libraries and Ivy League diplomas on their walls. Not just any Ivy—Dartmouth and Yale—hardy institutions where athleticism and the capacity for eternal bon vivant were equally prized as was the pursuit of knowledge. The atmosphere here was so foreign to Claire's sense of self, to her Mudville upbringing of meatloaf and discount warehouses, that she'd completely forgotten she had rights to this fantasy now, as John Harding's wife.

Marti stepped onto the scrubbed sidewalk. "When we were growing up in Hunting Hills, Haywire Falls was the only place to shop. Now there's Beachwood Place with Saks and Heritage Village. Higbee's used to be downtown in Cleveland, but it's gone now."

"That's John's whole point about the need to redevelop the inner city," Claire said. "That's what he hopes to do with this latest project, build retail so that business will move back from the suburbs."

This is getting boring, Marti thought, though she said, "It's sad, isn't it? It used to be that all the men like my father worked downtown. Now our husbands are stuck in either that office park or this office park. All of them right near Beachwood Place. And they don't even shop."

Claire felt an obligation to clarify John's position, to impress upon Marti the nobility of his mission to save Cleveland proper. However, as soon as she entered Board and Basket all serious sociological thoughts withered in the bliss of glistening Domestic Decadence.

Martha Stewart Claire was not. Still, even Martha Stewart's cellmate would have been mesmerized by the quality forged pots and pans promising evenly baked pies and creamy béchamel sauces. There were displays of white Cuisinarts and stainless-steel cappuccino makers and rugged French cutlery and whisks so small Claire couldn't conceive what they could be used for.

There were wicker picnic baskets brimming with red and white gingham napkins, marble wine chillers, fresh grapes and imported cheeses. Polished wooden cutting boards—too good to cut on—hung like artwork, their dark and light pieces sanded together. Thick ceramic white baking wear along with a huge selection of wines and crackers and stuffed everything—olives, artichoke hearts, figs—made Claire want to throw a Tuscan feast. On top of that, the whole store was filled with a heady perfume of garlic, lavender and rosewater.

It was inspiring, but also overwhelming. Where to begin?

"I love this stuff. Do you ever use it?" Marti held up a small bottle of *vinaigre de pomme,* which Claire quickly translated.

"Apple vinegar?" She checked the price. "Eight bucks! You can get apple vinegar in the grocery store for sixty cents."

"But this is soooo worth it." Marti placed the bottle in her basket. "I sprinkle it on watercress salads with pears and goat cheese. It's the only salad I make."

At that price, Claire thought, I'd sprinkle it on my wrist for a night on the town.

"This is what you need," Marti said, pointing to an eight-piece set of Mauviel copper cookwear. "Copper cooks everything evenly and it's French. I have them and I love them." Though she wasn't quite sure if she did. Have them, that was.

Claire checked the price, a whopping $979. "I can't buy these. John will kill me."

"No, that's where you're wrong. He'll love it." Marti waved over the boyish store clerk in a green apron to get a box. "The more you buy, the more your husband values you. Didn't you know? It's a Hunting Hills Wife Rule."

"Excuse me?'

Marti blushed. "It's nothing. A little joke Karen and Kit and Boots and I share. Hunting Hills Wives' rules. There's a whole list of them we cooked up one night. For example, one Hunting Hills wife rule is to always tell people you're reading quality literature, when you're actually swapping smut in book group."

"You have a book group?" For the first time since coming to Hunting Hills, Claire felt her despair begin to wane. Perhaps she had found an oasis in this desert after all.

"Boots runs it. Right now we're not open to new members. So, so sorry." Marti reached for a green jar of hot pepper jelly. "See this?"

She held up the jelly. "This is like a staple at every Hunting Hills party. You could serve cracked crab and caviar tapenade and still your guests would demand the pepper jelly over the block of Philadelphia cream cheese. I swear to god I could make it in my sleep." Marti covered her eyes and pretended to dump jelly over the cream cheese. "You better take ten jars, for starters."

Claire took ten jars. "I think I have more than enough. I'm not really used to shopping like this, so . . ."

"Isn't this precious?" Marti gently placed a small figurine of a pewter bull in Claire's basket. "It's a Belfiore Giuseppe cocktail pick set. John will think it's a gas."

"I don't think so." Claire gave it back to her. "At three hundred dollars it's a bit above my budget."

"Budget? Hah! Who has a budget?"

Claire decided to get out of there before she lost all her savings.

At the counter a middle-aged woman with dimples and an affected German accent introduced herself as Helena (which she pronounced "Elluhna") and proceeded to gush over every item. The jelly was "delicious," an "excellent choice." The Mauviel copper pot set Claire would not regret. "The best there is!"

Claire, it turned out, had "exquisite taste." Who knew?

What amazed her even more was that after each pepper jar had been wrapped in purple tissue and figures jotted down on paper (not in the cash register), Helena smiled and pledged that the bounty would be delivered to her house by the time Claire returned from shopping. Claire was left holding out her Visa in confusion.

"No need," said Helena, waving it away as though the credit card was dirty Kleenex. She glanced over Claire's shoulders to Marti with a look that said, "Explain . . . it . . . to . . . her."

"It's on John's account," Marti whispered, tapping her watch. "See the time?"

It was almost four. "So?"

"So you never walk in the house around dinnertime with your arms loaded down with bags, as though you've been doing nothing all day but shopping."

Claire was confused. Wasn't she supposed to shop? "But I thought you said . . ."

"You have the store deliver your purchases the next day when John's at the office. That way only you and your housekeeper are the wiser. Weeks later when John gets the bill or the accountant or whomever, no one will care." Marti winked.

"Is that a rule too?"

"You bet. It's a biggie."

Helena backed her up. "It's true. Listen to Mrs. Denton. She is our favorite customer. For her, Helmudt undt I would do anything, she is such a *Prinzessin.*"

The last stop was the Rose Shop next door to Board and Basket. "A must visit," according to Marti, who then went on to rip apart the store's owner Rose as "too pushy" and its merchandise as "real snoozers."

"Then why shop there?" asked Claire.

"You have to," Marti said, stopping Claire outside the door, "because if you don't, Rose will bad-mouth you to every personal shopper in town. You are going to get a personal shopper, aren't you?" She gave Claire the quick one, two, three, an abbreviated version of the spectacles-testicles-pocket-and-watch sign of the cross Claire had made three times a day as a student at St. Mary's of the Holy Torture. "You should."

"Really?"

"Definitely. Somewhere in you is a unique style that a good personal shopper can recognize and accessorize."

"I see." Once upon a time her "unique style" had been her ability to eek out juicy information from tight-lipped sources and then write up a gripping story. But she supposed no one cared about that in Hunting Hills.

"My personal shopper visits me twice a season, prunes my closet, and when she goes on vacation, like to Beverly Hills or Palm Beach or whatever, sends me back outfits you just can't buy around here. In between, there's the Rose Shop."

The Rose Shop emanated the serene quiet of a forgotten era. Its blue carpet and even paler blue walls, the raised dais and brocade love seat for viewing fashion models, held the aura of an Audrey Hepburn movie. As did the white silk padded hangers on which every dress, suit, blouse and gown hung, protected by a thick plastic bag. Marti rattled off the list of its better designers. Armani. Coco. Loro Piana. Chanel.

Claire, clueless, nodded as though she understood.

Botoxed so that her skin gleamed with tightness, Rose approached Claire and Marti with what Claire sensed was fervent desperation due to battling the encroachment of aggressive corporate retail. Violent rap did not blare from hidden speakers at the Rose Shop. The two demure clerks behind the counter did not wear microphone headsets or gab on cell phones. No thongs were on display and, unlike Abercrombie &

Fitch, everyone's shirt was on. Claire surmised that Rose's only hope of survival lay in tirelessly serving the new generation of middle-aged women whose mothers had once considered this tiny domain to be their personal connection to Jacqueline Kennedy.

It was doubtful Rose would have paid any attention to Claire had she arrived alone. It was Marti who added the flair, making sure to deliberately announce that Claire was John Harding's bride.

"We're just browsing," Marti said, coyly. "I'm giving Claire a rundown."

But Rose would not be put off that easily.

"I have the perfect suit for you. Perhaps something Italian. Luciano Barbera." She stepped back and studied Claire, her two red arcs for eyebrows raised in expert assessment. "Yes, you have a beautiful figure. It is the kind of figure men love. Curvaceous. Very womanly."

If that was code, Claire wasn't complaining.

"Here." Rose rushed off to a far rack. Shoving aside several dresses and glancing again to pinpoint her size, Rose selected a nubby cream wool suit that even Claire recognized as a Chanel. In a million years, she never would have imagined herself in a Chanel. Where would she wear it?

"With your hair and complexion the color is perfect. Don't you think, Marti?"

"Hmmm," said Marti, who was flipping through a display of Hermès scarves.

"Or maybe this." Rose handed the suit to an assistant clerk and moved on to another cream that was not so nubby. "A St. John." Rose held it to her. "St. John never goes out of style."

Soon Claire was in the dressing room, the size of her bedroom in Prague, and smoothing down the Chanel. It fit her perfectly, accentuating her waist without emphasizing her hips. Even the lining was silky and well tailored. She was a different person in it, an elegant, sophisticated woman.

I could do this, she thought, critiquing her reflection in a whole new way. Rose had been right, her auburn hair had never been so shiny and her green eyes so dazzling as in the Chanel. She was someone else. Claire Harding—until now she hadn't even considered taking John's last name—and now she was boldly saying it out loud. *Mrs. Claire Harding*. "Mistress of the Jesus Spanadopolous kitchen!"

If she could just dump her crazy puritanical work ethic, she could enjoy this world. She could wear boutique clothes and fill her new large house with all the lovely knickknacks they'd seen in Board and Basket. She could entertain and be charming. Learn how to play tennis. Flirt with John during their many parties. Have fun! Why not? Didn't she deserve it? Hadn't she slaved all her life, working steadily since she was sixteen? Was it so bad to simply be someone's wife?

"Nice," said Marti, letting herself in.

Claire bowed her head shyly. She'd been caught pretending, just like a teenage girl in the school bathroom.

"You can wear it to the next bar mitzvah." Marti ran her finger across her throat, indicating that the suit was death.

"You mean this is a no?"

"Even if you were Coco Chanel I'd say it to your face."

Claire was disappointed because she really did like the suit.

"Trust me." Marti held up a large pink silk Chanel camellia pin that Rose had insisted Claire try. "And avoid these like public restrooms. I once went to a party where three women were wearing camellias pinned on different parts of their dresses so they wouldn't look like they'd worn the same flower. As though no one noticed."

Marti then attacked the St. John, hanging unworn. "Rose insists St. John is back in style but it'll never be back in unless you want to look like your mother."

Claire thought of her mother who used to cut her own hair in the bathroom mirror. "Not *my* mother. Maybe yours."

Marti thought of her mother splayed on a Garfield pool lounge in an orange linen dress, a cigarette in one hand, a martini in the other, her long, brown legs expertly oiled. "OK, not my mother either. But somebody's mother."

"Boots?" suggested Claire.

Marti laughed. "Yeah. You're right." Then, giving Claire another look, said, "Hey. That Chanel is growing on me. It works for you. Get it."

"You think?"

"Absolutely. It fits your style."

Claire checked her cuffs. "I can't find the price . . ."

"Forget the price. Price doesn't matter. OK? Actually, I saw a new Prada that Rose hasn't had before. I think I'll go try it on. You know what?"

"What?"

"You're a lot of fun."

Claire smiled, warmth rising within her. "You too and thanks for dragging me away from Fran. I was beginning to develop a complex. An I'm-not-Boots complex."

"Any time. I'm like a retail therapist. I even do house calls."

After Marti left, Claire let out a little squeal of happiness as she slipped out of the Chanel and back into her regular clothes which she vowed to burn as soon as she got home. She wanted a whole new wardrobe. A sexy, young wardrobe. She wanted to spend every hour of the next week stocking her closets with sweaters and skirts and dresses and even skinny jeans and shoes and handbags and . . . everything!

Starting tomorrow she would work out until she was drenched in sweat and she would not eat one single gram of carbohydrate. Then she would call those stylists Marti had recommended and she'd be on her way to perfection. Manicured nails and kicky hair. She'd hire a cook and perfect her backhand. John would be ecstatic.

What about your journalism career? You worked twenty years to be a solid reporter.

Screw it. Claire contemplated the camellia. Newspaper reporting was her old life, and what a cruddy, dirty, messy life it had been, full of foul editors and irate readers. Now she was opening a new chapter. A new genteel identity. The wife of John. Close friend of Karen and Marti. They really weren't so bad, those two. Marti particularly was a blast. It would be good to have girlfriends again.

What about contributing to society? What about making a difference?

There'd be plenty of ways to contribute to society. She could do what all the other wives did, raise money for causes she believed in—AIDS, homelessness, battered women. She would join boards and actually have an impact instead of just writing about *other* people having an impact.

So you're selling out. You're becoming one of them, one of the rich and privileged hypocrites who is happy to raise money for a shelter but wouldn't so much as shake the hand of a real homeless person.

"Stop it!" She slapped her hand over her mouth. It was bad enough that she'd been conducting a running conversation in her head. Now she was talking to herself out loud.

"Everything OK?" Rose asked from the other side of the dressing room door.

"Absolutely," responded Claire, already adopting Hunting Hills' favorite affirmative. She opened the door and handed Rose the Chanel. "I'll take it."

"Excellent choice."

At the counter, Claire remembered not to pull out her Visa or ask for a total. Instead she made small talk as Rose continued to push her toward more items. Perhaps a Chanel scarf? Or have you seen this outrageous bag?

"What about the camellia?" Rose asked.

Claire considered the big pink silk flower. So what that everyone had one just like it. It was pretty.

"It's in the dressing room," Claire said, "wait a minute."

And before Rose could insist on getting it herself, Claire opened the door and found the camellia lying on the floor, abandoned and slightly crumpled.

"I give it two months, tops," Marti said.

Claire picked up the flower and checked behind her. No one was there.

"No, I mean it. I'm not exaggerating."

Her voice floated over the partition of the dressing room. There was a *zip* and it clicked that Marti must be talking on her cell phone while trying on the Prada.

"Oh, she's, you know, *nice.* She's just kind of blah. Not John's type at all. I swear he must have been hypnotized or something to marry her so fast. My God, she asked the price of ev-er-y-thing. She's, like, money obsessed."

Claire twirled the camellia between her fingers unable to help herself from eavesdropping.

"I am. I *am* trying to be welcoming . . . Lookit, Lisa, I cancelled my entire afternoon to take her out to, gawd, Board and Basket. So don't get on my case that I'm being catty. How would you like to spend your day at the fucking Rose Shop? I'm only doing it for John and Fran. Yes, that's right, Fran. She's in town for a day and she took me aside at the Garfield club and asked me to *do something about her* before she embarrasses John."

A lump swelled in Claire's throat.

"No, I do not think she's pregnant, though, now that you mention it, she does have a bit of a pot belly."

The pregnant comment was the clincher. Claire's chest heaved and she felt like she was about to faint. She wasn't sure if she was angry or hurt or, worse, the awful, painful combination of both. She felt like a sucker, that was true, but it wasn't only that.

It was disgust. Disgust for Marti and Fran and the rest of them who were so incapable of seeing a human being beyond her dress size and designer label. Disgust that they could be so bovine shallow. She sighed, opened the door and took the camellia to Botoxed Rose who'd been fearful that the silk flower might not be a go.

Chapter Nine

"Help me."

"It's 5 a.m. I'm not helping anyone." Josie yawned into the phone. Six months pregnant, she was as sleepy as a hibernating bear and just as grumpy when awakened. "Even if you are my best friend in the whole world. Go back to bed, Claire, and call me in two hours. I don't have to get up until seven."

Claire checked the clock above the mantel in John's library. Without her contacts in it was hard to see, but she was sure she hadn't called that early. "It's seven thirty, you dope. Wake up!"

"Oh, shit." There was the sound of scrambling and then a crash as Josie's alarm clock fell to the floor. "My dufus of a husband turned if off to let me sleep in. If you hadn't called I'd be late for the second time this month."

"You can thank me later. Just as soon as you take ten minutes to convince me why I shouldn't pack up right now and go home to West Virginia to take care of you and your baby-to-be."

Josie waddled to the bathroom, the portable crooked against her ear. "Because the average IQ in this town is body temperature and because the last exciting thing that happened here was word that Miss Claire Stark done run off and got herself hitched to a multi-multi-millionaire in a fan-ceee mansion."

Claire smiled to herself. "See, this is why I miss you. I miss normal people who wear ripped jeans and clip coupons and listen to Journey and swear up a blue streak."

"What the fuck are you talking about? I don't fucking swear."

"And I'm not locked in a gilded cage."

"What's the matter, Cinderella? Don't tell me Prince Charming is turning into a rat."

"He's no rat." Claire stretched her bare legs. "I'm still madly in love. He's still madly in love. The roof is off the house what with all the steamy sex we have. He's wonderful."

"What is it then? From what you've been telling me everything seems like gravy. Gorgeous, devoted man. Soul mate. Great sex. Not slaving on a newspaper anymore. My only questions would be, where do I sign and can I borrow your pen?"

Claire got up and closed the door so snooping Fran wouldn't hear. "Here's a quick quiz. What's the worst story you've ever heard?"

"That would be tiny Peter Kimic who saw his mother raped and her throat cut by Serbian soldiers when he was three and clung to her body for twenty hours until the neighbors tore him off." Josie didn't have to think twice about that answer. Like Claire, she'd been haunted by him since they'd met the boy at the refugee camp. "Why?"

"According to the wives here, it would be becoming a country club hostess after your rich husband slash heart surgeon doctor leaves you for a younger woman, his nurse."

"Well, duh. You spend all those years eating dinner alone while he's doing his internships and residency and, hell yes, you want him to be around when he finally starts bringing in the dough."

"You're missing the point, Josie." Claire left the library and followed the aroma of coffee to the kitchen where Dawn had just brewed a fresh pot. "The point is that I'm surrounded by a bunch of women who don't have a clue of what the real world is like."

"Don't be so hard on them. Let me remind you that you had no idea about Peter Kimic either, until I dragged your sorry ass overseas after your big relationship with Eric Schmaltz blew up and then your mother died. Before that, you would have been clueless too."

That was true. In the kitchen Claire waited as Dawn poured herself a second cup, adjusted the volume on her iPod, and then poured one for Fran, leaving Claire with the dregs.

"Put yourself in the place of this hostess woman," Josie continued. "You know the only reason she's a hostess is because she probably got married pitifully young with the expectation that her rich doctor husband would take care of all her wants and needs. Then she reaches middle age without one single valuable skill except maybe knowing the secret formula for the exact numbers of appetizers per partygoer and suddenly she's cast out into the cold."

Again Josie was right. Claire imagined herself as Patty Cox but all she could see was a spoiled, aging debutante who hadn't had enough gumption to venture out into the real world and land an honest job when her husband pulled the plug.

"Go on. I need more."

"It's like being sold a bill of goods. Here you think that if you're a good wife and mother, that if you hold up your end of the bargain, you'll keep your job. She has kids, I bet."

"Four. Two in college, which adds to the so-called tragedy."

"Okay, so she raised the kids. Shows up at the office everyday, so to speak, and still this jerk fires her. It's not fair."

"But this isn't 1958, Josie." Claire had given the matter a lot of thought the night before and, finding that John had no interest in discussing it, had waited for the sun to rise to call her oldest childhood friend to hash it out. "This woman's probably fifteen years older than we are. Postfeminist liberation and all that. Who of our friends do you know that still expects men to take care of us?"

"None of my friends. We were too stupid to figure out that we didn't have to get up and work every day if we just kept ourselves pretty and hooked a wealthy breadwinner."

"Come on, Josie, you really don't think that."

"The hell I don't."

Claire found the sugar in the back of the pantry where Elena the cook must have hidden it from John. "Do you mean to tell me that if you had to do it all over again you wouldn't have become a nurse? That you wouldn't be doing what you loved?"

"Hey, nursing has been fine up until now. But what happens when the baby comes? If I didn't have my husband's salary to live on for a while, I'd be stressing out on finding good day care and then spending every minute of my forty-eight-hour shift wondering if my baby was OK, if she was being held enough and loved enough. It sucks, Claire. Our generation has been sold a lie. Be all you can be, they told us. They never told us to examine the fine print for the exact cost."

Claire thought about this. "I don't know."

"What do your wives in Hunting Hills think? They do think, don't they?"

"I'm not sure. We've never gotten to that level of conversation."

"Shit, girl, then what are you discussing? Floor wax?"

"Close. Kitchens. Apparently that's my first assignment, to redesign the kitchen left over from John's first wife. Yesterday I spent six hours looking at kitchens and kitchen-related products." Claire did not add the comment she'd overheard from Marti. She had chosen to wipe that off the slate entirely to save herself an aggravating bout of depression.

There was a sigh from Josie's end. "I can't believe it's that bad."

"It's that bad. In a few hours I'm going to the all-girls prep school for the annual fall bulb and kitchen herb fund-raiser. Never mind that it's being held at 10 a.m. on a Wednesday morning. It's assumed that the bulbs will be sold to mothers, not fathers, and it's assumed that the mothers don't have jobs."

"What if you show up drunk?" Josie often was of the opinion that a good blowout could shake up any bad situation.

"Don't think it hasn't crossed my mind. Drunk, singing, naked. You name it. If I could establish myself early on as outrageous, people might leave me alone."

"And John would start having second thoughts."

"There's that."

"Though you have to admit it would be fun, to show up at the all-girls prep school drunk and naked before lunch."

"Drunk and naked at an all-girl's prep school is always fun no matter what the time of day."

Dawn's right iPod bud had popped out and, eavesdropping, she grinned as she wiped the stainless-steel sink.

"Listen," Josie said, "I really do have to take a shower and get going or Dr. Dickhead is going to can my ass. In the meantime, try to cut everyone some slack. You don't need to be stark Claire Stark on her white horse twenty-four seven, you know?"

"Is that what I am?"

"Sometimes. No offense. Just remember, they're people too, Claire. They look perfect I'm sure with their bony hips and haute couture, but you have no idea what's in their closets."

"Armani," Claire said. "It's what all the best-dressed skeletons are wearing these days."

Chapter Ten

Marti examined a lineup of twenty-one Brooks Brothers all-cotton, button-down, long-sleeve shirts and tried to determine if her husband had come home the night before.

She stared at the sleeves of white, blue, royal blue, white with blue stripes, white with gray stripes and, most unfortunately, gray. For the life of her, she could not figure which Denton might have worn to work.

In the dry-cleaning basket, he'd left a white one, but she couldn't discern if it had been the same white one he'd worn the day before. And the suits in gray, charcoal, black and navy were all a blur. So were the business shoes. They were like his black socks, completely identical.

She sat on the beige upholstered dressing bench in the middle of Denton's beige carpeted walk-in closet with its beige walls and beige-colored granite tables and felt very beige. Where the hell was he?

Not that she was worried. Hunting Hills wives did not worry. To worry would imply that you had doubts, that your life was not being lived to perfection as, of course, it was.

Besides, Hunting Hills husbands were risk takers. They sank their cash into risky ventures. They risked their lives skiing double black diamonds during the annual family Christmas vacations in Colorado or driving ninety miles an hour, zipping their Mercedes in and out of traffic on I-271. They risked their marriage by getting blow jobs in the office. They could not come home to a Nervous Nellie, wringing her hands and squinting at the lipstick on her husband's collar. It would ruin all the fun.

On her fortieth birthday Marti had made a vow to be happy, upbeat, adventurous, guilt free and optimistic for ever more. Barry was a big believer in optimism. "Be optimistic and you'll have something optimistic to be about," he'd taught her. He called his philosophy "smooth sailing." As in, from now on everything will be "smooth sailing."

Marti repeated the phrase over and over—*smooth sailing*. A delicious feeling of calm descended from on high. Yes. That was much better.

At nine o'clock when there wasn't any more for her to do, when clearly Denton wasn't going to call her, Marti took a shower. She dressed in a pair of Chip and Pepper jeans and a Lacoste orange and blue striped rugby top that, together, made her look sixteen. She'd already worked out that morning with Todd, who came every other day to do weights, and she had an hour to kill until the Holly School Annual Fall Bulb Fund-raiser.

She went down to the kitchen and got out half a yogurt left over from yesterday. She'd really like a piece of toast, but Marti had banned all bread a year ago because of its hypoglycemic effects. Still, toast with butter would have been just the ticket on a chilly October morning.

At nine thirty she phoned Lisa to plan when they should leave for the Holly fund-raiser. Lisa was an Uber Bitch who sliced and diced their friends and enemies with an almost bloodthirsty lust for gossip. Despite that—or maybe, because of that—she was also Marti's absolutely dearest friend.

Today, Marti was going to seek Lisa's approval of her potential affair with John. It wasn't that Marti couldn't act on her own. She could. But if you want a girlfriend's support when a relationship goes bust, especially when it comes to a cutthroat friend like Lisa, it helps to get her endorsement beforehand.

Girlfriends are like your Security Council in the United Nations, Marti thought. Trustworthy, powerful and at your side in an emergency. (At Trinity, Marti had graduated cum laude with a degree in international relations, a major that had failed to land her a French diplomat husband as she'd been sure it would.)

"I need to talk to you," Marti told Lisa on the phone. "I have a big crisis."

"You think you've got a crisis, Eloise's class is setting up a cultural booth at Holly's fund-raiser today. She's supposed to bring a dish from her native land." Lisa sounded hyper. Too much Nomadd probably. "And you know how hard that is for her. We're Welsh. It's not like you have much of a culture when you're Welsh. What am I supposed to do for cultural day when we're Welsh?"

Nomadd. Definitely Nomadd.

Lisa had discovered Nomadd a few years after marrying Ty. Though normally an easy-going Midwestern businessman who wanted nothing more than a family, a house and a set of buddies to golf with, Ty panicked at the possibility of marrying someone like his mother, a frowzy woman who'd been given to flipping through soap operas while lying on the couch 24/7. This explained why, when he came home early one afternoon and found his new wife in a pair of sweats asleep on the couch, exhausted and spent from caring for a colicy baby, he'd hurled his briefcase across the living room and then threatened to divorce her on the spot.

That's when Lisa realized that if she, a poor girl from inner city Cleveland, was gloing to make it in the polished fairyland of Hunting Hills, if she was going to hang on to Ty, the richest and most successful man she'd met so far, and compete with the natives like Marti Denton and Karen Goss, then she was going to need extra help. Something to keep her thin, on top of things. Something that would make her permanently perky.

Naturally, her thoughts turned to speed.

Only it wasn't so easy for her as for the other mothers who could simply steal their children's medication. Eloise was still a baby and not a particularly hyper one at that. So just as she would later lead a trend by purchasing the first pair of Diego Della Valle pebble-soled driving loafers, Lisa's diagnosis of *Adult* Attention Deficit Disorder had all the other Hunting Hills wives clamoring for their own AADD stamp and its chemical cure, Nomadd. The possibility of pure amphetamines in adult form was utterly irresistible.

Overnight, Hunting Hills became a much more efficient community. Bills were paid on time, children were no longer late for school, fun-raising was up 200 percent and the wives had never been thinner. They had no need to eat, no desire, really, thanks to Nomadd.

Marti promised she'd be right over, before Lisa who, genetically speaking, was anything *but* Welsh, overdosed.

Slipping into her Dana Buchman quilted leather jacket, Marti grabbed the keys to her Audi and waved good-bye to Rachel, the Dentons' cleaning woman. Rachel was Amish and like all the other Amish carpenters and cleaning women in Hunting Hills, she was bused in daily from Middlefield as a white alternative to "other" domestic help. "Other" domestic help, it was rumored, were prone to laziness and thievery, though it was not considered politically correct to say so out loud.

The Amish, who didn't shirk or steal because it was against their religion, arrived in a white van stuffed with men in long black beards who smelled of beef jerky and B.O. The women wore thin muslin bonnets and stared blankly as they passed the mansions, as though they weren't there at all.

The one problem with Rachel was that she was a technoaddict. She was obsessed with all things electronic, especially the washing machine and the dryer. Only the dishwasher made her nervous and she covered her ears when Marti ran the blender to crack ice.

Above all, Rachel loved the computer. She spent an hour every day on it, surfing the Web for info on her favorite TV obsession—*The Price Is Right.*

"Bye!" Marti called, waving to Rachel on the porch where she was shaking out the dog's bed.

Rachel nodded and then went back to her cell phone conversation. She was also totally addicted to her cell. It was one of the few approved electronic devices permitted back on the farm.

For the heck of it, Marti started her Audi, pulled halfway down the driveway and stopped. As she had expected, the blue of the downstairs television appeared in her living room. That was Rachel's other secret vice, TV. If Denton knew that Rachel spent at least two hours a day watching the tube, he'd have her fired.

But Denton wasn't around during the day. Denton never was around anymore. So as far as Marti was concerned, Rachel could watch all the game shows she wanted.

Likewise, Marti was within her rights to sleep with John Harding, to have a wild, public affair with him, so that Denton would, finally, have to start showing up for dinner.

Chapter Eleven

Lisa did not look nearly as hyper as she'd sounded on the phone when Marti found her repotting purple mums on her slate patio. Her brown hair flowed long and straight and she was fabulous in a pair of skinny jeans and a mysteriously nondescript white T-shirt. Was it Gucci? Chanel? It was going to drive Marti nuts until she knew, which of course she never would.

Lisa was one of *those* women. She refused to wear and tell.

Today, Marti was particularly green with envy because Lisa had a husband and she didn't, at least not one who came home and stayed home. Plus, now that Lisa was on Nomadd, Ty treated Lisa like a goddess, buying her emerald earrings she casually mentioned liking, treating her to surprise weekends in New York City and vacations in Barbados. When they were together, Ty couldn't keep his hands off her, stroking her hair, patting her rear. They'd been married for ten years and acted like it had been ten minutes.

You had to admire her, Marti thought. When it came to finding and keeping a wealthy husband, Lisa née Obuchowski, the daughter of a foul-mouthed garbage worker from Glendale, had devised a foolproof system.

Before meeting Ty, she'd run up her credit cards to acquire the "must haves" for any Hunting Hills wife wannabe: a great body, a designer wardrobe and a job in public relations. Lisa would have preferred hospital fund-raising, but it was too competitive. In cities all over America, there are fund-raising twinkies: educated, attractive women in their twenties working in the endowment divisions of major medical centers, clawing and scratching for a chance at that double whammy of marital bliss—either a rich doctor or a rich benefactor. Lisa had enough smarts to know that she was out of their league.

She ended up landing a gig as a flak for L'Plaza, a small, posh mall in the heart of Cleveland's downtown, and made the most of it, immediately compiling a list of Cleveland's wealthiest bachelors. Most names she gathered by culling business articles in the *Cleveland Citizen* or society profiles in *Cleveland Magazine* or simply by asking around. Then she proposed that L'Plaza host a series of charitable events, including a bachelor fashion show and auction featuring clothes from the mall's boutiques. Something for everyone.

Bachelor auctions are standard stuff for Hunting Hills wives wannabes. Hospital fund-raising twinkies know all about dressing up in a subtle-but-seductive Adrienne Vittadini suit. About showing up unannounced at the bachelor's office with a seemingly innocent and yet flattering request that he model a Hugo Boss for charity. There is no surer way to get the personal cell number of the hottest guy in town than by asking for it in the war against Chronic Wasting Disease.

Lisa did the hospital twinkies one better.

She researched and discovered that Ty Renfrew, a newbie to the bachelor list, had recently been divorced from his socialite wife, Sandra. Of course Ty had not stooped to a messy court divorce. It had all been neatly arranged in his lawyer's office. However, the simple declaration filed in family court had been enough for Lisa who, as luck would have it, showed up at his house a year to the day after the official split.

What happened next could only be described as a wannabe's windfall. Lisa discovered Ty in his garage, in his Lexus with the car running and the door closed. This was no wonder as Sandra had made it a point to tell everyone in Hunting Hills that she'd dumped Ty because, well, because he was a sex dud. Or, as she so tactfully put it, because he "ran on low test gas."

So deflated had Ty been over his public humiliation that he'd opted to off himself on the anniversary of his divorce. When Lisa found him half-conscious she knew her ship had come in. Pushing the 180-pound businessman aside, she backed the car out to the fresh air, gave him mouth to mouth and called a local doctor who specialized in being discreet. No 911 for her.

A few weeks later, she turned Ty on to a prototype of Viagra and allowed him to impregnate her on their first try. Never again was a disparaging word spoken in Hunting Hills about Ty Renfrew's virility. He couldn't marry her fast enough.

"Crisis over?" Marti asked, getting out and leaving her keys in the ignition.

Lisa waved a trowel, miraculously managing not to get so much as a spot of sphagnum moss on her. "I had a brainstorm. Zalika."

Zalika was one of Lisa's cooks, a big African woman whose husband taught at Case. Lisa used her once or twice a year for dinner parties. "Zalika cooks Welsh?"

"No. But that doesn't matter. She has a culture." Lisa stuck the trowel in the pot. "And a microwave."

"That's cheating."

"No, it's not. All the mothers are doing it. I was late getting on board. I really wanted Britta, but that conniving bitch Marcie Delvecchio had already roped her into making Swedish meatballs and Anka's making borscht for the Williamses. It's just like them to snag Anka, even though they know full well that I hired her first."

Not for nothing was Lisa referred to as the Uber Bitch.

"Thank god Zalika had some *nyama choma* in the freezer. Remember? I served it last New Year's."

Marti didn't remember but she lied and said it was absolutely awesome. That was another Hunting Hills rule: Always Proclaim Everything Terrific!

They got in Lisa's Lexus 470 and headed for Holly. During the entire five mile trip through quiet Hunting Hills streets, Lisa kept the speedometer at an average of fifty even though the posted max was forty. Nomadd again.

"Have you finished the book for book group?" Lisa asked. "It's not too bad, though the middle was slow."

"I'm almost done." They were reading *Jane Eyre,* part of their books-we-should-have-read-in-college-but-we-partied-too-much-instead series. After *Jane Eyre* they'd be back to their usual erotica. First up, *100 Strokes of the Brush Before Bed.* It bordered on child porn because it supposedly had been written by a seventeen-year-old girl, but it was considered acceptable as the book was Italian and, therefore, *tres avant-garde*.

Though Marti, like all the wives, preferred the smuttiest books they could find, she'd been pleasantly surprised by how much she was enjoying *Jane Eyre*. She felt especially sympathetic toward the madwoman in the attic, the Creole "drunkard" Bertha Mason. As a sophomore taking Introduction to English Fem Lit at Trinity, her heart had gone out to Jane. Yet Jane now seemed like such a manipulative simpleton. What woman with half a brain would buy the line that a man as rich and handsome as Mr. Rochester would still be single?

"So what's your big issue?" Lisa shouted, now whizzing through intersections and past stop signs. There were no traffic lights in Hunting Hills. Hunting Hills hadn't come to that, though it had come to lots of fender benders.

"Denton's gone missing again," Marti said. "I think. I'm not too sure."

Lisa checked her blinding white teeth in the rearview as her right tire jumped a curb and nearly nicked a fire hydrant. "Focus, Marti. Be specific. What do you mean, missing?"

"Missing like I don't know if he's been home." Marti gripped the door handle. Maybe she should offer to drive on the way back.

"Did he leave one of his Post-its?"

"No."

"When was the last time you spoke?" Lisa rubbed her index finger across her gums. The speedometer was sixty-five. Sixty-five in a thirty-five-mile-an-hour zone.

"Last night. He came into bed and kissed me on the cheek." She bit a nail, uncertain. "Or maybe it was a dream."

For no reason in particular Lisa slowed the SUV to an acceptable speed and stared out the window.

Marti followed her gaze, searching for a cop. The three-man Hunting Hills police force rarely pulled over its own residents. Mostly they patrolled to keep out the riff as well as the raff. Still, perhaps Lisa hadn't tipped them adequately last Christmas and now she was on their naughty list.

"What's wrong?"

"Nothing's wrong. I'm looking at Val. He's with the new baby, strolling it, has the beard thing going." Lisa sighed at the sight of Kit Vicker's husband with the Unpronounceable Ethnic Last Name, wheeling his fifth child on the street, as there were no sidewalks in Hunting Hills. "Sensitive new dad studs. Is there anything sweeter in the whole world?"

Marti was tempted to slap some sense into her. "You ninny. Val will sleep with anyone and anything. It's not like he's off the shelf."

"Yes he is. Whenever Kit gives birth, for six months he's out of commission. He becomes all loyal and domestic and soooo sexy." Lisa rubbed her arms. "Just gives me the chills how cute he is. Look, he's rolling back the quilt and kissing her." She lowered the window and waved.

Val, his jet hair so long it curled at the nape of his neck, his black eyes glittering and bright, blew her a kiss too. Despite Kit's efforts to squeeze Val into a suit and get him a job "cold calling" at Ty's commercial real estate firm, her Italian-born husband rarely put in a full day of work. He was often seen wandering around Hunting Hills biking or reading while walking and smoking or snoozing by their swimming pool.

This, he once explained to Marti, was the European way. European men had no difficulty living off their wives' trust funds, unlike the American men of Hunting Hills who required both office and salaries as props or, as Val called them, "hang-ups"—and very foolish ones at that.

"He's eating through Kit's family money," Marti said. "He has no pride."

"Kit's family money"—(rubber/Akron)—"is all you can eat. He'll never finish it." Lisa licked her lips. "Is your mouth dry? My mouth's dry. We should go to Starbucks right now."

Marti reminded her about cultural day and the fund-raiser at her daughter's school.

"Oh, right. Holly." Lisa shifted into drive. "I've been getting distracted lately. Maybe I should up my medication. Do you think I should up my medication?"

"No." Marti wanted to get through this Denton business and segue into John and whether, being an ignored wife and all, she was finally free to let John have his way with her. "John," she began, until Lisa interrupted her again.

"So is John's new wife really a frump like you said? Or is she just very maternal? That's the way Boots put it, that John clearly went for Claire because Fran couldn't mother worth shit."

"Kind of." Marti hoped Lisa's foray into Claire gossip was the start of their John conversation. "She wants to work at the *Cleveland Citizen* as a reporter. She told everyone that, right in front of John. And she was serious."

"Oh, dear. How did he take it?"

"Bad, I think. You know John. Never blows up but simmers at a low boil."

"Hmm."

"She's all wrong for him. Very wrong."

Lisa cocked her head. "Then again, you're not entirely trustworthy when it comes to sizing up John's women. Are you?"

"What do you mean?" Marti grabbed the dashboard as Lisa cut in front of a FedEx truck.

"I mean, you and John have always had the hots for one another."

"We have not!" Marti acted shocked, though she was thrilled. At last they were getting to the good stuff. "John and I are friends and that's it."

"Don't play coy. You know how John feels about you. He finally came out and said so at my pool party last summer, that you were perfect for him and it was such a shame he was only getting around to realizing it."

That wasn't *exactly* what John had said, but Marti was savvy enough to know that if she had corrected her, Lisa's radar would have detected Marti's obsession and she never would have heard the end of it.

Lisa turned right onto Woodruff Road, one of the most beautiful streets in Hunting Hills. The ancient maples that lined it were just past peak, forming an autumnal canopy over the street.

"But that's water under the bridge, isn't it?" Marti said, throwing out one more line to make sure. "I mean, I'm married and now John's married. Case closed."

"Puhleeze. Ty's parents had affairs growing up and so did John's from what Boots told me." Lisa sipped a diet Red Bull from her cup holder. "For that matter, so did yours."

Marti had been thirteen, far away in Wa-ho-wa-ka, a wilderness camp in Canada's buggy lake district, the summer of her parents' sexual experimentation. She never had a clue until years later when she overheard two women gossiping in the Union Club ladies' room at the Assembly Ball, Hunting Hills' annual coming out party.

What Marti overheard was that in the summer of 1976, her mother, Kiki, had slipped off for a weekend with Arthur Cronin, the family lawyer and close friend since childhood, to see the Tall Ships sail into New York City Harbor. After her father, Herb, found out, he sought solace with Ginny, Arthur's wife. Solace he'd apparently been seeking regularly on Thursday nights during Arthur's Christ Church vestry meetings.

The significance of the vestry meeting trysts had not been lost on Marti. Even at a very young age she'd been aware of the resentment her father, a Jew, had felt about suppressing his lox and kreplach heritage for Kiki, who insisted their children be raised Episcopalian, including Christmas with all the trimmings.

Meanwhile, Kiki's explanation for the affair had been that "life is so much more difficult when you're a shiksa married to a Jew. I just wanted a lobster for once." Her mother's admonition against marrying a man like her father was how Marti came to marry her Assembly Ball date, a chinless former fellow Sunday school student named James Denton III who had no problem eating shellfish or decorating a Christmas tree as long as he wasn't expected to pitch in.

Other than Marti and Denton's marriage, the parental affairs had had little effect on the Swan and Cronin families. No one moved out, no one got divorced, not one plate was thrown. Kiki, a regal tower of bleached blond hair and leathery dark skin, took pride in this, in how civilized the couples remained. She continued to send Christmas cards to the Cronins and the two families often spent New Year's Eve together as well as other major celebrations. Marti remembered, vaguely, Kiki and Arthur doing a polite cha-cha on the Garfield dance floor during her wedding reception, Ginny and Herb smiling and shuffling next to them.

This was how affairs were conducted in Hunting Hills, how they'd always been conducted. Like country club dances, with husbands and wives switching and shuffling, yet always ending up in their air-locked luxury sedans, groggily ambling home together when the party was over.

"As long as you don't stray outside Hunting Hills, it's not really an affair. Think of it as taking your friendship with John up a notch." Lisa turned at the gate marked THE HOLLY SCHOOL. "Besides, it doesn't seem to me that Denton's being much of a husband. For all you know he already has a woman on the side. That's why he's never home."

"Really?" Marti tried to imagine Denton having an affair, rendezvousing at a hotel, tipping the bellhop and ripping the clothes off his mistress. She thought of him spouting corny clichés like, "My wife doesn't understand me," or "Marti never lets me do this at home." Of him having wild sex doggie style or in a hotel Jacuzzi and decided, nope. That wasn't her blue-suited, dental-floss-packing, Skittle-munching husband.

"I don't think he's having an affair," she said. "He's too Republican."

"Whatever. I get bored talking about Denton twenty-four seven."

At the entrance to the Lower Campus, a baby blue Chevy Caprice was parked with Zalika behind the steering wheel. Lisa pulled into the visitor's space, killed the engine, whipped off her Versace shades and gave Marti a meaningful look. Marti noticed that Lisa's pupils were tiny black dots.

"OK. Now that I've given you the green light, when are you going to get it on with John?"

Marti felt kind of busted, but she didn't let that bother her. "The only thing holding me back is that I don't want to hurt anyone. I don't want to open my family circle to bad karma." Another Barryism.

"Bad karma my ass." Lisa waved at Zalika, who was now out of the car, a foil-covered casserole in her hand. "If anything an affair will be good for you. A genuine growing experience that'll make you more magnanimous, a better wife and mother."

Lisa removed a paper from her purse. It said ELOISE RENFREW, THIRD GRADE HERITAGE: SWAHILI. "If you and John finally quench this thirst you have for one another, he'll be psychologically free to settle down and you'll stop being a middle-aged frustrated hausfrau."

"But . . ." It wasn't the sex she was after, Marti wanted to say. It was love and devotion. The way Ty was devoted to Lisa.

"You haven't kept yourself in shape, killing yourself to look like you did when you were in high school only to have your husband ignore you. You're forty-three. You're just hitting your sexual prime." She gripped Marti's arm earnestly. "Your body is *crying out* for physical attention, for god's sake. Answer it!"

My goodness, Marti thought, catching a glimpse of her smooth face and plucked brows, her youthful reflection in Lisa's heated side-view mirror. Her body *was* crying out for physical attention.

"Why don't you call him right now? Set up a date to meet him at the Heritage Village Starbucks." Lisa picked up her phone, scrolled through her address book and found John's office number, called his secretary who patched her into him right away.

"Here." Lisa handed her the phone. "Talk to him."

Marti wanted to object, but Lisa was already out of the car, retrieving the casserole and taping on the ELOISE RENFREW. THIRD GRADE. HERITAGE; SWAHILI sign. Then she went inside, carrying the African dish as proudly as if she were a member of the Kusu tribe herself.

Chapter Twelve

"I know what you're dying for," Karen said. "I know exactly how you feel."

"You do?" Claire stepped into Karen's boxy Mercedes SUV. It wasn't nearly as indulgent as she'd have expected a Mercedes SUV to be. For one thing she'd thought there would be leather. "What am I dying for?"

Karen gripped Claire's knee. "My kitchen."

"Your kitchen?"

"I know, I know. Everyone talks about it. How flighty Karen ripped out a gorgeous 1920s restaurant-equipped Marky Tart original and put in a complete environmentally safe, chemically free kitchen. It's OK. Let them talk. Generations from now when they're dying of respiratory illness and their grandchildren sprout fins, they'll wish they'd listened to me."

"Honestly. No one's mentioned your kitchen."

Karen pushed back a lock of her long black wavy hair which was loosely bunched in a ponytail low on her neck. Karen's hair was very intriguing in that the fine wisps of gray salted throughout it looked natural—as if she alone among the Hunting Hills women had eschewed coloring—yet they were so flattering and artistic that Claire decided they'd been professionally applied. Gray highlights. Was such a thing possible?

"Aren't you redoing your kitchen?" Karen asked.

"Fran wants me to. I was thinking . . ."

"Then let's go look at mine now. You know, I'm such a believer I feel like preaching the good news." Karen raised her hands off the steering wheel. "Alleluia. I have been saved from V.O.C.s."

"V.O.C.s."

"Volatile organic compounds. They're the worst."

In the seven-minute ride to Karen's secluded mansion, Claire learned more than she'd ever wanted to know about V.O.C.s, about the urea-formaldehyde glue used in particleboard that polluted the air and, according to Karen, was single-handedly responsible for the increased rates of asthma among children. "Though, really, who has particleboard these days? No one I know."

Claire was sure she'd grown up around particleboard and, suddenly, her breathing seemed a bit more labored.

"I'm telling you, the chemically free kitchen of today is like the lead paint scandal of the sixties. Before you know it, everyone's going to be throwing away anything that's glued or finished. Those varnishes are killing us all."

Claire padded stocking-footed (Karen had made her dump her shoes in the garage—too many germs) into Karen's immaculate Dutch blue and white kitchen with a walk-in pantry, large Sub Zero, wine cooler, computer area and bar even though, as Karen quickly pointed out, neither she nor Bob drank. At its heart was a massive Wedgewood-blue four-oven Aga cooker, which put pay to Fran's wimpy two-oven demands.

Claire said, breathing in easier now, that the kitchen air was indeed "very fresh." Possibly it was because nothing had ever been simmered, sautéed, fried, boiled, poached or baked in, on, or around the ten-thousand-dollar Aga.

"Bob hates clutter," Karen mused, wiping a smudge of nothing. "If everyone were smart they'd have a kitchen like this."

"I don't think," Claire said tentatively, "that everyone can *afford* a kitchen like this."

"Sure they can, if they make it a priority. Solid wood and single-slab granite are musts."

"Maybe you should write a letter to the Cleveland Housing Authority."

It had been meant as a joke, but Karen didn't take it that way. "Yes, maybe I should. Okey-dokey." She jotted a note to herself and stuck the Post-it with WRITE HOUSING AUTH. RE: VOC on the computer. "Want to see the rest of the house?"

The rest of the house took another half hour, and that was with a cursory popping of heads in and out of rooms. Claire could barely recall what she'd seen, aside from hygienic neatness and simple grandeur. It was the sense she had more than any particular design. The carpet beneath their feet was thickly padded and comfortable. The ceilings high and the doors solid core. Cut glass knobs. Real brass handles. Marble sinks and genuine mullioned windows. Every item was of quality.

And then there were the walls and walls of photos, mostly of the Goss family engaged in Vigorous Outdoor Activities. The Gosses at a tropical beach, Bob and Karen with their arms around each other, their two sons, Chip and Birch—Claire somehow managed to keep a straight face at that one—on surfboards, their sun-bleached hair tousled and salty. Bob and Karen in state-of-the-art Goss Outdoor Outfitters hiking paraphernalia climbing Mount Washington in New Hampshire where Chip was at Exeter. Bob and Karen and the boys white water rafting through the Grand Canyon, parasailing in Seattle, skiing in Vail.

Claire said, "I'm exhausted just looking at these."

"We have fun," said Karen, who had mastered the Hunting Hills understatement.

"How did you and Bob meet?" Claire had become fascinated by the women and how they were inversely beautiful to their husband's ugliness, Bob with his balding pate and stocky stature and glasses, being one such example.

"You know, I can't remember how Bob and I met." Karen squinted, thinking back. "We've always kind of known each other, or of each other. Then, the Christmas break I came back from Skidmore, I bumped into him at a party here in Cleveland. I'd just broken up with this jerk in college and Bob was so nice and polite in comparison. Though he did have this four season rule."

Claire studied the next picture. Bob and Karen and the boys deep sea fishing on an immaculate white boat on turquoise water. "Four season rule?"

"He said he wanted to see me in all four seasons to make sure I was sexy spring, summer, fall and winter. I invited him down to Key West for spring break, just so he could check me out in a bikini. I was worried because Martha Crew was also in the running and he'd spent a week with her on Cape Cod."

"But Bob chose you."

"I guess so because he proposed the following Christmas. Though, when I think back on it now, I bet that was the only reason I said yes."

Claire lifted her gaze from the photos.

"Because it was like I had won a prize and I had to accept. That never occurred to me before. Wow. And to think that I didn't even love him at the time."

Claire decided to change the subject before she heard any more personal confessions. "Does Chip like Exeter?" she asked brightly, not really caring one whit.

"No." Karen led the way to the greenhouse located off the kitchen.

"But Bob says that if Chip wants to get into Yale, which he does of course, then he's going to have to stand out from the Cleveland crowd so he can't go to Tate. That's why Bob arranged to have him sent to Zimbabwe last summer and to the Writer's Retreat in Vermont the summer before that, to flesh out his résumé."

They entered the humid and airy greenhouse which was packed with plants and smelled of deep, moist earth. It was a brilliant idea, the greenhouse. Just the ticket for chasing away the Cleveland blues.

"It hasn't been a picnic for Chip, giving up so much of his free time, and I worry about him traveling overseas with all the terrorism." Karen went directly to a wooden table that held palettes of bulbs and herbs. "But Bob says I mother him too much. If Chip were at home, he says, he'd be a nancy boy with me hovering around him. I don't think so because when Chip's on vacation he's out with his friends and barely spends five minutes with me. That's the thanks I get after breastfeeding him until he was three."

She held up a pot of kitchen herbs. "Mind giving me a hand with these? Every year I donate more and more and never think how I'm going to schlep them to Holly."

"What have you got here, Karen?" Claire studied a pot filled with long-stemmed greenery.

"This is an Aruba oriental lily, a chionodoxa, a Ziva paperwhite narcissus and some organic kitchen herbs. Lavender, basil, thyme and, what you're holding, oregano."

Claire reached out and touched the spiked leaves of the oregano. "That's not oregano, Karen. That's pot."

"Pot?" Karen blinked. "You mean marijuana?"

"Cannabis." Claire fought the impulse to burst out laughing. Perhaps this was Chip's other extra-curricular activity.

"Oh, how could I have been so stupid." Karen smacked her forehead. "Of course that's my sensi hash. I always get those two mixed up. Wait a sec, will you? I've got to get the oregano."

Claire was dying to dig a bit deeper into Karen, the perfect wife and mother with the THC loaded sensi hash stash, but on the way to Holly her cell phone rang and Karen insisted she answer it.

"It might be John."

It wasn't John, it was Eric Schmaltz, the *Cleveland Citizen*'s executive editor and her former flame from West Virginia. The number one guy she'd been trying to avoid since understanding how hurt John would be if she worked there. As she'd feared, Eric hadn't improved in the many years since their fling had ended. He seemed not to give a damn that she was married—newly married at that.

"Why aren't you in the newsroom right now undressing me with your beautiful eyes?" He was puffing on a cigar. Claire could tell by the way he was talking through clenched teeth.

"Because I'm on the way to the Holly School for the annual bulb and kitchen herb fund-raiser," she chirped cheerfully, so Karen, who was doing a poor job of pretending to be more interested in the autumn morning, wouldn't be the wiser.

"Would you like me to shoot you? Because that's what I'd want done to me if I was on the way to the Holly School fucking bulb and herb whatchamacallit."

"I'm looking forward to it," she lied.

Clunk. Clunk.

Claire flinched as Eric hit his receiver against something hard. "That's better. Now let's try this again. When are we getting together?"

"I'm afraid my schedule's packed. Seeing as how I've only been in town a week and as I'm *just married*."

"Don't give me this just married crap, Stark. That is, if you still call yourself Stark. You haven't gone over to the dark side, have you? You're not some creature called Mrs. Harding, are you?"

"No. I'm still Stark."

"Excellent. So, listen, I have a proposal and you can't say no because if you do I'll make it my personal mission to hound you day and night until you give in."

Claire braced herself.

"I have to be on your side of the tracks this afternoon. Don't ask why. Rest assured it's for something expensive and stupid and I figured that it would give me a chance to meet you on your turf. How about that hideous new mall they've built over there? What's its name? Heritage Village."

"Heritage Village? Don't know it."

"Ask one of your ladies at the bulb show. They probably have it programmed into their dashboard GPS. Meet me at three and I'll be out of your hair. You can't expect me to not want to see you, Claire. My god, think of those nights in the composing room when you stripped off . . ."

"At three." Claire was eager to cut him off before he recalled her youthful indiscretions on the paste-up boards. "And then you'll be out of my hair. Promise?"

"No. But three it is anyway."

"Where?"

"The Starbucks. You can't miss it. It's loaded with suburban housewives just like you."

Chapter Thirteen

Heritage Village was not so much a mall as an artificially created, yet upscale "lifestyle community" with a real working Main Street (complete with meters whose quarters went to charity), heated sidewalks and, thank heavens, valet parking. It was far enough away from Hunting Hills so as not to taint its quaintness, yet close enough that should a Hunting Hills wife have a last minute need for, oh, a Viking Butter Warmer, it was hers for a fifteen-minute drive and a ninety-five-dollar charge on her Visa.

Claire drove around and around the glorified shopping mall, completely confused by its layout until she gave up and parked the Avis rental Dodge Shadow behind Ann Taylor. She straightened her black wool pants and brushed off her matching jacket. She'd decided that looking professional might put Eric in his place and, to that end, chose a beige shell with the most unflattering cut and highest neck she could find.

Starbucks. Starbucks. There was one on every corner in America, right? Even on fake corners. She ran her finger down the list of shops and found it. Super, she was at the wrong end. She checked her watch. Five after three. Already late, as usual.

She did a quick march through what appeared to be a Disneyworld for shopaholics, past Crate and Barrel, Talbots Kids, Talbots Womens, Talbots Mens, Talbots Petites, Talbots Accessories and just plain Talbots. She inhaled the aroma of frying garlic from a dozen restaurants, past Le Gelateria, Janie and Jack and the huge Joseph Beth Bookstore feeling slightly guilty for not telling John what she was up to.

It wasn't a stretch to understand why John didn't want her working for the *Cleveland Citizen*. Never mind that Eric was her first real love, a heartthrob of such dynamic proportions in the *Wheeling Register* that the librarians in the newspaper morgue would fight each other to pull clips for him. He was witty and irreverent with the kind of Mick Jagger swagger that made women faint.

At the impressionable age of twenty-six, when a woman's thoughts turn to marriage, Claire had been roped into helping Eric with a detailed investigation into the county sheriff's department. Her job had been to sift through a decade of financial records searching for evidence that the sheriff—who drove a sixty-thousand-dollar car and took five vacations a year—had been siphoning money from the till. She'd found the proof, thanks in part to a very helpful ex-wife, and Eric spun gold out of her straw. Not only was he gorgeous but, dammit, he could write a mean sentence, too: a deadly combination for any woman who appreciated fine men and fine prose, though not necessarily in that order.

On their last night of copyediting the first series installment, Eric had insisted they celebrate with a drink, pulling out a very nice bottle of champagne from their editor's private office mini-fridge. Unaccustomed to real champagne or men who stole it from their editors, it didn't take long for the exhausted Claire to find herself in Eric's arms, his skilled lips sending shivers up her neck between murmuring seductive words about how great a reporter she was.

Their passionate affair lasted five weeks with Claire naively assuming that she had met the love of her life, that they would go off together like comic book characters, two dedicated journalists on a mission, unveiling corruption and raising babies. That she would be His Girl Friday.

Until she discovered that he already had a His Girl Friday. Eric's true love was a former Southern beauty queen and current White House staffer to whom he'd been engaged for a year and who—wouldn't you know—had been out of the country during the sheriff investigation. Eric's sheepish explanation to Claire was that, actually, they'd split before she went overseas for her job.

But when his fiancée returned from her goodwill mission to China, Eric broke Claire's heart with the news that "he was going to try to work it out with his ex," a line which Claire later discovered he'd used so often that it was penned on the men's room wall.

Humiliated, devastated, pissed, Claire was ready to take drastic action. Plans involving minor explosives were not excluded from her list of options. For years she was forced to face Eric every day as he first married, then divorced, the Southern beauty queen, after which he returned to relentlessly hitting on newsroom ingenues.

Claire was about to take another job in Chicago to get away from him when her mother received a diagnosis that would change both their lives. Cirrhosis of the liver. Claire ended up watching helplessly as her mother, a lifelong closet alcoholic, slipped into dementia while each of her organs—liver, kidney, spleen—clicked off slowly.

Dying from alcoholism is a fearsome way to shuffle off this mortal coil. The alcoholic is usually tormented by regrets and horrifying nightmares as the brain is inundated with toxins that a normally healthy liver would have removed. Claire was a fixture at her mother's bedside, calmly stroking those beloved wrinkled hands which had comforted her as a child and which, for self protection, were lashed to the bed. One night, after her mother had sunk into a coma, Claire quietly got up to go home for some well-deserved rest.

"Good night, Mom," she'd whispered, drained. "I love you."

She flicked off the light and heard a small voice.

"I love you too, Claire. Forever."

Claire turned to see her mother in the dim light smiling at her peacefully, all anxiety and torment gone from her face. A few minutes later her mother's heart stopped and Claire collapsed.

It was big-hearted Josie who rescued her friend from the depths of depression with a proposal that they blow out of West Virginia and go to Macedonia to volunteer at one of the newly established Bosnian refugee camps. Claire didn't exactly know where Macedonia was, not to mention the Stankovic camp, but she accepted anyway because neither was anywhere near Wheeling, West Virginia or Eric Schmaltz.

The last she saw of Eric was of him leaning over a college intern, a sweet-faced girl who'd been hired to write obits for a summer and whom Eric would eventually invite to share a bottle of champagne "borrowed" from their editor's office.

"You're thinking what a scoundrel I was. I can tell it from here."

Claire looked up to find Eric waiting for her, leaning against the Starbucks with a manila folder tucked under his arm. Though she was married and in love with her husband, she was startled to find that the sight of Eric still made her pulse race.

He hadn't changed much despite the years of interns and champagne. His brown hair was not as long, more styled, with touches of gray here and there. He wore rimless glasses which only made him appear more dignified than he really was. He was fit and cocky and grinning. In short, he was, as usual, dead sexy.

"Fuck you," she said, glad to get it out of her. "I was too polite to say that when I should have."

"Yet, not too polite to screw me in paste-up." He shrugged. "Go figure."

Quick. She'd forgotten how quick he was. "Before we talk you should know that I've made up my mind." She clenched and unclenched her fists for strength, trying to remember the exact speech she'd rehearsed over and over. "I can't write for you. I know this is not what I indicated on the telephone from Prague and for that I'm sorry. But after considering where I am and what John wants, I don't think the *Cleveland Citizen* is the place for me right now."

Eric said nothing for a few minutes. "What's the matter, darling? Still in love with the old Schmaltz?" He made exaggerated goo-goo eyes at her and Claire held back the urge to slap him.

"Hardly."

"Then perhaps you're worried that I'll be too much of a temptation and, of course, you're right. I am still loaded with charm."

"That's it." She turned to go but Eric caught her arm.

"I'm sorry. I should know better than to tease a newlywed. Come on. Have a cup of coffee with me at least. What harm has a cup of coffee ever done anyone?"

She threw up her hands. He was impossible and she was about to really tell him off when the door to Starbucks opened and she stopped dead short. There was John, hand in pocket, reading the *Wall Street Journal* in line.

"Shit," she said, yanking back Eric. "We have to go someplace else."

"Why?"

"The line's too long."

Eric glanced over her shoulder. "Yeah, you're right. How about we go up the so-called street to Joseph Beth Books. Won't be half as crowded. Much nicer atmosphere."

"I really shouldn't be having coffee at all," she said as Eric took her by the arm. "There's no point in it."

"Oh, would you cut it out already. Jesus, Claire, what happened between us was over a decade ago. The Berlin wall was still up. Bush was in office . . . On second thought. By the way, have I told you that you look great?" He kissed her on the cheek. "You've only blossomed with age. Like wine or blue cheese."

Claire tried very, very hard not to smile. Eric Schmaltz could be a two-timing bastard. A lothario. But like many two-timing bastards and lotharios, he could be irresistibly charming.

She followed him through the expansive bookstore to the back café. This was a trend she'd missed while living in Prague, the transformation of bookstores from places where you just bought books to majestic centers of CDs, DVDs, couches and fresh-ground Colombian.

They stood in line squinting at the coffee choices. Latte. Cream. No Cream. Milk. Two Percent. Skim. Soy. Cappuccino. Decaf. Caf. Half caf. Claire was too woozy from it all to make a choice so she let Eric choose for her, a role he was only too glad to assume.

"OK, so what's the deal?" He ripped open a brown unrefined sugar packet and dumped it in the coffee. "John Harding can't stand the *CC* because it's anti-business and anti-Cleveland and filled with lefties and Democrats and he wants his delicate wee wifey to stay home. Is that it?"

"Stuff it." She dumped in half-and-half. "It's more like this: that your sloppy reporters screwed over his father with their abominable fact checking, ruined him until he was just a shell of his former self and even caused his death."

"Please. Don't hold back."

"I mean it, Eric. I checked John's allegations myself by talking to the guy who used to have your job. Sam Winship. He said that two rookies, straight out of J school, concocted facts out of nothing in order to get an above-the-fold, front-page story. That's why Winship eventually fired them."

"But you have to admit that there was a smidgeon of truth there, Claire. Hardco Enterprises tried to bribe a couple of politicians to expedite approval on their Hough Redevelopment Project. That's been proven."

She pointed a finger at him. "Hold on. It was true that Hugh Harding's partner offered the bribe without Hugh's knowledge. Hugh Harding didn't operate that way and he severed ties with the partner as soon as he learned about it."

"Before my time, cookie. You can't crucify me for my paper's sins."

"No. But I can respect John's pain enough to stay away from your rag and work elsewhere." Claire felt hot and her voice must have been raised because two women reaching for the sugar packets backed off. "Plus, has it ever occurred to you to do a story about how John's company is investing in small, high-risk entrepreneurs who are rebuilding the inner city? He's not supporting Wal-Mart or liquor stores. He's backing groceries."

"Excuse me. Did I just hear you say he's packing groceries?"

She glared at him. "You heard what I said."

"Bad joke. Listen, Claire, I have to tell you you're right. I apologize." Either Eric Schmaltz was being sincere—a rarity—or he had perfected his acting skills because he came off as truly contrite.

"It's not me you need to apologize to. It's John." she pouted.

"Good idea. I'll do that."

"Really?"

"Sure. Let's sit down and maybe we can sort this out so we can be friends again." He found a couch hidden behind PERSONAL DEVELOPMENT which offered quiet privacy. Eric slid his arm along the back.

Claire sipped her latte, trying to regain her prior outrage which Eric had diffused so quickly. He'd always had an uncanny knack for doing that, whether it was in calming the ballistic girlfriends who'd just caught him in bed with another woman, or irate sources who were angry that he'd uncovered hidden lies. She could see why he'd been promoted to executive editor.

"I have to tell you that when I got your letter saying that you were moving here to get married, I was thrilled. Not about the marriage part. That sucked. I totally disagreed with that. No, I'm talking about the you moving here part. I can't wait for us to work together again. And wait until you hear the assignment I have in mind. You're going to be chomping at the bit."

Curious, Claire found herself hesitating. "I'm serious, Eric. I can't . . ."

"Wait. Before you leap into another lecture." He reached into the breast pocket of his gray tweed jacket. "I have a little gift for you." He handed her a tiny black plastic folder, the old-fashioned kind that came automatically with checkbooks, only this one was the size of her Visa. "Go ahead. Open it."

Inside was a set of official *Cleveland Citizen* white business cards. In raised lettering was her name CLAIRE STARK. CLEVELAND CITIZEN STAFF WRITER.

"So you can get straight to work," he said.

"You've gone too far. I can't take these." She slid them back to him.

"Sure you can." He slid them back to her. "Not like anyone else can use them."

"Including me." She took a deep breath on the long shot that oxygen would sharpen her wit against Eric's biting tongue. "I can't work for you or with you. Ever."

They were silent for several minutes, drinking their coffees and planning strategy.

"Diana Plimpton," he said, cocking an eyebrow.

The name brought back a rush of memories. "Pardon?"

"Don't tell me you've forgotten the Socialite Slayer."

"I always hated that moniker. Diana killed one man, her husband, and that was by accident. Though if you ask me, he deserved to get in the way of her frying pan. What made you bring her up?"

"She's in town."

Claire was surprised by this. "I thought she was in the West Virginia Correctional Institute for Women."

"Turns out she was quietly granted parole by the West Virginia Board of Parole last month. Her sister, Daphne Sturm, has taken her in and West Virginia was only too glad to send her home to Ohio. To your backyard."

"Hunting Hills?"

"Daphne and Diana are Hunting Hills natives, dontcha know. Old

Holly School alums, in fact. Diana used to teach there after she got out of Wellesley. It's where she met her ill-fated husband."

"Ill-fated, my ass!" Claire declared, recalling Diana's account of how Kendrick Plimpton, headmaster to the prestigious Baylor Preparatory School for Boys in Greenbrier, West Virginia, used to repeatedly assault his wife, including locking her in the basement during winter nights and burning her with cigarettes—in discreet places, of course, so that no one would catch on.

As the wife of a highly respected educator, Diana never reported her abuse to the police or left her husband but, as many women of her class do, kept up appearances by pasting on a happy face. That was until one night after Kendrick returned from a faculty party smashed and threatening to beat his wife to a pulp. Diana let him have it with a frying pan. She was convicted of manslaughter despite a series of articles Claire had written detailing her plight.

Claire was so caught up in her recollections, which still summoned feelings of fury, that she hadn't noticed Eric's obvious pleasure over her reaction.

"I thought you'd be interested," he said with a nasty grin.

"Interested in what?" Though she knew exactly what he had in mind.

"Calling up Diana and requesting an interview. She won't talk to anyone at the *Cleveland Citizen*—which is no shocker considering the hacks I've got working underneath me—but I know she'll talk to a pro like you. You were her biggest advocate."

He'd snagged her. Claire sat back against the rich leather couch, defeated. She would have interviewed Diana Plimpton in a heartbeat given any other situation. Meeting Diana again, free and out of prison, would provide much needed closure to a horror that had haunted her from her own days as a budding reporter.

"She's dropped her married name, which is to be expected. She goes by her maiden one, Darcy. Daphne and Diana Darcy. Parents must have run out of other letters in the alphabet. Either that or they had a perverse fondness for the letter D. I have the number in my top left pocket. If possible, try to arrange a photo shoot too."

"I can't." Claire twisted a paper napkin in her lap. "I have to confess that you have really piqued my interest as you knew you would, Eric. But I just can't do that to John, write for the *CC* that is."

"Oh, brother. I can't stand women who stand by their men." Eric shook his head in disgust. "Would it help if I called him and apologized?"

"I doubt it."

"Well, then there's no choice. I'll have to get mean."

She turned to him, alarmed. Eric had been known to go to impossible lengths for a story. Once, to gain access to classified documents, he'd taken Polaroids of a U.S. senator frolicking on a beach with his mistress. Unfortunately, his tricks worked, which meant that Eric saw no reason to quit them.

"What do you mean by 'mean'?"

"You know. I'll think of something."

"You wouldn't dare." It crossed her mind to dangle the possibility of a lawsuit, should he try anything, but she knew that a legal threat would only make Eric more motivated.

"Don't you get it?" he said, bowing his head toward hers. "It's not the story I'm after. It's you."

Chapter Fourteen

Marti could not believe her eyes. One artificial Heritage Village block away from her and there was John's bride already in cahoots with another man.

She scrutinized them behind her sunglasses. *Seems Saint Claire's not so virtuous after all.* She reached in her Fendi purse and flipped open her cell phone, pressing speed dial #3.

Lisa answered on the first ring. "Don't tell me you're chickening out."

"I might." The reception was incredibly poor considering Lisa was only in the parking lot, serving as back-up driver and personal motivator. "There's been a complication."

"You can't. Think of what Barry's been telling you. Be the opening to the universe."

"Yeah, well, my opening just closed."

"What's wrong?"

"Claire. She's right there at the door to Starbucks."

"Get out!"

"Honestly."

"Do you think John invited her?"

"Doubtful. She's with another man. And they're tight."

"Tight?" Lisa gasped. "How tight?"

"Rendezvous tight." Marti loved the word rendezvous. She loved the whole rendezvous concept—that it was French and suggested clandestine activity. That you could slur it. "Definitely, rendezvous."

"Wait until Boots hears. This could back up her theory that Claire is only after John's money. What's she doing now?"

Marti watched as the two strolled arm and arm. "They're walking away together. He's got his arm around her and he just kissed her, though only on the cheek. Oh, and he has a folder."

"What kind of folder?"

"I don't know." Marti searched for the right terminology. "Oak tag."

"I haven't heard anyone use the word 'oak tag' since I was in second grade. You mean 'manila.' "

"Whatever." Marti checked her watch. It was already after three and the last thing she wanted to do was irritate John or, worse, have him leave Starbucks and hook up with Claire. "They're down the sidewalk now, so I guess I'll go through with it."

"What would she have a folder with her for?" asked Lisa, who, thanks to Nomadd, had a tendency to get stuck on minor points.

Marti, unable to spare another minute of speed-fueled speculation, hung up, flipped a lock of hair behind her ear and headed to Starbucks.

She didn't feel so crummy now, knowing that Claire had a man on the side—and so soon. Possibilities popped into her mind. Maybe this man and Claire were conspiring to rip off John. Maybe they'd known each other for years, since elementary school. Just like John and Marti and Denton and Karen and Kit and Ty and Boots. Maybe they were already married.

Who knew? Did John?

John was in a *tres* perfect double-breasted gray suit, his dirty blond hair artfully unkempt, reading the *Wall Street Journal* and looking very impatient when she arrived at Starbucks fifteen minutes late.

"I'm soo sorry." She kissed him on the cheek, her lips lingering a scooch longer than necessary. He smelled of Clinique aftershave. Sporty, masculine. Claire was a fool to let him out of her sight with a woman like her around. "I got tied up. And not in a good way."

This was a total lie. Lisa had insisted Marti could not go to Starbucks in a Lacoste rugby shirt, even if its jaunty youthfulness bespoke of false innocence.

After much deliberation in Marti's closet, they chose a White & Warren V-necked cashmere shirt in absinthe, a black denim pair of Seven jeans and Marti's absolute favorite Etro Brooch pumps. The outfit was designed for kicking around town, though all totaled, at a thousand dollars she might as well be kicking around Rodeo Drive.

It worked. Seeing her in it, seeing how slim and young and breathtakingly sexy she was, John's frown melted into his famous boyish grin.

"I understand totally." He held her at arm's length, drinking her in. "You look terrific. Not nearly as sad as you sounded on the phone."

This could be bad, she thought, better snap into action. "I'm doing the best I can." She gazed up at him with her baby doll eyes.

"Oh, Marti." John brought her to him and she rested her head on his shoulder. "It'll be OK."

"I know. It's just that . . . I want to do the right thing."

("Above all," Lisa had said, zipping through traffic, "John cannot think you are out to seduce him. You've got to act torn, yet drawn to him. Let him conquer you.")

John's first victory was to snare a triple vente, half caf, skim latte. He sat her down in a maroon leatherette chair by the gas fire. It was a superb choice. Warm and intimate, yet hidden from the street—or rather fake street—outside. All signs pointed to success.

He surreptitiously checked his watch again and took her hand. "Tell me the whole story. When did Denton leave?"

"Well, here's the deal. I'm not sure he *has* left." She sipped her coffee, its miniscule amount of caffeine triggering a tiny headache.

"I thought on the phone you said . . ."

"It's just that he's not around. It's like he's disappearing." She adjusted her gaze from baby doll to limpid, which was not easy to pull off without a mirror as she did not know if her eyes were actually limpid or more bugged. "Every night I go to sleep, alone. And every morning I wake up, alone."

John rested his chin on his fist like *The Thinker*. "Alone, huh?"

"Alone."

"And during the day?"

"He's around sporadically. I saw a flash of him at Lois's away game in Oberlin yesterday. Lois talked to him but I didn't. He goes to work before I wake up and comes home long after I'm in bed."

Marti's knee gently brushed against John's. "I call him at work but he doesn't return my calls. Or when he does, I don't ask where he's been because"—this had been Lisa's suggestion, so Marti would avoid coming off as a shrew—"I don't want to be a nag. I've never been a nag, you know that."

"I do." He let his knee rest against hers. "It's one of the reasons why Denton's so lucky to have you. I've always thought that of all of us at Tate, he ended up with the best deal. You know how I feel."

"Oh, please." She cocked her head.

"No. It's true."

"If it's true, then how come you ended up with Boots?" Fishing now.

"Because you were going out with Steve Shapiro all through high school."

"We broke up at graduation."

"And then, before I could get my foot in, you were with Denton. You never gave me a chance."

"Never say never." She kissed him again on the cheek.

John didn't seem to mind. Any moment now, he would bring up last summer, Marti was sure of it.

And so he did. "Do you remember that party at Renfrew's last summer?"

"Hmmhmm." She leaned forward to reveal an eensie weensie bit of cleavage.

"That was the night that changed my life." He gazed at her meaningfully.

"I know," she whispered. "I've been thinking about it too." It was all happening so fast! Faster than Lisa said it would.

"It's why I fell in love with Claire."

Marti nearly dropped her triple vente half caf. "Claire?"

"Claire. You made me realize it was time for me to stop being such an ass, to take another chance at a real relationship. Maybe marriage."

"Claire?" Marti chirped again, her confusd brain unable to communicate anything else. Why wasn't he reminding her of what he said, of her being the perfect woman, her in the moonlight, blah, blah, blah? "Claire?"

"Yes, Claire. You know? My wife? Tall redhead." Now it was John who seemed confused. "Apparently you two went shopping the other day. She came back with several jars of pepper jelly."

"Oh, yeah." Marti pretended as though she and Boots and Lisa and Karen hadn't been dissecting her nonstop since. "She's extremely nice." Marti would have to steer him off this track and fast. "I think I just saw her a few minutes ago. Outside."

"Here?" He lifted his chin and looked toward the street. "I wonder what she's up to. You don't think she was looking for me, do you?"

Definitely they were going way, way off track. "I doubt it." An evil impulse came over her which Marti, having spent the morning under Lisa's influence, was not powerful enough to resist. "She was with another man. In tweed."

"Ahh." John stirred his black coffee and seemed to draw into himself, becoming thoughtful and silent.

What kind of wife, Marti wanted to know, made her husband so morose? Wives were to uplift and boost the men in their lives, the providers, to praise and, in moderation and when necessary, tell little white lies. Without wives men would be lost. They would be plagued with doubt and do very poorly at work, earning measly bonuses and wearing ties stained with lobster butter.

"Something wrong?" she asked.

"No," he said quickly. "I'm just thinking about Claire. Want to know a secret?"

Yes! thought Marti. "Sure," she said casually.

"I think I've made a mistake."

They were the words she'd been waiting for. The words she'd instinctively known all along. "How so?" she asked, playing it cool as Lisa had taught her.

"Marrying Claire so fast and bringing her here. It was all wrong."

Marti gently placed her hand on his strong thigh so that her pinky finger slid daringly toward his crotch. "It's OK, John. You haven't been married *too* long. Besides. Most mistakes can be corrected."

"I don't know if I can correct this one." He massaged the bridge of his nose, an adorable quirk of his, and Marti's heart went out to him. This man, the love of her life, was in pain. How easy it would be to ease his suffering by letting him know that she, at last, could be his. That he could have her, the Cadillac, and not Claire, the Chevy.

"I'm being stupid." He sat up and finished his coffee. "You called me to help you with Denton, not talk about Claire."

"That's all right. We can talk about her if you want."

"No. We shouldn't."

"Really. It's OK."

He stood and brushed off invisible crumbs. "Come on. I'll walk you to your car. We'll talk on the way. I usually come up with bright ideas when I'm walking."

This invitation presented all sorts of difficulties. For one thing, Lisa, Uber Bitch, was in her SUV waiting for her. Marti did not want

John to see Lisa. He would know right away that something was cooking.

"Actually, I was planning on doing some shopping. The bookstore," she added in a last minute bit of brilliance. "I'm almost done with *Jane Eyre*." John the bookish intellectual would appreciate her reading Charlotte Brontë, whereas Denton would have heard, "I'm almost done with *Jane Eyre,*" and immediately thought lesbian porn.

"*Jane Eyre*? That's impressive." He helped her on with her coat. "How come you're reading Brontë?"

"The book group." They were outside now and the air, with its pseudo European aromas of freshly ground coffee and sautéed garlic, was almost romantic. Perhaps almost as romantic as Prague, Marti hoped.

"Boots's book group? I thought all you guys read was blue prose."

Blue prose? What was he talking about? "This month we're reading books that we should have read in college, but partied too hard to get around to."

For the first time that afternoon John laughed and Marti felt as though she'd achieved something.

"What's next? *Moby Dick*?"

"Lord no. That's a boys' book."

"A boys' book, eh?" He smiled down at her. "How is it that despite Denton's neglectful treatment of you, you can still be so sweet? You always manage to make me laugh, Marti. Always have."

Marti bowed her head. "Come on, John. You know how I feel. I'd," she lifted her eyes to him, this time with longing (baby doll and limpid having paved the way), "I'd do anything for you."

"Anything?"

"Anything."

They stopped at Joseph Beth's big dark green doors. "Then I have a very dangerous request," he said. "And I hope you won't think I'm overstepping my bounds."

Marti's fingers tingled. She wished Lisa were there to hear every word. "Shoot."

"Get Boots to invite Claire to her book group. I know she's all hung up on keeping it exclusive, that she won't even include Karen, but it would do a world of good if Claire could see that there's an intellectual underpinning to this vapid hell hole I've brought her to. How about it?"

It had been instant devastation. A blow that hurt like a slap, not only to her but to Hunting Hills and the Greater Cleveland Area which Marti definitely did not consider a "vapid hell hole." However, raised to maintain a brave face in the most trying of circumstances, she refused to let her disappointment show through. "I'll do what I can," she said.

"Thanks." And he bent down and kissed her softly and gently one last time on the cheek, which gave her just enough hope to devise Plan II.

Chapter Fifteen

The next morning Denton sat on the edge of the king-sized bed and studied his Ermenegildo Zegna suit under the muted overhead light. Was it green? It looked kinda green. Goddamn Marti. She was always doing that, buying him green suits. She'd say they were gray or charcoal but she lied.

They were green.

Why didn't she stick with Brooks Brothers instead of this Italian crap? You knew where you stood with Brooks Brothers. Navy. Black. Gray. Simple. Uncomplicated.

Unlike his life.

"Almost ready?" a woman's voice called from the bathroom.

"Pretty soon." Denton checked his watch. Gucci. It was 5 a.m. and all the world, meaning Marti, erroneously assumed he was off to work. That's what he loved about this arrangement. The lying.

If lying was an art—and Denton had come to believe it was—then he was a Grand Master. No one could pull off a lie like he could, whether it was insisting to a waitress that he'd given her a fifty when he'd actually handed her a twenty, or telling Marti he was out for drinks at the Union Club when really he was screwing another woman or . . . more.

Much more. So much more that if he were ever found out, if anyone had the slightest inkling, he'd be ruined. He and his whole family. Fuck that, he and everyone he knew.

God that was great.

Denton loved the way a lie could spontaneously roll off his tongue, how the listener would nod in earnestness, foolishly trusting that every word he spoke was true. He was proud of his professional polish, the unique details he added that lent credibility. Or how he had never, ever forgotten a single lie, starting with Mrs. Cameron, his childhood neighbor.

Denton had been eighteen, a freshman at Tufts (alma mater to P. T. Barnum, "sucker born every minute") and in need of cash for a motorcycle. Mrs. Cameron had been sixty-two and flush. The lie was simple. Denton called her from his Carmichael dorm room with a sob story about raising money for a fictional roommate named Stan who suffered from a deadly form of leukemia.

Mrs. Cameron zipped off a check for a thousand dollars and Denton was on his way.

Just the other day he thoughtfully sent a note to the Florida community where Mrs. Cameron had retired, thanking her for the kindness she had shown twenty-five years before. It included an update of Stan, a healthy father of two living near Portland, Maine, and a bit about his quiet vocation in woodworking.

"On this twenty-fifth anniversary of your generosity," Denton's note concluded, "know that your contribution was put to its best use, bringing happiness and joy that hadn't before seemed possible."

He did not mention that the happiness and joy ended up wrapped around a telephone pole on the Fresh Pond Highway.

Best of all, though, Denton loved pushing the lie, the thrill of narrowly being caught and slipping by on a whisker. For example, getting head at 5 a.m. There was not one aspect of rolling out of a nice, warm bed and dragging himself to a neightor's on a dark, cold morning that was appealing. Not one thing. Not even a perfectly executed blow job.

Except that for the first time they would be doing it in her house, on the bed where she and his best friend slept, her kid down the hall, the neighbors who knew him as Marti's husband only yards away. That was what made this morning awesome.

It was now five after five. Denton craned to see what the hell was going on in the bathroom. Why was she taking so long?

He caught a glimpse of himself in the full-length mirror she'd propped up against the wall. Another one of her creative "aids." Damn, with his hair still sandy blond and his skin still smooth he looked young. Affable. Trustworthy. With a fine layer of baby fat around his face, but not fluffy like Bob Goss or balding like Ty. Harding might have had him beat when it came to physique, but Denton had him hands down when it came to wealth. Fuck him.

"How are we doing?" Lisa appeared from the shower, a towel wrapped loosely around her enhanced figure. She had cleverly draped it in such a way that he could sneak a peak of her navel set in her flat stomach, catch a glimpse of her artificially filled breasts. Her hair was wet and slicked back from her smooth face. Boy, she looked terrific. Ageless. And, for once, speed free.

He reached out and Lisa took his hand. "Shh. We have to be quiet."

"I know," he whispered, loving it.

Lisa hadn't gone after Harding and she could have too, since he used to reign Cleveland's list of wealthy bachelors. No, she went after him. Jim Denton. Boss Broker. Why? Because Lisa knew that he could take her places. He could take her out of this Cleveland morass, this white-bread purgatory of Hunting Hills forever. And once he'd confided to her that those were his plans, to blow this town in style, to go to Manhattan or L.A., there was no stopping her pursuit of him.

She'd seduced him, slipping her long, tapered fingers down his pants under the table at La Trattoria, Marti a few dangerous seats away, flashing him her manufactured boobs during her otherwise soporific pool party last summer.

Denton smiled at the memory of Lisa's churning legs in the underlit sparkling water, the way she'd spontaneously lifted her flowered bikini top, looking over her shoulder to make sure Marti was deep in conversation with Harding.

The memory triggered a slight tingling between his legs. Finally, it was working. It was really working. The prescription pasted to the bottle had warned to take one, but when did Jim Denton ever follow directions? Directions were for hose boys.

All he knew was that he was not about to wait for a goddamn hour while the Viagra made its way through his system, slowly unlocking blood vessels like a dotty old school janitor. Besides, he didn't need the stuff, really. It was merely a matter of streamlining. If you could buy a faster, easier and better way to do something, then Jim Denton would pony up. That was his personal creed and that's what he'd told the doctor. The doctor immediately understood since he too had graduated from Tate where the omnipresent motto of "Fidelity, Integrity and Trust" sounded more like the name of a bank than a moral maxim.

Lisa placed his palm on her bare stomach and Denton felt the tingling unleash into a full swell. *That's my man,* he thought, feeling big and masculine. Energized. Like the bunny.

The thick cream-colored towel dropped in a heap to the cream-colored carpeting. (Very expensive. Marti had tried to talk him into buying the exact same carpet, but he'd balked. It was an outrageous amount to pay—fifty-five dollars a square yard.)

In the mirror he could see Lisa's nicely rounded ass, the way it curved melon-like to the thighs, so smooth and firm he didn't know where to begin. He ran his fingers over it. Lisa moaned and the bulge between his legs grew.

"Let's see what we have here." Lisa leaned over and unzipped his pants, issuing a squeak at her discovery. "Oh, my. Aren't you something?"

Denton felt proud. He let Lisa pull off his trousers and remove his suit coat. She undid his tie, dangling her breasts in face. (He suddenly remembered that they had floated in the pool. How funky was that?) He licked her pink nipples as she unbuttoned his shirt. She hung his clothes carefully so as not to wrinkle.

It was great to be a rich, white male, he thought, lying on his back, hands behind his head as Lisa kneeled before him, taking advantage of American pharmaceutical research. As a broker he'd had his doubts about the drug companies. Merck had been a bust, MRK dropping from forty-five dollars a share to twenty-five dollars. Ditto for Pfizer, the genius behind Viagra; PFE had slipped from sixty-five dollars to fifty dollars in the past year.

Denton exhaled a groan of pleasure as Lisa's technique kicked into action. He worried that he was so loud he might have awakened her kid. He didn't want to dash the moment. He didn't want to go limp.

But he wasn't losing his hard-on, was he? Denton lifted his head. Lisa was bobbing up and down exerting herself and his man of the moment showed no sign of relenting. He lay back and relaxed again, really let himself go.

Denton went to his happy place. Aventis. AVENF.PK on the stock exchange, fifty-five dollars to ninety dollars over a fifty-two week period. God had he been brilliant to get in on the ground floor of that puppy. He felt a sweet, pure surge as he imagined AVE's stock chart, felt himself rising, rising, rising right along the Y axis in a steady slope of capitalistic consummation. *Yes!*

He closed his eyes, spent.

Lisa spit into the towel. "How was that?"

"Seven point five." They had a scale. Ten, naturally, being best.

"Seven point five?" She was indignant. "But I put in a twist."

That was true. The twist was nice. "Seven point eight then."

"Ugh." She got up and ran to the bathroom to brush her teeth and wash her face, gargle with industrial strength mouthwash.

"Mom!" A tiny voice inquired from the other side of the locked bedroom door.

His eyes popped open. Lisa jumped out of the bathroom, fumbling for a robe. "In a second, honey." She glared at Denton, naked and sated on the bed. "Get out!" she mouthed, pointing to the bathroom.

Denton hated kids. Not his. Just everyone else's. He slowly got up and proceeded to gather his suit, his shoes with his socks stuffed into them neatly. He looked down. He was still rock hard.

"Mom? What are you doing in there?"

"Just a minute." Lisa was in full panic mode, falling over herself to pull on a pair of jeans. "Come on!" she hissed to Denton. "Hurry."

He stumbled to the bathroom and Lisa slammed the door. He locked it from the inside to be safe. As he buttoned his shirt and knotted his tie he listened to the conversation between Lisa and her ten-year-old, a boy or a girl. He never could remember.

"Where's Dad?"

"He's on a business trip. Now, let's get some . . ."

"But I heard him."

Lisa laughed nervously. "You must have been dreaming. Want some yogurt? I've got organic banana."

They clattered out. Denton stepped into his boxers and discovered he had a problem. A real problem. His man would not give up.

Damn. It had to be the Viagra. Well, that could be remedied. He sat on the edge of the cold iron tub and thought the worst. He thought of Marti and Lois, what they would say if they found out he'd been sleeping with Lisa Renfrew for the past three months. This had no effect.

He thought of his mother and his overweight childhood maid Bethesda who could deflate a basketball, she'd been so ugly. He thought of his nasty third-grade teacher Mrs. Cafferty and he thought about how much the Indians sucked.

Still, he remained upright.

Fuck. Denton grabbed a white washcloth and ran it under the cold water. He'd scheduled a breakfast meeting with Marguerite Grayson, eighty-two, the last remaining heiress of the Grayson department store empire and one of his most valued clients. It would not do to salute Marguerite from below.

He clenched his jaw, braced himself and draped the freezing washcloth over his rigid offender. At that moment Denton knew what it would be like to freeze to death and how awful that would be. There was a quiet knock on the door.

"Coast is clear," Lisa murmured. "She's in the den watching cartoons. Now's the time."

Denton let her in. Lisa's gaze dropped immediately to the white washcloth that hung on his rack.

"What are you doing?"

"I've got a problem." Denton pointed south. "What the hell am I supposed to do with this?"

"But I thought you . . . I know you . . ."

"I did." Denton placed his hands on his hips. "It's that goddamn Viagra. No wonder Pfizer's tanking. The stuff is crap."

"How much did you take?" Lisa couldn't stop staring.

"Four."

"Four Viagra? You're supposed to take only one. That's what Ty does."

Denton tried not to let himself get exasperated. "I'm not Ty. I wanted it to work fast so I doubled the dose. I thought the dose was two."

"Oh, no." Lisa covered her mouth and stifled a laugh.

Denton was not amused. "What?"

"Well, don't get upset. You'll be OK."

But Denton *was* getting upset. He couldn't help it. "Tell me!"

"You don't have to go to the hospital or anything. Not unless, you know, you stay stiff for four hours."

"Four hours!"

"Shhh!"

"Don't *shh* me." He tore the washcloth off and threw it into the sink. "You mean to tell me I have to walk around like this for four hours."

"It won't be so bad. You can zip up your pants, can't you?"

"So what? It'll still be obvious."

"Blow off the morning, then. Tell your secretary you're going to Dayton or something. Isn't that what you usually say?"

Denton started pacing back and forth, he and his human metal detector. "I can't. The client I'm meeting is very touchy. If she thinks I'm blowing her off she'll move her assets. Her sixty million dollars worth of assets. Goddamn Marguerite Grayson."

"Marguerite Grayson?" Lisa arched her brows. "Isn't she ancient?"

"Eighty-two."

"And never married?"

"Probably still a virgin."

Lisa shook her head. "Well, you can't stay here. You'll have to think of something. You'll have to lie."

Denton looked down again. It might have been his imagination, but he was getting stiffer. And longer. *What am I going to do?* He thought, desperately. *Everyone will see. I'm like. . . .*

Pinocchio. It was the only word he could think of. Pinocchio. The boy made out of wood. Like him.

Chapter Sixteen

Barry was right. The "John Affair," as Marti had come to think of it, had been the perfect pick-me-up, just the right distraction to take her mind off Denton and the old boring question of whether he was or was not trying to flee. Whether he was so-called disappearing. Really, the entire issue was fast becoming a drag.

In contrast the John Affair was like a Caribbean retreat for the soul, maybe the Sandy Lane Resort in Barbados only without having to wade through customs. Marti felt the same anticipation as if the travel agent had been called, the flight booked and the hotel suite reserved. Now all she had to do was study the brochures and count the days until takeoff.

Already she was feeling the affair's therapeutic effects, its calming, yet energizing, transformation. As Lisa predicted, the John Affair was going to be *good* for her. Marti's only question was how come she'd waited so long.

Take the morning after John kissed her at Starbucks—*their* Starbucks. Marti didn't wake up until the decadent hour of 9 a.m. and for the first day in weeks hadn't bothered to search for clues to see if Denton had come and gone. She no longer cared!

As if to prove how free and liberated she was, she marched straight downstairs for a cup of coffee. Buck naked! Like she was twenty-three and living in an apartment in SoHo or something.

Rachel in her black skirt and long-sleeved white blouse had been watching TV and folding linens and when she saw Marti, she got off her cell and said, "Mrs. Denton. The landscapers are right outside! They'll see you."

To which Marti had simply tossed back her hair and replied, "Lucky them."

Lucky them? Never ever in a million years would she have said "Lucky them." More proof that the John Affair was A-OK. Like Lisa said, the fling would make her magnanimous.

So magnanimous that Marti actually helped bag some of her groceries at Heinen's—and not just because doing so allowed her to stand closer to Derek, the Adonis of Bag Boys. Studmuffin in Aisle #3. Derek who wore a circular stone on a thin leather strip around his neck, who ran a knock-off Outward Bound course for underprivileged children and who, his mother told her, was destined for Princeton crew. My god she loved Derek.

Truly, though, the bagging thing had been a big step. It showed that she was hip to the youth, that she was not confined by stupid boundaries like who writes the checks and who bags. Boundaries like who's married and who's not. That whole "forsake all others" part.

Wasn't monogamy a fairly recent concept among the upper classes anyway? Husbands and wives commonly took lovers without getting divorced until as recently as the twentieth century. Look at *Jane Eyre*.

Which brought her to Boots's book group, one of the touchier aspects of this whole John Affair. She and Boots had almost come to blows over it the day before.

"I can't allow Claire in," said Boots, tossing a saliva-soaked tennis ball for the umpteenth time at Bedo and Alys. "Karen's been on the waiting list forever. It would be a disaster if I took Claire first."

They were at Marti's house, in her flat backyard with its trampoline and fenced-in garden and swimming pool and tennis court. Marti did not especially look forward to Bedo and Alys crapping on her lawn, which was wet from a good Lake Erie-effect drenching, but it was the sacrifice she'd have to make if she wanted Boots to grant John his favor.

Surely Boots owed him this.

Boots and John had dated steadily since eighth grade, except for the "tennis summer" Marti had shared with him in high school. His proposal on a snowy Christmas Eve during Boots's senior year in college—John at Williams, Boots at Middlebury—came as hardly a shock to their parents or anyone who knew them. Christ Church had already penciled in their wedding for the last weekend in June.

There were no fewer than six major engagement parties for the couple. Boots received tons of gifts and promptly replied with thank-yous on embossed cream stationery with a proud flourish of Mrs. John Harding—a signature she'd practiced on her textbooks for eons. The wedding on a warm, azure day was fragrant with pink roses and baby's breath, which hung in garlands throughout the white tented reception area on the sloping lawn of her aunt's "cottage" in Haywire Falls.

After their trip to Bermuda, John and Boots rented an apartment in Greenwich Village where he planned to start his novel while Boots worked at Sotheby's. But then, much to Boots's secret pleasure, John was called back to Hunting Hills to clean up the scandal that had rocked his family. His father promised it would take no more than three months.

Three months turned into six months, during which John's father died uttering his last wish that his only son take over his venture capital company and restore the name and mission of Hardco Enterprises. Of course John agreed, though, deep down, he simmered with resentment. He hated all business in general. To him business was greed and theft and avarice.

But Boots was thrilled. One week after the funeral, she put a down payment on a spectacular new house in Hunting Hills. She told John that it would be ideal for the babies their future surely held. Hunting Hills and the Midwest in general was a safe and secure place to raise children, unlike dirty Manhattan with its super exclusive private schools and questionable park system, she explained.

In Hunting Hills their children could benefit from the fairy tale childhood each of them had enjoyed—the Christ Church nursery school, egg rolling contests on the wide green lawns of the country club, solid Holly or Tate educations. Plus, they'd have friends galore. Now that Marti and Jim Denton were engaged, they'd be having kids, and newlyweds Bob and Karen Goss were moving back too.

Once John hesitantly came around, Boots threw a big party.

There were no babies, however. Instead, their future held Gwen and Rhys, Boots's first pair of Pembroke Welsh corgis, yipping donations from her godmother Dora of Bloomfield Hills, Michigan. Boots fell madly in love the way a mother instantly attaches to her infant and no one—including John—and nothing else—including the prospect of real children—could come between her and her dogs. She insisted the puppies eat dinner with them, often feeding them biscuits held in her own tiny mouth. She took them everywhere, even in her purse and even to bed.

It was the beginning of the end of her marriage.

Soon it became clear that John, who had counted on fathering a boy and a girl, or at the very least humans, could count only on having sires and bitches. He did not want sires and bitches. There were enough bitches in his life, for one thing, and talking to the self-important, overrated, stunted dogs was pointless. He and Boots parted amicably two years and five days after their blowout nuptials, with Boots soon hooking up with Sven Larson, the famous Swedish Vallhund trainer who took a dim view of spaying, neutering and all prophylactics in general.

Boots found herself pregnant within weeks of her divorce from John, forcing her and Sven to sneak off to Vegas where they were quietly wed. But as Hunting Hills loves nothing more than naughty antics, the new couple was heartily toasted upon their return. Boots moved into the same "cottage" where she had married John and awaited the birth of Ingrid, a red-faced, howling, colicky baby whose nonstop cries drove Sven back to Sweden with a quickie divorce, a termination of parental rights and a promise never to set foot in America.

Only John could calm the distressed child. Night upon night he paced the wide-board floors of Boots's antique home, rocking and soothing Ingrid, running the vacuum or taking her for rides in his Porsche 911 until she conked out. Later he taught her how to ride a bicycle and tell the difference between vertical and adjacent angles. He lobbed Ingrid her first tennis ball, cajoled her into her first high dive and put her on her first horse—a pricey error.

In that way John became the father Ingrid never had, which was why she called him "Daddy" and he thought of her as his daughter and why Boots expected him to set up a trust fund for her. Yet he never reconnected with Boots on the principle that she was incapable of truly loving anything that did not have four paws, fur and a snout. Plus, it wasn't like he was hard up for sex. Women threw themselves at John Harding. He was the biggest catch in Cleveland.

"Anyway, I don't like her," Boots said. A faint drizzle began to fall and Boots pulled her British Barbour around her. "I still think she's after his money. Ingrid's money."

"You might be right. I saw her with a strange man the other day at Heritage Village. He kissed her and put his arms around her." Marti left out the insignificant detail about the kiss being no more than a peck. "I told John about it and he got all glum."

"Wow." Boots threw the tennis ball as far as she could into the woods. It made Marti retch to see Boots clutch that ball even though she'd read somewhere—*Jane Eyre* perhaps?—that dog saliva was supposed to be sterile. "Then something must be up if he's down about her already."

"If we invite her to the book group we can, you know, prod for information." This had been Marti's goal all along. "Then we could have a better idea if the marriage will last."

Bedo dropped the ball dutifully at Boots's feet but Boots did not pick it up. Instead she stood there, jaw lowered, looking at Marti aghast. "Oh my god. It's happened."

"What?" said Marti, thinking Boots was referring to her dog, that maybe it had finally given up on its incessant fetching.

"You are going after John."

Marti's throat tightened. She hadn't considered out how Boots might take the news of her affair. Alas, there was no point in hiding it. Their love—John's and Marti's—was not the kind of passion that could be denied. Though you couldn't blame a girl for trying.

"No I'm not. John and I are old friends. Why would I be going after him now?"

"Because he's married."

"So?"

"So you're the ultimate consumer, Marti. If a sweater's marked down and on display, you won't touch it. But if suddenly something disappears from the market, like iPods last Christmas, then you kill yourself trying to find one. Remember how you were thinking of driving up to Canada to get one for Lois?"

This was, sadly, true. Marti thought about what Boots said as Bedo and Alys repetitiously went back and forth, their small doggy brains on autopilot, fetching and dropping, fetching and dropping.

"Are you saying," Marti began after some reflection, "that my interest in John is nothing more than my urge to buy an iPod?"

"Ah, ha! So you admit that you're interested in him." Boots held the chewed green tennis ball aloft.

"Yes." Marti kicked the soggy turf with the toe of her Wellington. "I think . . . I think I'm in love."

"It'll never work." Boots was blunt, not jealous. Just plain matter of fact. "John's a bookworm. He's not into money and acquisitions like Denton and, face it, that's what turns you on. You admire the way Denton wheels and deals and maybe even . . ." Boots stopped. She knew when too far was too far.

"Has it ever occurred to you that maybe now that I'm in my forties I'm ready for a change? I am. I want a man like John who is sensitive and thoughtful and who's not at the office twenty hours out of every day." Marti said this last line with a choke in her voice, which surprised even her.

Boots flung the ball as far as she could into the woods, the two dogs scrambling into the underbrush like idiots. "I'm sorry. I'd forgotten about how Denton's been ignoring you."

"It's like I don't exist except to keep the house running and . . ." Marti bowed her head, not eager to go on. She thought of another Hunting Hills wife rule. Be Perky. Wives must always paint a perky picture about their husbands—the biggest, smartest, most adorable breadwinners ever!

"OK." Boots nodded resolutely. "Then let me give you a tip. If you're really serious about pursuing an affair, you've got to hire Mrs. Distal."

Marti ran over her mental Rolodex, trying to place Distal, Distal. "Who's she?"

"She's *the* personal shopper for when you're having an affair. She not only puts together a fantastic wardrobe, but she's very savvy when it comes to bill paying."

"Bill paying?" peeped Marti, who was unaccustomed to the task.

"You don't want Denton getting all nosy about a two-thousand-dollar Dolce & Gabbana satin stretch dress that he's never seen. A Mrs. Distal is a must."

Marti tried to imagine Denton caring about her at all. It was hard for her to conceive that even a two-thousand-dollar Dolce & Gabbana would spark his interest. She could see him sitting at his home office off their bedroom upstairs, opening the bill, squinting at it and shrugging, putting it aside for the accountant to pay.

Just then Marti remembered something awful and she had to grip Boots's arm. "You must not tell Jesus."

"Why would I tell Jesus?"

"He's doing Claire's kitchen."

"I know. Fran had me ask him. He's booked, but he'll make room. For my sake." Boots treated Jesus like he was Brad Pitt or George Clooney, a celebrity far out of reach of most mortals. "Frankly, I thought it was about time."

"That John kissed me?"

"No, that someone redid that kitchen. I don't know what I could have been thinking with the yellow and blond oak."

"But what do you think about John kissing me? He did so right after he asked if I could get you to invite Claire to the book group, to show her that we're intellectual and everything and not a bunch of ditzes."

Boots leaned down, grabbed the tennis ball and tossed it so it hit a tree with a *splat.* "If John asked, then I'll do it. But we have to make sure that under no circumstances does Karen find out. Understand?"

"Understand." Marti would call Claire that afternoon, right after she invited her to the party she was throwing in the honor of Claire and John's marriage. It was an inspired idea, seemingly generous and welcoming, totally innocent. The theme of the party would be Late Blooming Love. Everyone would be required to think of the names of couples who had married late in life.

No one would have the slightest idea that while they were laughing and drinking and misbehaving, somewhere she and John would be alone, consummating their love at last.

It was decided that the party would be on a Friday. Claire had accepted and Marti could tell even over the phone that she was ecstatic that someone had decided to celebrate their marriage. The book group invitation went over well too, though Marti felt that Claire was not appropriately thrilled that she had used her influence to get her in. Claire had already read *Jane Eyre,* had written a paper on it in college—a no name place called West Virginia State of all places—but promised to reread it by the book group's meeting on Wednesday—as though that were necessary.

Karen and Bob Goss were coming to the party. So were Lisa and Ty and Kit Vickers and her husband, Val, and a bunch of other people whom Marti thought of simply as The Clients, meaning they held accounts with Denton.

Only Denton hadn't R.S.V.P.'d. No surprise there. She couldn't find the guy. For that matter, no one could. It was reaching crisis proportions. It was extremely *annoying*.

On Wednesday, the day of their book group meeting and two days before the party, the phone had rung nonstop. First it had been Tim Watson, one of Denton's buddy brokers at Anderson Brothers. Tim had been polite and genial, though there was a rather rude tone of impatience to his questions.

"Where's Denton?" he'd asked tersely, after they'd run through the list of formalities. *How's Lois? Where's she thinking of going to school? Is Ava coming out at the Assembly Ball this year? Who's her escort?* "We have a situation at the office."

Marti didn't know what, exactly, "situation" meant, though she'd lived with Denton long enough to know that "situation" was stock broker code for "deep shit."

"Honestly," she'd told Tim, "I have no idea."

"Well, we have a situation with Marguerite Grayson. Denton stood her up last week and he hasn't called her to apologize or reschedule. Hasn't even dropped her a line. She's extremely upset."

As though this were somehow her fault. "You've tried his cell, of course."

"Of course. Come on, Marti. We need to know." Tim wasn't being so nice now. "Denton left a message with his secretary that there was a supposed medical emergency. I'd think you'd know if there was a medical emergency."

"You'd think," Marti had replied, giggling. "But you don't know Denton. He doesn't tell me anything. I'm completely clueless."

Tim groaned and hung up.

Marti hoped that was the end of that and proceeded to fax her updated menu to Luis at the Red Dawn Grille, her absolute favorite caterer for small events, especially when Luis himself served the sushi and his wife, Janelle, made the drinks. Janelle was a gas. She used to live in California. The menu—designed to keep everyone light and happy and drunk—went like this:

Cocktails:

Ginger Margaritas (Lisa's request)
Cosmopolitans
Sammy Davis Jr. Cosmos made with Red Bull
(candy eyeball optional)
Martinis made with Absolut (for Denton)
Stewart's Root Beer (for Bob Goss, whose drug of choice
was not alcohol)
Filtered Water (for Karen, she was such a drag)

Appetizers:

Oyster and Artichoke fritters in cornmeal batter with
horseradish cream
Baby Octopus Salad (icky, but Luis insisted)
Planters Peanuts and Cocktail Weenies
Hot Pepper Jelly over Cream Cheese, Ritz Crackers (de rigueur)

Dinner:

Bites of Cold Smoked Duck with Pine Nuts and Citrus Reduction
Sushi Galore!
Hamburgers, Plain, No Lettuce or Tomato or Cheese,
Heinz Ketchup Only (Bob again)

Wines:

A 2000 Clos du Val Reserve Cabernet Sauvignon
A Piper Heidsieck Cuvee Sublime
And, for fun, a sparkling sake. Okunomatsu Junmai Daiginjo "FN"

Marti was watching the desserts fax by—Homemade Peach Ice Cream with Balsamic Syrup / Tropical Fruit Salad, when the machine stopped and the phone rang.

"Hello, Marti. This is Dick Anderson. Sorry I had to break in. It's an emergency."

Even Marti, who'd been preoccupied by what to wear when she got John alone, had enough presence of mind to know that when Richard Anderson, the president and CEO of Anderson Brothers, calls you at home, a "situation" was really a "SITUATION."

"Hi, Dick," she chirped. Dick liked her, or so she'd been told. "I suppose you're calling about Denton."

"We have a crisis on our hands, Marti. We have to find Denton right away."

"As I told Tim, I don't know where he is. I haven't seen him in days."

"In days? Where's he been?"

"He's been here, I guess. We've just been like two ships passing in the night, except we've been passing in the day. He gets up before I get up and comes home after I go to bed. We haven't even spoken."

Dick cleared his throat. "I don't mean to get personal, but are you two having marital issues?"

"Oh, no. We're fine."

"Though you haven't seen him in days and you don't know where he is."

"Right." Marti wished he'd get on with it so she could fax in the rest of the menu. That peach ice cream tended to be a very popular dessert and already she was late ordering.

"Do you know who Marguerite Grayson is?"

"Absolutely. She's on the Cleveland Museum Board with me. She's got a selection of furs you would not believe. Minks. Foxes. A white leopard. And she's so politically incorrect she has the guts to wear them. I love Marguerite. She's a hoot."

"Marguerite is very upset with Denton. Do you understand that?"

"Uh-huh." Perhaps chocolate. If she didn't have something chocolate for dessert, Bob Goss would be a stinker the rest of the night.

"Now, you know I appreciate Denton. He's our top-earning broker. That's why I made him manager of the office last year. That's a position of trust, Marti. Denton has to be his own guardian. As office manager he oversees himself. OK?"

"OK." Why was he telling her this? Blah, blah, blah, blah, blah.

"So when the office manager leaves a client like Marguerite Grayson sitting by herself at the Stouffers, picking over her eggs benedict and coffee, naturally I worry."

"Don't do that, Dick."

"What?"

"Worry." Marti circled Dark Chocolate Mousse Torte with Raspberry Rosemary Roumelade on the Red Dawn Grille Menu. "It's not good for you. It churns up all the toxins in your system. Extremely bad for your skin. And heart. You have to pay attention to your heart, Dick, especially since you sit all day."

"Aren't you worried?"

"About your heart?"

"About Denton."

"No. That'd be silly."

"Marti, I'm worried that you're not worried."

"Don't worry. I never worry. We don't worry in Hunting Hills."

Dick didn't even bother to say good-bye. Marti faxed in the rest of her menu and went upstairs to take a shower. Tonight was book group night. Get through that and in forty-eight hours John would be hers.

She changed into a black Juicy Couture velour hoodie and matching stretch pants, something comfortable for the casual fall night in Boots's den, and waited for Lisa, a copy of *Jane Eyre* on her lap, along with a bottle of Pinot Grigio. As she had in the shower and every minute since John's kiss, Marti indulged in the fantasy of the two of them together, perhaps by the fire, perhaps in bed. It didn't matter, as long as she had his full attention.

"Mom?"

Marti looked up to see Lois with an open cell phone in her hand.

Lois was wearing her weeknight homework outfit—a pair of pink flannel drawstring harem pants that rode a brazen three inches below her navel, along with a spaghetti-strapped T that showed ever-y-thing.

"I called your name three times. What's wrong with you?"

"Is it John?" Marti asked. "Is he on the phone?"

"John who?"

"John Harding."

"Ingrid's dad?"

"Uh-huh."

"No. It's *my* dad. Your husband." Lois thrust out the phone, her hand over the receiver. "He sounds in one of *those* moods."

Marti got on. "Hello, Denton." Forever mindful of the Hunting Hills wife busy rule, Marti injected, "I'm just about to go to my book group. What's up?"

"Jesus, Marti. I need you."

Marti shooed Lois who shuffled off to the refrigerator, opened it, and stared at the bare shelves vacantly, apparently not finding carrot sticks, bottled water, tofu and yogurt the slightest bit appetizing. Lois settled for a gigantic bowl of Frosted Flakes—without milk.

"Is there something wrong, Denton? You sound upset."

"What are the signs of a heart attack?"

"What do you mean?'

"Think, Marti. You know this stuff. Is it," on the other end he exhaled and inhaled deeply, "pain on the right side or the left side? I never can remember."

"You're not having a heart attack. You're not even fifty." Denton could be such a hypochondriac. "You're too young."

"I'm not too young. Ken Johnson was forty-three when he dropped dead in the shower, hit his head on the steam valve and Mary came upstairs, thought he'd been shot there was so much blood."

"Yeah, but Ken Johnson sat on his ass all day long."

"So do I." There was more inhaling and exhaling. "Sit on my ass and make money."

"You don't. Sit on your ass, that is." This was part of another Hunting Hills Wives Rule: Never imply that your husband is not the ultimate breadwinner. "I mean, you're very active. You work out. You play golf. Tennis three times a week."

"I don't, Marti. You make it sound like what I do for a living is a hobby. You have no idea how hard I work. I work like hell to keep up your lifestyle. Christ. There it goes again."

"What?"

"That pain in my neck."

The glow of headlights penetrated the den. Lisa had arrived to pick her up for book group and Marti felt torn between her husband who might, or might not, be dead within minutes and Lisa, who insisted on punctuality.

"Just come home, Denton."

"I can't come home. Not tonight."

"Why not?"

"I'm in New York. At the Ritz."

"The Ritz? What are you doing there?"

"You know. I left a message."

Impossible. Marti had listened to the machine all day and checked the Krups for messages first thing this morning. Besides, when had he gone to New York? And what for?

There was a short, quick beep outside. Beeping was legal justification for murder in Hunting Hills, but Lisa could be temporarily forgiven, seeing as how she had ADD.

"Listen, Denton, I've got to go. But first I have to ask you a very important question."

"Can't stop now, Marti. I gotta go."

No way. She was not going to be the hangupee again, not after the Holly School humiliation. "Wait. Hold on."

He didn't hang up.

Marti took a deep breath. "Can you make it Friday night? I'm throwing a dinner party. For John and Claire, to celebrate their wedding. The theme is Late Blooming Love. You haven't met Claire but she . . ."

Beeeeep. Marti examined the screen. CALL WAS LOST!

Damn he was good.

Chapter Seventeen

John was ready to give up.

He'd done everything he could. He'd coddled her, bribed her, cajoled her. Brought her presents—an Indian silver ankle bracelet, a pair of Russian amber earrings—and even paid for the insurance on her car. Occasionally he'd lost his patience and launched into lectures (what some might call rants) about responsibility and maturity and the need to take hold of one's self.

And, still, Ingrid was unreachable. She was, John feared, lost to him forever.

The turning point came during one of their calculus tutoring sessions. John had been using them as an excuse to be alone with Ingrid for at least an hour every other night, as a way of rescuing her from the academic apathy into which she had been sinking fast. Boots was perfectly willing to go along with this arrangement since her contribution to Ingrid's education went no further than appearance. She'd provided Ingrid with a classic study—a computer, library, work area and, of all amenities, a stereo and mini fridge. Other than that, Boots didn't care a whit. Style over substance, that was Boots.

"OK, let's say *f* represents time, with both the *X* and *Y* axis in the positive quadrant," John began, carefully drawing a pencil along the pale blue line of the graph paper. "You do understand that *f* is the function of real to real numbers, right?"

"Uh-huh." Ingrid flipped through a *Teen People* and stopped at a particularly helpful hint: "How to Be a Doorway Diva."

John leaned over. "How to be a doorway diva? What does that mean?"

"You wouldn't understand." She filed a white-tipped French manicured nail as her gaze moved from "How to Be a Doorway Diva" to "Drive Him Wild with the Ultimate Hair Flip."

John tapped his pencil on the desk and fought the urge to rip the magazine out of her hand, to let her know how rude and inconsiderate she was being. Here he was, a newlywed no less, giving over his precious few free evenings in a futile effort to spark what little flame was left in this kid's pursuit of knowledge and what was she doing? Reading "The Art of Listening: Pretend You Care So He Will."

"Ingrid," he said sternly, barely able to recognize what had once been a chattering, bright-eyed girl who used to spout off all sorts of theories—why frogs croaked, why the stars twinkled, why crickets sang and why Mommy liked to be alone with her accountant. This creature in front of him was nothing more than a composite of corporate advertising. Pantene hair and Revlon shine. Max Factor eyes and Bonne Belle kissable lips.

"Ingrid! This is important. You have a test tomorrow."

She shrugged and tossed aside the magazine, yawning. "I'm beat from hockey practice. They made us do suicide sprints. Are we almost done?" She yawned again.

That was it. He slammed the calculus book and turned off the calculator. He was so mad, so frustrated that had he been her real father he would have grounded her, yanked all her email and IM rights, pulled the plug on her "must have" TV and put her Jeep Cherokee on blocks. But he wasn't her real father. He was the worst of all possible worlds—the authority figure without any power.

"I'm going home," he said, pushing his chair away from the desk.

"Why?" Ingrid blinked. "Am I done studying?"

"Ingrid, you haven't even begun to study. All you've been doing is reading a magazine."

"I need to transition. Mom says everyone needs to transition. That's what the cocktail hour is for."

John opened and shut his mouth. So *that* was it. No wonder she was yawning. Boots was right. Ingrid did have serious, serious problems. He sniffed the air. "Have you been . . . drinking?"

"No." She wrinkled her nose. "Yuck. That's your generation, not mine."

"Then what's this about the cocktail hour?"

"It's only a metaphor. My life is very stressful. Adults don't realize that, how hard it is for us teenagers. Especially girls. There's a lot of expectations society puts on us that we have to live up to. It's exhausting."

"Sure, if you keep reading that crap." He picked up the *Teen People* and flung it across the study so that it hit a can of Diet Red Bull—Boots's other contribution to the "academic process."

"The only expectations you should care about are the ones you put on yourself," he said, attempting to keep his tone reasonable.

"What if I don't have any expectations?"

"Then don't expect much from life." He got up and took his coat off the back of the chair before leaving the study without even saying good-bye.

Claire's simple advice to him had been to remember what it was like to be seventeen. Well, he remembered what it was like to be seventeen and what he remembered was being athletic, strong, full of energy and enthusiasm and reading anything he could get his hands on—Dickens, Hemingway. *National Geographic,* for Christ's sake.

This kid could probably list the forty-eight lipstick tints in Clinique's line and not one state capital. Not even Ohio's.

Boots, who was getting ready for her book group, was in the kitchen fixing mini sandwiches with her maid, Bella, when he passed by.

"Everything go okay?" she sing-songed.

He wanted to point a finger at his ex-wife and blame her for turning Ingrid into an automaton, a ditzy, brainless Barbie doll of a girl, but he didn't. "I give up," he said. "I can't do this anymore."

Bella sighed.

"I know *exactly* how you feel, John." Boots stopped slicing cucumbers. "It's my fault."

John set his lips firm.

"I can read your mind. I should have sent her to Hotchkiss."

Hopeless, he thought. Hopeless from the get go. "Good night, Boots." He went outside, grateful for the light drizzle that had begun to fall, cooling off him and his temper. It was an unseasonably warm night for the first week in November and there had been many years before when the drizzle easily could have been snow. The rain was soft and gentle. Nice.

Boots had great woods behind her house, not like the dinky clusters of trees which passed for woods in Hunting Hills. She was lucky that her grandmother hadn't parceled off the fifty acres and sold them for development. Having the forest, the stream gurgling nearby and the pond on the marshy field made the "cottage" feel special.

His hope had been that by growing up here, Ingrid would learn to appreciate nature, and for a while she had. By age nine she could identify several indigenous, intriguing plants. Trout lilies, Jack-in-the-Pulpits, trillium and wild blue phlox. In the spring she found frogs and tadpoles and saved several newts from drowning, though she was never able to find the elusive marbled salamander, a mysterious and rare creature in Northern Ohio.

She did, however, learn to spot the song of a bluebird and once John helped her build a nesting box for a pair who actually raised three babies. That had been the spring of her twelfth year, the last spring John could remember Ingrid walking with him in the night woods to listen for the varied cries, the barking or spitting, of the large barred owl.

Let it go, he told himself, opening the passenger side door of his Z3 where a box lay, wrapped. It was something Claire had handed him to give to Ingrid, before he left for work that morning. He'd completely forgotten it.

"You better open it first, to see if it's OK," Claire had said, a mischievous twinkle in her eye. "I don't want Boots all over my case."

John ripped off the plain white paper and read the note Claire had carefully penned, as opposed to her usual illegible scribble. His heart leaped. Claire might not have the fashion sense or society savvy of Marti Denton, he thought, but she was unique in her own right. Marti would never have bought something like this for Ingrid.

He opened the box, assembled the contents and grabbed a thin rope he kept in the back. Then, not eager to face Boots's disapproving looks or her snide remarks, he went around to the back of the house where through a window he could see Ingrid in the study, still reading the *Teen People* he'd flung across the room.

"Ingrid!" he hissed.

Ingrid concentrated on the magazine, every once in a while leaning into the computer to type an IM.

"Ingrid!" He picked up a small handful of stones and flung them to the window, where they made a sound much louder than he'd expected.

This startled her and she squinted outside to see who was causing the racket. "Daddy?"

"Come on. Put your sneakers on. I have a surprise for you."

"A surprise?" She smiled and ran out of the room. Two seconds later she was by his side in her sweats and sneakers, trying to peek at what he was holding behind his back.

She wasn't adequately dressed for tromping into the marsh, but

John wasn't about to send her back in. Ingrid would be gone in a flash if she suspected that they'd be heading into the woods.

"Follow me," he said, taking her hand.

"Where are we going? What's that in your hand?"

"You'll see."

"It's dark and it's raining." Her delight was waning. "We don't have a flashlight. My hair will get frizzy."

"Come on." He held her smooth, still childlike hand firmly as they followed the field to the edge of the woods, to the pond.

"You're not, like, a serial killer all of a sudden, are you?" she asked.

"Ingrid."

"Because I saw this movie on TV called *The Stepfather* about this guy who'd marry into a family thinking they were perfect and then when one of them screwed up, like maybe I'm doing in calculus, he'd kill them and start over."

"Geesh, Ingrid. Can't we forget about TV for once?" He stopped at the pond and unraveled the rope from the cylindrical cage.

"What *is* that?"

"It's a minnow trap. You throw it into the pond and it sinks to the bottom. The fish or whatever go in, but they can't get out, like a roach motel." He showed her how the funnel-like ends prevented fish and eels from escaping.

"Why do you have it?"

"Do you remember how we used to search for the marbeled salamander?"

"No." Ingrid looked back at the cottage which stood like a dry haven emanating warm, golden light. "Can we go back now?"

"When you were a little girl you used to have a trap like this and every spring night you'd throw it into the pond and in the morning you'd check for the marbled salamander. You'd catch tadpoles and minnows and all sorts of other salamanders, but never a marbled one and do you know why?"

"Why?"

"Because unlike other salamanders, the marbled salamander mates during the fall. That's the only time it goes into the pond. Claire found that out."

"Oh." Ingrid seemed disappointed to hear Claire was part of this. "Was the trap her idea?"

"Not exactly. I've been telling her about what you were like when you were younger, in your Wellingtons and your raincoats. You were a budding botanist, Ingrid. Boots worried you were going to go wild."

Ingrid giggled. "Me? I don't think so. The only place I go wild is at the mall."

He handed her the rope connected to the trap. "Come on. Throw it in. Maybe we'll get lucky."

Ingrid gingerly took the trap and the rope and after several unsuccessful tries, managed to toss it into the pond. After it sank to the bottom, she and John talked for a few minutes about the barred owl and how it eats other owls and he was gratified to learn that she hadn't forgotten about the spring when they built the blue bird house, which still stood in the middle of the field, graying, rotted and too dirty for the finicky birds.

The rain picked up and they walked back to find Boots at the door, fussing and fuming about mud and dirt and Ingrid neglecting her homework. That she had found another way to irritate her mother added some appeal to the minnow trap which Ingrid found herself checking the next afternoon.

The catch had been disappointing. A worm and weeds. Ingrid decided it needed bait and that night filled it with bread only to be rewarded with a few small fish the next morning. She thought maybe protein would be the ticket and started with cheese, gradually bracing herself for a few night crawlers, which she gathered from the driveway.

Checking the minnow trap moved from mild amusement to obsession. Ingrid would drift down to the pond each day, sometimes standing for several minutes as she poked the mud with a stick, thinking about stuff. About boys and school and college and her future. She found incredible peace in the pond, a peace that seemed unattainable in her room at home.

At some point she completely forgot about the minnow trap, which was about the same time when she finally remembered the person she really was.

Chapter Eighteen

With each day that passed after their Heritage Village meeting, Claire became more and more certain that she had taken the right step by giving Eric the heave-ho. It was a relief to have her rejection over with and even though Eric kept telephoning—he seemed to find it hysterical that she had a housekeeper to play interference—his calls had dwindled in recent days and she regained hope that he would leave her alone.

She never told John about her rendezvous and if by chance he had spied her at Heritage Village as she had spied him at Starbucks, he was discreet enough to say nothing. Perhaps he sensed what she felt, the lifting of a suffocating pall, and was simply thankful for it. With Fran out of the house, Claire and John got down to the business of being married, both of them enjoying the most trivial aspects of it thoroughly.

Elena was given an additional night off so that the two of them could cook together. On those nights, John would come home early from work and drive Claire to the local racquet club where she had started taking lessons, making slow but steady . . . Skip that, *very slow* progress.

"See now, usually you want to keep the ball in the court," John said as she hit a lob that sailed over the netting.

"Fuck!" she screamed, forgetting that crude swears, especially at high volume, were not considered examples of sporting-like behavior.

"We can do that later. For now let's try your backhand."

And so it went, usually ending with John zinging a few serves that showed what a stud king player he really was.

Afterward they would take showers and stop off at Heinen's, picking up fruit for the next morning and whatever hit their fancy for dinner that night. Sometimes John would pick out three ingredients—more often than not healthy vegetables like red peppers or whole wheat pasta—and Claire would deep-six his efforts with a gruyère sauce or anchovies.

They would talk about what they'd read in the *New York Times*—carefully avoiding any mention of the *Cleveland Citizen*—or what Claire was reading besides *Jane Eyre* as they sipped superb red wine and chopped and sautéed and listened to the Beatles or Springsteen or, John's pick, Thelonious Monk (whose eclectic music, confidentially, made her teeth hurt).

It was amazing how much they had to learn about each other and yet how much they already had in common. The Beatles, for instance. It had been craziness that Claire had married a man without first checking if he loved "The Ballad of John and Yoko," as luckily he did, or if he believed in life after death and whether the current White House administration was a bunch of bozos. (They differed on this last point. Claire was sure that she could bring him around once she disabused him of several myths while he privately assumed she would see it his way once he enlightened her.)

Miraculously, none of this—not the politics, the food, the crappy tennis or even their existential differences—mattered one whit. They were truly in love. More importantly, they were old enough and wise enough to appreciate it. A rare constellation of events indeed.

The rest of Claire's life started falling into place too. She made it her routine to wake with John in the morning and make coffee while he went for a run. When he came back they scanned the papers, she reading various items of interest while he shaved or knotted his tie. After he left for work, she drove to a gym far away in Mayfield Heights so she wouldn't run the danger of embarrassing herself by collapsing on the cross trainer in front of a perky Hunting Hills wife.

The pressure to fit in with Hunting Hills society did take its toll, however. At Fran's insistence, Claire finally relented on her appearance. She had her auburn hair highlighted and her nails done and her bikini area professionally waxed—an experience she decided violated the Geneva Convention's protocol on torture. She upgraded her wardrobe at Bloomingdale's and Saks where personal shoppers buzzed about her once they discovered that her last name was Harding and that she was John's wife.

John approved of Claire's new polish, though he was so leery of her possible feminist backlash that he carefully kept his praise to a subdued, "If it makes you feel good, then I'm happy," instead of the alternative, "Thank God you finally had your crotch waxed!"

Even her social calendar showed improvement. Marti Denton of all people offered to throw a party to celebrate Claire and John's marriage, though Claire was even more touched to learn that Marti had weaseled her into Boots's book group, which John noted was a bigger honor than the party as Boots was an out-and-out snob. Perhaps Marti wasn't so bad after all. Perhaps they would grow to be friends. Perhaps, Claire thought, monkeys will fly out of my butt.

Still, Claire vowed to keep an open mind and she finished *Jane Eyre,* even prepared a few thoughtful questions, and baked mini mushroom quiches for the occasion. She had just pulled the quiches out of the oven, gingerly placing them on a cooking rack, when there was a knock at the back door. Waldo the Saint Bernard, who had become protective when John was out of the house, let out a threatening low growl at the silhouette of a tall man with humongous shoulders.

He knocked again. Tiny prickles ran up Claire's neck. The alarm system was off and she was so secluded in this house no neighbors would come to her rescue if she were in trouble. Plus, John was tutoring Ingrid in calculus and wouldn't be home for at least another hour.

Eric, she thought, *and he's really pushing it.*

"Claire?" The man on the other side of the door said. "It's OK. It's George Rico."

She swiped a large butcher knife and hid it behind her back. One year volunteering in a Bosnian refugee camp and twenty as a single woman and she no longer greeted Jehovah's Witnesses without weaponry.

"John sent for me," he said. "Sorry I'm late."

Clutching the knife and holding back Waldo, she opened the door to a tall, blond beefcake who was unlike any Jehovah's Witness she'd ever met. He possessed such long full hair and defined muscles that he could have modeled for *Bloom Off the Rose,* the tattered historical romance hidden under her pillow upstairs.

"I'm George Rico," he said again, as if that was supposed to be significant. Over his shoulder was a large blue gym bag.

"George Rico?" She didn't remember John mentioning a George Rico.

"No." He smiled patiently. "Joriko. J-O-R-I-K-O." He flexed a bicep. "With the weights?"

It clicked. Joriko was the personal trainer Marti had listed in her dos and don'ts, though Claire couldn't remember if he was a do or a don't.

"I was scheduled to be here a half hour ago to start our workout. Got held up by another client. Long story." He rolled his eyes and pushed past her, completely unfazed by the knife Claire was clutching, just in case.

Like in case she wanted to use it on herself. How devastating! John had hired a personal trainer. A personal trainer who looked like a Swede and had a Japanese, one-word name. Was she really that bad? *Wait,* she thought, *for the sake of what's left of your self-esteem, don't answer that.*

"I'm about to go to my book group. I don't know if we have time to . . ."

"You can't wear that," he said, ignoring her protest. "Do you have a yoga set?"

"Pardon?"

"Sweats."

"Sweats?" The very word was self-fulfilling. "I have Spandex stuff I wear to the gym."

"I mean sweats, sweats. I know John has some." Joriko dropped the bag. "Come on." Clearly, he'd been here before because he made his way easily up the back stairs, two at a time, to John's suite of his and hers walk-in closets, dressing room, bath and bedroom.

"Hold on." She hustled after him. "How do I know you're not a robber or something? A rapist."

Joriko stopped at the closet doorway, a look of genuine hurt on his face. "If I were a rapist, don't you think you'd be raped by now?"

She found his answer illogically comforting.

He yanked open the bottom drawer of John's California Closet and pulled out a pair of old-fashioned gray sweatpants, the kind that do no favors to any woman, unless that woman happens to be Christie Brinkley and even then those favors have to be airbrushed. "I'll meet you downstairs. In the weight room."

There were no iffs, ands or butts. Actually, there was a butt. Hers. And it happened to be a couple sizes too big.

Claire wiggled into the gray sweats, donned one of John's T-shirts, refused to look at herself in the full-length mirror and ran to the basement. Joriko's sandy mane was in a ponytail and he was doing push-ups. One-handed push-ups. The very sight of it made her ill.

"Perfect." He stood and wiped off his hands. "We'll start off with some stretching, move into twenty minutes of aerobics and then some weight work. Sound good?"

"No." She caught sight of her sweat-suited body in the wall of mirrors. "All right, yes."

"Excellent." He rolled out a mat and from somewhere produced a large red inflatable ball. "Ever done this before?"

"Beach ball? I think so."

"No, this." Joriko lay on the ball, the muscles of his super flat stomach—or, rather, abs—defined and rock hard. He launched into a quick set of mind-bending crunches.

What evil genius had thought up this torture? Claire wanted to know.

"You try it." He tossed her the ball, which was so big it nearly knocked her over.

Claire imitated Joriko and promptly fell off, flat onto the floor. "Woops! Maybe we should move on. How about arm circles? I like those. I was very good at them in elementary school."

"You have to try again."

She was beginning to despise Joriko. Joriko with the fru-fru name and the fru-fru hair.

Joriko repositioned the ball, leaning over her to do so. She could tell he was trying to make eye contact. Like a petulant child she refused to play along.

"Just want to make sure you're secure," he said. "So you don't fall off again." Joriko's large hands slid up her chest, his thumbs grazing the sides of breasts.

Claire was petrified. *Oh my god, he's got his hands up my shirt.* Joriko didn't seem to give it a second thought.

"Start out slow and build up. We're working on your abdominals. Right here."

She gasped as he placed a hand on the bare spot between her T-shirt and sweatpants, a good inch or so south of the navel. It was so . . . daring!

"You don't mind me touching you?" he asked with a footnote of amusement.

"I didn't even notice," she fibbed.

"That's too bad because I want you to notice. I want you to focus on my hand. Those are the lower muscles, the ones you want to strengthen."

He was right. She couldn't help but focus on his hand. His hand was warm and, as she rolled up, somewhat down her pants.

"You're not breathing."

"I can't imagine why."

This lasted for a mesmerizing eternity until Claire was dizzy with lack of oxygen. Joriko then ordered her to lie face down on the mat while he bent her leg toward her head. This time his hand was right below her ass, before it slipped around and briefly stroked her inner thigh, causing Claire to let out an involuntary, "Yip!"

But it wasn't until they'd finished with the boring treadmill and were in the middle of endless bicep repetitions, that things really got interesting.

"Stop!" He had one hand between her shoulder blades and one hand under the flabby part of her upper arm, to make sure the weights were working on the right muscles. "What's this?"

Claire dropped the weight gratefully. Her arm was killing her. "What's what?"

"Right here." Immediately, Claire was in excruciating pain as Joriko palmed a tender spot, one inch from her spine. "Does that hurt?"

"Ahhh," was all she could manage.

"Hmmm. I'll need to take a look. Take your shirt off, please."

Now confused in addition to being in pain, she whispered, "How come I have to take off my shirt?"

"Please. I won't look. This is important."

"Then close your eyes." She was Caleb Stark's daughter, after all.

Claire checked to see he had closed his eyes before yanking off her T-shirt and unclasping her white cotton bra, holding them against her chest out of modesty.

She hoped it wasn't cancer. Like every woman around her age, she lived in mortal fear of undiagnosed cancer that could have been easily treated if she'd *just been vigilant*. That what's made being forty such a drag, all that constant vigilance.

"OK, you can open your eyes now," she said.

"Sit down in front of me." He collapsed into a lotus position.

She complied and studied their reflection in the mirror. Joriko removed the ponytail, shook his hair free, closed his eyes and examined her back, pushing and pinching various muscles. They made a funny pair—her alarmed, clutching the T-shirt to her tits, and him all Mr. Romance. It was kind of amusing . . . until he delivered his diagnosis.

"There is a shadow on your soul." His voice was definitive.

"There is?" Was that like a spot on a lung X-ray? "What does that mean?"

"You've suffered a trauma. A severe loss."

She didn't respond. The statement could have been a trick—what woman at her age hadn't suffered a severe loss? But it could also have been kind of creepily insightful. It wasn't the loss of her mother—though Claire missed her every day. It was another loss that was consuming her every waking thought.

It had happened at the refugee camp. Josie and she had been there all of a month when one night Claire developed severe cramps and a high fever suggesting a virulent bout of pelvic inflammatory disease. PID was not what you wanted to contract in a place with flashlights for examination equipment and outhouses for sanitation. Claire chose to endure the pain on her own and with the help of a bitter herbal tea brewed by local women, she slowly recovered.

When she left the camp and began work in Prague she saw a well-respected gynecologist who confirmed her worst fears. The untreated PID might have left scarring, scarring that could make it difficult—if not impossible—to someday conceive. Worse, his dire predictions were proving true. After nearly three months with John, during which neither of them used birth control, Claire still wasn't pregnant—a condition she optimistically chalked up to the vagaries of age.

Joriko started massaging her back. "When the soul experiences a trauma, part of it flies off and hides. It's why people who've been in car accidents don't remember the crash. It's the soul's attempt at survival."

OK, she thought, keep going.

"The rest of the soul misses this missing part and there can be emptiness and bad luck and sickness until that part of the soul returns."

OK, she thought, you're nuts.

"But this. Right here." He pressed the painful muscle again. "This is trapped energy. Someone has been sending you bad energy and it is stuck in your body."

"Owww!" She flinched as he pressed it again. "I thought that was from my computer. Bad ergonomics."

He ignored this. "Who would be sending you bad energy?"

"I have no idea. Frankly, these days I'm grateful for any energy at all."

Joriko didn't get the joke.

Claire had a feeling he wasn't big in the humor department.

"You have to remove that energy or your hiding soul will not feel as though it is safe to return. Your future will be dark."

"Dark?" Hardly. "Actually, I think my future looks pretty bright."

"What you see as your future in the present cannot be because your present actions are the product of an incomplete soul. The future, therefore, is an unattainable illusion."

She took a few seconds to unravel this. "Because of the missing soul thingy?"

He nodded sagely. "It leaves an emptiness that creates meaningless desires and frustrations. I sense that you have been disappointed with your professional life recently and that you irrationally assume that people you've just met don't like you."

Claire bit a nail. Both were true.

"And of course you do not fully reach orgasm."

She leaped off his lap. "Excuse me?" She considered slapping his smug, ponytailed face. "I'll have you know I orgasm just fine, thank you."

"How do you know?" Joriko shrugged casually, completely unperturbed. "Does the dawn know dusk? Does black know white? Does life know death?"

"What? That makes no sense."

"There's no point in being ashamed, Claire. It is all the same. It is all about trapped energy you don't want and missing energy you need. The pain in your back, your loss, your insecurity, your inability to . . ."

"Watch it!" She held up a warning finger, though she wasn't sure if that was for what he was about to say or the insecurity remark. "Let's just stop right there."

Part of her was dumbstruck. Appalled. Then again, part of her wanted to say, *How did you know?* But she just couldn't. It was too wacky and the suspicious journalist in her was already convinced that Joriko—"Joriko" of all names—was a flim-flam man. She was curious to learn how much John had paid for this snake oil salesman.

"And I suppose you're just the man to free that energy."

"I can help."

He held out his hands. Claire shied away.

"It's not like that. I'm a healer. It's a gift." He grasped her hand and looked into her eyes. She tried to wiggle free, but he pulled her onto his crossed legs, and for some reason she let him. He turned her so once again her bare back was to him.

"Let me show you," he said calmly.

Sliding aside her hair, he closed his eyes again and let his hands drift gently over her, not quite touching her skin. It sounded kooky, but she could almost feel a force, like magnetism, in the thin space between his hands and her back.

What followed was a mystery. Claire vaguely remembered Joriko laying her down as he chanted softly, his lips tracing a line from hip bone to hip bone pausing at certain points to suck.

"What're you doing?" Alarmed, she tried to sneak a peek.

He pushed her head away. "Acupuncture," he said. "Kind of."

When she came to, she was on the mat, the T-shirt still underneath her.

"Do you feel that?" He pressed that tender spot near her spine.

"No." She lifted her head. "It's gone. You got rid of the pain."

"Yes. But there's much more that needs to be healed, Claire."

"Like what?" She couldn't believe she'd asked.

"Finding your lost soul. You will need a power animal for that. Do you have a power animal?"

She thought hard. Power animals. Power animals. She had power brakes and power steering. PowerPoint on her computer. But no power animals per se. "I have a stuffed bunny, does that count?"

This elicited a laugh, finally. "You should ask to dream about your power animal. Or look for him, or her. Only your power animal can retrieve your soul." He sat back. "Is there something else you'd like to ask?"

She turned her head and curled her toes. This was so embarrassing, worse than being at the ob-gyn's and discussing the benefits of cranberry juice. "The, uh, stuff you said before about . . . you know."

"Hmmh." His hair brushed the part of her back that moments before had been sizzling in agony. "I think you will notice a change right away. You're very receptive."

"I know." She sighed. "That's my problem."

"That's not your problem. That's *your* gift. But we've done enough for today." He got up and she heard him snap the elastic over his hair. "Right now, it's late and I'm still behind schedule."

She watched him gather his weights and towel, stuffing them in the blue gym bag. He really was handsome, for a shaman. Not often you come across a shaman who looks like Fabio. The shamans she'd met in Europe came up to her shoulder and smelled like cooked broccoli.

"Do you go around releasing energy for everybody?"

"Not everybody." He zipped up. "Usually, I work on increasing muscle mass and aerobic efficiency. By the way, don't forget to alternate those reps. Three sets of fifteen one day, one day off." And with that, he left.

So this was the perk of affording your own personal trainer-slash-shaman, she realized. Not a perk the average woman got hopping up and down with Richard Simmons and *Sweatin' to the Oldies,* was it?

Claire flipped over and discovered she was exhausted, physically and spiritually spent. As she drifted off, plunged actually, into the deep abyss of a satisfying cat nap, it became crystal clear to her why the Hunting Hills wives were so incredibly fucking fit.

Claire startled awake to the sound of footsteps upstairs. Her watch said seven thirty-five, the usual time when John came home. But he was at Ingrid's.

She needed sanctuary. The bathroom! Yes. It was right off the workout room and there was a sauna and a steam shower, which could wash her free of all Joriko's musk scented acupuncture oils. Claire gathered up her sweats and flipped on the water. She stripped off what was left of her clothes and jumped under the warm spray.

She anxiously studied her belly. Five reddish purple marks ran right along her bikini line—or what would have been a bikini line if she'd been daring enough (OK, fit enough) to wear a bikini. Evidence of Joriko's deep massage. Like a fool, she ran a bar of soap over them on the off chance that they could be erased. But the washing was useless. The hot water only made it worse.

"Hey. Can I come in?" There was a polite knock on the bathroom door.

Cripes. It was John after all and he'd be sure to notice the marks right away. Claire rinsed off and grabbed a thick white towel. She had no choice. She'd have to come clean.

John, the personal trainer sucked me dry. I hope you don't mind.

"Joriko must have really worked you out," he said, entering the misty bathroom. "Made some comment about you being very receptive."

"You don't want to know." She peeked into the workout room. "He's not still here, is he?"

"No. He left. He was in one hell of a rush. What were you two doing?"

The steam floated past them, out the door. John loosened his tie in the heat, an ordinary gesture that Claire, like most women, found irresistible. "Promise not to get mad?"

"Why would I get mad?"

"Look." In the protective safety of the steam, Claire opened her towel. John's gaze dropped right away to the line of hickies. She braced herself for a torrent of jealous rage.

"Geesh. I hope he's had his shots."

"You don't mind?"

"It's Joriko. He's a flake. I trust you both but . . ." He ran a finger along the line. "What's this all about?"

"My infertility." As soon as she said it she choked on the word. Somehow, in saying *infertility* out loud it had solidified her condition, made it real. She found herself in John's arms, sobbing into his shirt and gushing about how sorry she was and how he knew he always wanted to have children and first Boots wouldn't and now she couldn't and it was such a mess.

"Stop, stop," he soothed, pushing back her damp hair and kissing her forehead, her cheek and her neck. "It's OK, Claire. I love you. *You.* You're my wife. My friend. My lover. You have to start believing me when I tell you that."

Then he kissed her so deeply that his belt buckle pushed into the tender skin below her navel, made all the more tender by Joriko's treatment. So, of course, Claire had to unbutton his belt before moving up to his shirt, her fingers fumbling along, desperate as she was to have all of him.

"All I've ever wanted," she said through her tears, "all my life was a baby. And I put off getting married and having children for my career and now it's too late."

It was feminist heresy. Her ears burned to hear herself say it. But, goddamnit, it was true. She had always wanted to be a mother, though the fuckup hadn't entirely been her fault. She'd wasted too much time with men like Eric Schmaltz, wimps afraid of real commitment, and of course no one was to blame for nasty viruses or bacteria or whatever it was that had made her so sick.

"A baby," John whispered in her ear, sending shivers reverberating through the entire length of her body. "That's all you want? A baby?"

"More than anything." She pushed the shirt off and ran her hands over his smooth shoulders, tanned and, in some parts, freckled. "Is that stupid? Are we too old?"

"No. No. No." He kissed her again, his hair and face damp now from the steam. "God, you're wonderful. You're so good and pure and strong. We'll have *our* baby Claire. Some way."

The words, the way he said *our baby,* made her feel felt ripe and moist, lush and desirable.

Feel don't think. She thought of what Joriko had said. *Let go*.

John lowered himself, planting kisses between her breasts and down to where Joriko had been working his acupuncture only moments before. Claire moaned as her eager husband parted her legs and his tongue seduced her expertly. She ran her fingers through his hair, trying to pull him up, but instead he gently held her against the wall, persisting until her mind shut down completely and she, for a change, could summon only raw, determined craving.

They ended up in the sauna, making love in the dry heat on the hot cedar benches, though neither of them noticed the heat or even where they were. Claire couldn't recall sex like that ever before and she grudgingly gave Joriko his due. Perhaps he'd been right about her to begin with.

She rested her cheek against her husband's hard chest and listened to the steady pounding of his heart as one of his hands played with a lock of her hair. So this was it. This was marital bliss.

"Do you know when I fell in love with you?" he asked.

"You said it was love at first sight. When I showed up at your office door in Prague wearing that ratty old Burberry and holding a notebook."

"No. That's when I first *lusted* after you, because you were the living incarnation of a Roy Lichtenstein drawing and I've always had a weakness for big-busted redheads in desperate situations."

She smiled to herself, wondering if that's really how she'd come off.

"It's different for men, love versus lust. Lust is much less complicated."

"So I understand." She traced her finger along the fine hairs on his inner thigh. "Okay, when did you fall in love with me, then?"

"That night I came to your apartment in Prague and your drunken landlady . . . What was her name again?"

"Mrs. Krozan."

"Mrs. Krozan kept pestering you with her dog and her homemade moonshine. What I couldn't get over was how that old bird, a hard-bitten former New Jersey bar owner who's probably a son of a bitch to most people, adored you. She sincerely wanted you to be happy to the point of pulling all these pranks to get me to stay."

Claire lifted her head. "You knew?"

"We take his pants somehow? She must have said that at least five times."

Claire giggled. "I can't believe that's when you fell in love. I was hoping for something more romantic. When you saw my exquisite taste in literature, perhaps."

"That is romantic, you closet Stephen King freak. Not everyone can bring out the best in people. But you do, Claire. That night I saw you inspire what little loving there was in Mrs. Krozan and every day since you've brought out the best in me.

"That's what makes you different from the women I grew up with, the women I often wondered if I might be in love with. Sometimes they were extremely tempting. Still, in the end, I thank the stars for what paltry wisdom I had to wait for you."

Claire suspected that there was a heavy story behind that statement. Possibly something having to do with Boots. But all she said was, "I've got to go. Already I'm late for the book group. I do love you though."

She kissed the tip of his nose and let it be.

Chapter Nineteen

"The thing about champagne," Marti philosophized as Boots filled her glass for the third time, "is that some people can handle it and some people can't. It's gen . . . gen." Boy, it was hard to say that word. "Genethic."

"Genetic," corrected Lisa, amused.

Lisa was sitting on Boots's tooled leather hassock in Boots's historic registered library, smoking a cigarette. As a rule Hunting Hills wives did not smoke. They did not drink to excess or eat fatty cheese either. But all bets were off in Boots's book group. The rules, as Marti pronounced with a tipsy flourish of her hand, were out the window!

"And what happens here, stays here," Marti added out loud.

"Who are you talking to?" Lisa asked.

Marti pondered that. "I have no idea."

"Where's Claire?" asked Boots, removing the lead wrapper from another bottle of Moët.

(Lest anyone get the wrong idea that this was some high-end British affair or gross Beverly Hills shindig, it just so happened that Jesus—

Boots's Jesus—had been given a case of Moët by a thankful client, the wife of a liquor distributor, who was thrilled by her Mediterranean dining room and worried that writing the Second Coming a forty-thousand-dollar check couldn't begin to pay for his services and by that she was not referring to his upholstery samples.)

"I don't know." Marti checked her watch. "Maybe she got lost."

"You gave her directions, didn't you?" asked Kit Vickers in her permanent black headband and pearls, sucking back the bubbly. Kit was a former Alpha Theta Alpha who could really pack it away.

"Of course." Or had she? Marti couldn't really recall.

"It doesn't matter. She probably got them from John," said Lisa who was very, very smart, Marti thought, and well dressed too.

Lisa's long brown hair hung straight and flat, yet was somehow bouncy. Her silver gray cashmere sweater cardigan and shell—definitely not your mother's twin set—clung to her fortified bust as a six-hundred-dollar sweater should and on her feet were the most adorable boots. Marti had made a mental plan to steal her boots. She'd been working on it since glass number two.

"Well, are we going to talk about this book or not?" asked Kit, holding up *Jane Eyre*.

"Speaking of talk, guess who I talked to yesterday?" Boots uncorked the bottle with a *pop!* "Justine Frakes."

Marti racked her brain trying to place Justine Frakes.

"The guidance counselor at Tate," Lisa explained, seeing Marti's confusion. "You wouldn't know since you don't have boys."

"Right." Marti debated whether to break her six-month fast and have a butt.

"She told me on the QT—and you absolutely cannot tell anyone I said this . . ."

The women leaned toward her eagerly.

"That Chip Goss has a 10 percent chance, at best, of getting into Yale."

"Oh!" Kit covered her mouth. "Karen's going to be bullshit."

"Forget Karen," Lisa said. "What about Bob? He's been buying that poor kid Yale T-shirts since before he was born. He'll have a heart attack."

"Denton's having a heart attack," piped up Marti. "He said so on the phone tonight. Pass me a cigarette."

Lisa tossed the pack of Marlboro Lights but Marti—who, as it turned out, genetically could not handle champagne—dumbly watched the pack fly past her.

"What do you mean, Denton's having a heart attack?" Lisa asked. "You didn't bring that up in the car."

"I forgot." Marti found the pack under a lamp.

"Where is Denton anyway?" asked Boots. "Everyone's dying to know."

"New York. At the Ritz." Marti lit up, waving the match. "He's faking. I know he is. And if he isn't then at least he's in New York. There are great hospitals there. Not as good as the Cleveland Clinic, but close."

Lisa stubbed out her cigarette. "Did he happen to say what led up to this heart attack?"

"No. Though I think there's a lot of pressure at work. People from his office called all day long looking for him. Dick Anderson said Denton stood up Marguerite and hasn't been seen since."

Lisa twirled her champagne, eyeing the tiny bubbles, her professionally plucked eyebrows furrowed in artistic concern. More concern than Marti showed, Boots noted, and she quickly changed the subject lest Pandora from Glendale decided to open her box of secrets.

"Denton will be fine. Of course he'll be fine. And, if not, Marti will handle it." Boots refilled Lisa's glass slowly. "Getting back to Chip Goss, Justine said that his going to Exeter actually worked against him. He should have stayed at Tate because it's in Ohio, not the East Coast, and his extracurriculars are mediocre."

"He went to Nigeria," Marti said.

"Zimbabwe," Boots corrected.

"Same thing."

"Everyone goes to Africa. It's the inner city where you need to be. Or published by fifteen." Boots was an expert on Ivy admission requirements, especially now that Ingrid was a senior at Holly. Starting with Ingrid's preschool, an exclusive Quaker institution in Chardon, Boots had been ahead of them all when it came to knowing what was required to get into Harvard, Princeton, Swarthmore, Amherst, Middlebury and Williams. Her top choices, though they were becoming less attainable now that Ingrid wasn't showing up for class.

"If Chip Goss can't get into Yale then Lois is going to end up at fucking Cleveland State," Marti mumbled. "Her grades are the pits and her extracurriculars amount to giving her boyfriend head."

Kit cleared her throat and Boots said, "There's nothing wrong with Cleveland State" to cover for Marti who clearly had forgotten that Cleveland State had been Lisa's alma mater.

"There's lots wrong with Cleveland State. It's a pit. Only complete and total losers go there." Marti still wasn't catching on.

Thankfully Bedo and Alys started barking their heads off, indicating that someone was at the door.

"I hope it's not Ingrid." Boots grabbed the cigarette pack and stuffed it under a seat cushion. "I promised to pay her one hundred bucks a cigarette."

That was stupid, Marti thought. Why would Boots pay so much for a cigarette? Even the fancy ones were only seven dollars a pack.

Boots's maid, Bella, a trim black woman from Hough who would have no truck with women misbehaving, led in the rosy faced and glowing Claire, who clutched a worn copy of *Jane Eyre* and a foil-covered plate.

"I brought mushroom quiches." She handed them to Bella, along with her coat.

"They won't eat 'em," Bella said under her breath. "All these girls want to do is get liquored up."

"You're just jealous that you have to work and you can't party," Boots said.

Bella shrugged and marched off with the quiches. Boots introduced Claire to Lisa and Kit and then poured some champagne. "If you mind the smoke . . ."

"No!" Claire eagerly took the glass. "Actually, I'd love a cigarette. I haven't had one since I met John. He's such a health nut."

Interesting, thought Marti, sitting up.

Boots wagged a finger at her. "I thought you had potential. John's not the type to fall for prudes. Now you can see why we can't invite Karen."

"She doesn't seem much of a prude to me," Claire said, pulling a chair into their circle.

The women exchanged knowing glances and laughed.

Boots handed her a glass of champagne. "Don't get us wrong. We like Karen. We really, really do. She's a sweetheart."

"A better mother than any of us." Kit lifted her glass in a toast.

"But she's just so . . ." Boots frowned, searching for the right word.

"Stuffy," said Marti. "Everything's organic this and filtered that. She's no fun at all. If she were here she'd dump all our glasses and snuff our cigarettes."

"I'm not so sure." Claire was recalling Karen's greenhouse. "It's been my experience that the people who are the stiffest on the outside tend to be the wildest on the inside if you give them a chance."

"Like John?" Marti couldn't resist.

Claire lit a cigarette, gripping the chair to steady herself as the slug of carbon monoxide hit her brain. "He's not that stiff."

"Except when you want him to be." Boots kicked Claire's ankle gently. "Right?"

Claire blushed.

Marti was dying. Absolutely dying. Two women from John's intimate world. One who had been his wife; one who was. And here she was, Marti Swan Denton, his true *amour,* the only woman he'd ever really wanted, forced to live a lie. Forced to hide their passionate affair. It was more than she should have to bear.

"What's wrong with you?" Lisa whispered. "You look like you're going to puke."

"I'm putting on a brave face." Marti practiced smiling wanly.

"Get over it. He's not yours yet."

"Yes he is," Marti hissed back, catching herself when Boots darted her a dirty look.

"It was a delight to read this again." Claire thumbed the book. "I got so much more out of it than I did in college."

"You read that in college?" Kit asked.

"Didn't everyone?"

"CliffsNotes," Kit said. "My parents spent twenty thousand dollars a year for me to read CliffsNotes."

"I liked that drunken woman," Marti shouted, suddenly unable to remember Bertha Mason's name or how to control the level of her voice. "Who was she?"

"Marti Denton." Lisa put a finger to her lips.

"Oh, you."

"You know, I also had more sympathy toward Bertha Mason." Claire put down her glass. "It's odd because when I first read the book and Bertha's brother showed up at Jane's wedding and led them to the attic, I remember crying, I felt so sorry for her. But now I'm curious as to what it was that made Bertha go mad."

Marti hollered, "He locked her in an attic. That's what made her go mad. Wouldn't that make you go mad?"

"No, Marti," Kit said quietly. "He locked her in an attic *after* she went mad."

"No way!"

Boots said, "It's true. Read it again."

"The third time? What are you trying to do? Drive *me* mad? I swear he locked her in and then she went loopy."

"That was the whole point!" Kit was nearly out of her chair. "It was the only way to handle her. She was out to ruin him and in the end she did."

"You don't know what it's like. It would drive anybody nuts. I know because Denton once locked me in the attic." Marti sipped some more champagne and when she looked up from her glass she found the women staring at her. "He wanted me out of the way. For the Super Bowl. That's all."

Somewhere in the house the phone rang and the dogs barked again. Bella appeared at the doorway to the library and motioned for Boots, who left the room to get it. After she was gone they were silent, thinking about Marti running around the attic during the Super Bowl, her hair wild and untamed like Bertha Mason. A woman badly in need of a good hairdresser.

Marti was beginning to have doubts about mentioning the attic incident. She definitely had violated the rule about dissing one's husband. "It wasn't that bad, really. I found a box of photos and some empty photo albums still in plastic. I'd been meaning to get them organized anyway."

"I'd have punched his lights out if he'd tried that on me." Lisa had a hand on what passed for a hip.

"Why would he have locked you in the attic?" Marti asked. "You're not his wife."

Lisa flipped her hair. "Forget it."

Marti didn't like it when Lisa flipped her hair. It was so show-offy. But she did like those boots. Yes indeedy. Lisa wouldn't say where she'd bought them, only that they were from Italy so absolutely Marti would have to steal them. Maybe she could spill champagne on them and sneak them in her purse. It was crazy, but it might just work.

Boots returned and shut the doors of the library. Her face was ashen.

"What is it?" Kit asked anxiously. "Is Ingrid OK?"

"Ingrid's fine." Boots's lips were slim lines.

"The dogs?" Marti bellowed.

"It's Karen." Boots could barely get out the words. "She's downtown in the police department and she's too afraid to call Bob."

"What happened?" Claire asked, the stash of sensi hash coming to mind.

"She wouldn't tell me anything except that she's OK and she's been involved in an incident, if you can believe that. Karen in an incident. It doesn't make sense."

"Well, what does she want us to do about it? We're not lawyers," said Lisa the Uber Bitch.

"She wants us to drive down and get her." Boots began wringing her hands.

"Now? At eight thirty?" Lisa shook her head. "That's Karen, for you. She's so *needy,* not to mention inconsiderate. Doesn't she know we're in book group?"

"Of course she does. That's why she called here." Boots searched under the seat cushions for the cigarettes, forgetting that Claire had had them last.

"You didn't say we would, did you?" Lisa asked.

"I didn't know what to say. I told her to call Roy Phelps but she was dead set against it. She said he's the last person she wanted to know."

"Not Roy?" Marti said. "Why?"

"I have no idea. She refused to even give me a hint as to what this is about. It's odd. Very, very odd. It was so . . . awkward."

Boots shook out a cigarette. Kit poured herself some more champagne and Lisa examined her manicure.

Claire was stunned. Were these women going to do nothing? Were they just going to sit here, idly gossiping while a woman they considered their best friend was left to languish in the police department? Perhaps she'd been mugged or . . . worse.

"Maybe we should call Karen's dad," Marti suggested after a few minutes. "He used to be a lawyer."

"He's eighty," Boot said, nervously flicking an ash. "And in a nursing home."

"Then what *are* we going to do?" Kit asked.

Boots inhaled and exhaled deeply. "I haven't a clue."

"I think you should go get her," Claire said gently.

There was a collective drop of perfect jaws. Clearly, Claire had no idea what she was suggesting. She was new in town and wasn't aware that the Cleveland PD was where prostitutes and drug dealers and all sorts of urine-soaked individuals hung out. One did not go down to the Cleveland Police Department without a lawyer, certainly not at night.

"You don't know where the Cleveland Police Department is," Marti said. "It's in the heart of downtown. To get there you've got to drive down streets I wouldn't drive down during the day. You could get carjacked."

"Plus," Boots added, "we've been drinking. If we show up, we could be busted ourselves."

"Then I'll go myself." Claire stood. Bella, who'd been listening with interest, went to get her coat.

"You can't go. You don't even know where it is," Lisa said.

"I've got a map. I'll figure it out."

"I'll go with you. You can't go alone." Boots stubbed her cigarette.

"Boots, you can't," Marti said. "What if someone sees you?"

"Karen called me. It'll be weird if Claire, whom she's met twice, shows up and no one else does. Plus, what if she finds out that Claire was at the book group and she wasn't? She'll be ballistic."

This, Marti had to agree, was the best point made so far. If there was one good reason to fetch Karen from that hideous fortress called police headquarters, it was so she wouldn't hear about Claire's book group invitation she'd been able to wheedle out of Boots.

"Then I'll go too. After all, I was the one who twisted your arm to let Claire in. If Karen asks, I'll tell her that I had ulterior motives and that you really preferred her, but that Claire had to be at the top of the list because . . ."

Marti slapped her mouth. Boots and Kit were aghast.

Lisa, though, loved it. “Good going, Bertha Mason.”

“I mean,” Marti started, her champagne addled brain searching for a way to eat her words.

“You meant that I had to be on the top of the list because I’m John’s new wife and you were eager to include me,” Claire said graciously, barely able to hide her own amusement. “It was very kind of you, Marti. No wonder John speaks of you so fondly.”

To which Lisa simply raised her glass.

Chapter Twenty

Denton was bored so he made a list. It went like this:

THE RITZ	vs.	THE EMPRESS
24-hour room service		24-hour drug delivery
Pillow-topped beds		Quarter-operated massage
In-room hi-speed Internet		In-room hookers
Marble facade front desk		Plexiglas check-in counter

Denton was not in New York

Where he was, was in the Empress Hotel, across the street from the Trailways bus station and around the corner from the Tenth Street Precinct in bee-utiful downtown Cleveland. His third floor room, decorated in various shades of slime green, came saturated with the smell of stale cigarette smoke and spilled beer, which filled his nostrils as he lay on a towel on his cruddy double bed, mindlessly popping Skittles and listening to his neighbors go at it.

The clinks of ice and a woman's laughter in room 307 had turned to slurred accusations and then to several disturbing thumps near his headboard. Meanwhile, in 311, rap music pounded so hard that the laptop on his desk had almost bounced onto the floor. Only the flies on his ceiling seemed impervious.

The Empress was not a place where Sherry, Anderson Brothers' exclusive travel agent, would book him and that was exactly why he was there, waiting for Dr. Murray.

Matt Murray was Denton's psychiatrist and as a policy he did not make house calls, much less sleazy hotel calls. But Matt Murray was also Denton's classmate from Tate, about the only Jewish guy Denton knew growing up besides Stan Green, whose father was a judge.

Because Murray was a Tate alum he was loyal to Denton. So loyal that when he received Denton's hysterical call about the eternal erection and his crushing heart attack, Murray excused himself from a dinner party with people he genuinely enjoyed to rush over to the Empress to be with Denton, whom he genuinely disliked.

Denton knew Murray would come because, as they said in Hunting Hills, that's what you got with Jews. Dedication. A WASP wouldn't leave a dinner party. He'd be too drunk. But not Jews, Denton thought. They're there for you. Like his wife, Marti. She was a Jew, or rather, a Jewess. Though she didn't admit it.

Even so, Denton wouldn't let the sober and loyal psychiatrist into his hotel room until Murray slipped two forms of identification under the door and soothed him with reassurances so that Denton finally unlatched the three locks.

"This is crazy," said Murray, who was famous for his unorthodox sense of humor. "What are you, nuts?" He was about to toss his coat on the bed when he spied something crawling and thought better of it.

"So, tell me," he said, folding the coat over his arms. "What's going on with us today, Jim?"

Denton scurried to the bed, to a spot he'd had picked out since 4 p.m. when he checked in. "I think I'm dying," he proclaimed, leaning against a pillow and closing his eyes. "I think I'm having a heart attack."

"Then let's get you to a hospital." Murray was a behaviorist, none of this Freudian digging into the murk of penis envy and Oedipus complex for him. He grabbed Denton's wrist, took his pulse, then felt his forehead. "I don't think you're having a heart attack. I think you *feel* like you're having a heart attack, but that doesn't mean you are. We've talked about that many times, Denton, the difference between truth and fiction."

Denton palmed his own forehead, trying to see for himself whattell-tale sign was missing that would lead Murray to determine his heart attack was fiction. He liked to know where he messed up on his lies.

Murray glanced around the depressing room. No suitcase. No booze. No signs of drug use, prescription or otherwise. Just a large red open bag of Skittles on the desk next to the IBM laptop. Denton must have come here straight from work, he deduced. Problems on the home front.

"Did something happen with Marti?"

"No," said Denton, not offering more. Denton liked to have information coaxed out of him, an attention-getting trick established in childhood that Murray found to be one of Denton's more irritating qualities. And that was saying something, as Denton had a lot of irritating qualities.

"Was it something with work then?"

"Not *exactly.*"

Murray held back a sigh and leaned against the TV. "Lisa?"

"Kind of."

"Please, Denton, you have to meet me halfway." Murray threw his coat over the television and loosened his tie. "I left a party, including a succulent Cornish game hen and an excellent Northern California Pinot

Noir, to travel all the way downtown in the pouring rain just so I could talk to you."

Denton pouted.

"I'm charging you triple time. Plus mileage. If that matters."

That mattered. Denton quit playing around. "I think it's coming to an end."

"What's coming to an end?"

"You know."

"You mean the lying?"

"What are you talking about? I don't lie." Denton swung his legs over the side of the bed so his back was to him. "How can you say that?"

"Do I need to bring down the cone of confidence?" This was a technique Murray had borrowed from the 1960s sitcom *Get Smart*. He'd found that if he encircled Denton in an imaginary "cone of confidence" that Denton would actually tell the truth, at least what for Denton passed as the truth.

But tonight Denton didn't require the cone. He was ready to spill, starting with last week's rendezvous with Lisa and ending with the erection that just wouldn't stop and how he'd been too mortified to show up for his breakfast meeting with Marguerite Grayson because he was certain she'd see that he still had a stiffy.

"She's pulling out all her money." Denton went to his trusty laptop, which displayed Marguerite's many Anderson accounts, some of which had been marked CLOSED. "She's already transferred close to twenty-five million and I know she's coming back for the other thirty-five. The only reason she hasn't is probably because Dick Anderson has spent the past week on his knees offering his first born, begging her to stay. If she doesn't listen, I'm sunk. Anderson Brothers is sunk. Do you know how many other accounts I've had to dip into in order to cover her? Too many to count."

"I see." Murray rubbed his cheek. It never failed to astound him the dollar amounts Denton rattled off. They were so high that initially Murray suspected Denton's lying was pathological, until he saw the records himself.

"I mean, it's not like she was going to use it, old Marguerite." Denton pulled back a curtain from the inky window and surveyed the blinking streetlights of Cleveland's deserted downtown, all its residents having fled to the suburbs for the night. "She doesn't have any kids and it was just going to go to the museum or the SPCA or some such trust. That kind of money is wasted on a woman like her. Do you know she buys most of her clothes from the Goodwill?"

"Is that so?" said Murray.

"She lives on thirty grand a year. That's what her accountant told me. Thirty fucking grand. It comes from growing up in the Depression. She saves her tea bags just like Rockefeller. It's disgusting."

Denton shook his head, dismayed that Marguerite Grayson could be such a traitor to the Hunting Hills cause of rampant materialism. "No, I was perfectly within my rights to do what I did. Besides, I was only protecting her by fixing her statements. If she knew how much money she'd lost in the Recession she'd have dropped dead years ago."

"Therefore you view your cooking the books, so to speak, as more of a merciful white lie than, oh, outright fraud," Murray concluded, trying to get to the heart of Denton's circular reasoning.

"There's nothing wrong with a merciful white lie. If you asked if I liked your tie and I said yes, you'd feel better even though, personally, I think it's tacky and cheap."

Murray fought the impulse to glance down at the navy polyester tie with white and yellow interconnecting loops that his eleven-year-old daughter had picked out for him five Father's Days ago.

"But what about the money you've shifted from Marguerite's account already? For example," Murray pinched his nose, trying to block the stench rising from the dirt-caked floor, "wasn't there some developer who needed his eighteen million for a project, though he only had two million? Didn't you give him some of Marguerite's cash?"

"That was nothing. Money is fungible. I was going to put it back as soon as the market went up."

"But it never did go up, did it? At least not to 1990s standards."

"So what?" Denton again sat before his laptop. He typed in his password to close out of his Anderson account and stood up, robot-like, emptying a large, colorful handful of Skittles into his mouth. "Most of these people never touch their money. What I am is a redistributor of wealth. Temporarily transferring it from those who have it to those who need it. Like Robin Hood."

Not exactly, thought Murray, intrigued by Denton's spin. "What about giving to the poor?"

"Everyone's poor at some point. Poverty is meaningless."

Murray didn't bother arguing.

Denton was a hard case, the closest Murray had come to violating his oath as a psychiatrist by going to the authorities. If Denton had been a child abuser, a psychiatrist would have been mandated by state law to report his confessions to the police. But Denton was an abuser of rich old ladies, of neglectful millionaires, not children, and there were no laws requiring Murray to report his patient's crimes. On the contrary, according to his professional ethics, he was barred from doing so.

The one solace was the possibility that, through treatment, Denton could comprehend his problems, exit the cycle of abuse and own up to his misdeeds. It was this dim hope that motivated Murray to drag himself from the dinner party with the fine Cornish game hen and superb Pinot Noir and over to the Empress Hotel. That and a general concern for his old classmate's well-being.

"Now do you understand why I'm cooked?" Denton fell back on the bed, so distraught he no longer cared about contracting cooties from the skanky spread.

"All right, Denton, let's try and work through this." Murray slid out a brown plastic chair and sat down. "Let's go back to the moment when you discovered that your erection was not subsiding."

"Ohh." Denton crossed his legs at the memory.

"Do you honestly believe—now think about this, Denton—that Mrs. Grayson would have noticed your condition?"

"Are you kidding? It was huge." Denton held his hands a foot apart in demonstration of the monstrosity. "Everyone would have seen."

Murray smiled to himself. Ahh, the inflated—no joke intended—male ego. "OK. Let's say it was noticeable."

"A fucking ramrod is what it was." Denton shoved in another handful of Skittles.

"I'm sure."

"Really. I swing a club." Denton stood and proceeded to unzip his pants. "Here. I'll prove it to you."

"Won't be necessary," said Murray, averting his eyes. "Nevertheless, what would have happened if you *had* gone to your meeting in such a state? What would have been the worst outcome?"

Dr. Murray was always instructing Denton to imagine the worst outcome. This was the part of therapy Denton liked the least.

He zipped up his fly. "I don't know. Maybe Marguerite would have been horrified. Maybe she would have screamed. That's not really the point, though. The point isn't what *she* thought, it was what *I* thought. I couldn't go to her like that. That's not the way I was raised."

Interesting he should refer to his childhood. From what Murray knew, Denton had been pampered and praised from the womb. His mother believed he walked on water and his father wouldn't let anyone—not a teacher or fellow student—utter one word against him.

Once, when Denton had been mocked for missing a goal on the Tate soccer field, Denton Sr. had marched across the field and stood before the parents of the taunting child, demanding both an explanation and a handwritten apology.

"I'm going to posit an idea, Denton, and I want you to hear me out."

Denton looked up anxiously, his mouth smudged bright Skittle green and red. He yearned for an excuse that would let him off the hook, the kind of excuses Mother used to make.

"What I'm wondering is if maybe, just maybe, your reaction to your erection was an hysterical response to suppressed emotions. In other words, that your perception that everyone could see your erection, which arose during an extramarital sexual encounter, was actually the manifestation of overwhelming feelings of guilt."

"What guilt?" asked Denton.

"OK. Regret."

"Regret is for pussies."

Murray cleared his throat. "Really? Don't you regret cheating on Marti?"

"Marti expects it." Denton searched his bag for a rare blue Skittle. "She knows what I am. I'm a successful man who works hard and makes a shitload of money. Sex on the side is one of the perks. Marti's not dumb. She's well aware that I troll other waters."

"And she's fine with that."

"I didn't say that. I just said she expects it."

"What if you found out that Marti was, as you say, trolling other waters?"

"Impossible." Denton knocked back a blue and red. "You don't know Marti. She'd never sleep around. She was a virgin when we got married."

"Well then, how about this? How about the guilt you feel for bilking Marguerite Grayson?"

Denton aimed a finger at Murray. "Hey. I did not bilk Marguerite Grayson. That's what I can't stand in talking to you about this, Matt. You don't understand the financial world. All I did was shift money around. Happens every day. You think that just because your bank statement says you've got fifteen grand in your checking account that you actually have fifteen grand in your checking account?"

"I'd like to think so."

"Then, pardon me for saying this, but you're a pea brain."

The abuse, Murray recognized, was part of Denton's illness, though Murray hadn't the foggiest idea what illness that was. Would that there were a DSM III classification for terminal assholeness.

Denton crumpled the red bag and tossed it toward the wastepaper basket, missing it by a yard. "I hate stupid people. Especially when they're stupid about money."

Murray leaned forward. "Recall for me the first word that popped into your head the moment you realized that the erection was not going down and that there was no way you could face Mrs. Grayson."

Denton examined his foot. He picked at a callous and flicked the skin to the dusty carpet.

"There was one word. It was from a movie, my favorite movie as a kid. I loved that fucking movie."

"And that movie was?"

"You promise not too read too much into this? Because, really, it was just a flash of a thought, like thinking about going to McDonald's or whether the Mercedes was due for an oil change."

"What was it, Denton?"

"You won't laugh?"

"I won't laugh."

"Swear?"

"Swear."

"Pinocchio."

Dr. Murray tried very, very hard to keep a straight face.

Chapter Twenty-one

As soon as Dr. Murray left believing, wrongly, that Denton had momentarily been assuaged and that he would be checking out of the Empress Hotel forthwith, Denton once again plugged the connection of his hotel room phone into his laptop and dialed into Anderson Brothers.

The process took a ridiculous length of time. There were several hang-ups and finally, frustrated to the max, he left his room, rescued his Mercedes from the lot and braved the dangerous streets of deserted Cleveland to search for a Cumberland Farms that sold big bags of Skittles. Regular and Sour flavored. Denton bought four.

On the way back, while ripping open the big red bag with his teeth and listening to pumped-up rap music (in an effort to blend in with his surroundings, like audio camouflage) Denton hallucinated that Lisa Renfrew's Lexus LX 470 zipped through a red light at the intersection of Superior and East Fifty-first Street. He knew it was Lisa's because of the license plate—IM TYRD—a sampling of Lisa's rather pedestrian punditry of her husband's name, Ty.

But what would she be doing in downtown Cleveland at nine o'clock at night? It wasn't as though the Indians were still playing or an art gallery was opening. It was too late for that. What if she were searching for him? What if she wanted to run away?

Denton parked the car under a streetlamp outside the Empress and poured out some more Skittles, thinking about Lisa. He loved Lisa in a different way than he loved—or rather *had* loved—Marti. Marti was his high school sweetheart. She'd saved herself for him and borne him two beautiful daughters and designed a lovely house but that was it. They were over now.

Marti didn't know it but he'd moved on long ago. What he needed at this stage in his life was a woman who had grand plans, like him. A woman with whom he could become someone. A woman who wasn't afraid to leave Hunting Hills and all her silly little schoolgirl friends. A woman who knew exactly what it meant when he said the end would justify the means and who was willing to back him up 120 percent of the way.

Lisa was that woman. Ambition was in her bones. Denton had always admired her hard-luck tale of growing up poor and unschooled in Glendale and how she'd put herself through Cleveland State and elbowed her way into Ty Renfrew's heart.

Sure, Ty hadn't been the most attractive banana on the bunch. He'd begun balding at twenty-three. He was too short for a man and a bit of a putz when it came to style, preferring white bucks in the summer and Rockports in the fall. He had erection problems. The only things he did have were money and connections.

But this is where Ty and Lisa parted and where Denton and Lisa bonded. Ty, like Marti, was satisfied to remain in Hunting Hills, to raise grandkids and work on his golf game, partying with the same people every Fourth of July, attending the same Christmas open houses year after year. It was death. Pure, crystal death.

He and Lisa wanted more. They wanted to get as far from Cleveland as fast as possible. They talked about it all the time. Maybe California or some place like Fiji where it was sunny and warm and free; anything but Cleveland, which was damp and gray and where everyone had a stick up their ass.

Hang in there, Lisa, he thought to himself. *We're almost outta here.*

Though not quite yet. Right now he was at the Empress with its bulletproof Plexiglas counter and Defcon-5 security.

The fight in Room 307 had stopped, cheering Denton somewhat until he heard the moaning and banging within as he passed the door. Animals. He let himself into 309, triple locked the door and rushed to his computer to check his access to his Anderson Brothers account. Yes! He was in.

After submitting his password, Denton closed one eye, as though to shield himself from what the screen might reveal, and scrolled through the Grayson account. Indeed, the news was not good. Grayson had withdrawn her remaining thirty-five million which, technically, she didn't have. Thank God, he'd been on the ball and had seen it coming, making certain to transfer money from everyone else's account earlier in the day.

The resulting numbers were depressing, like jetsam in a low tide. Over the past three years Ty Renfrew's various holdings had slipped in total value from twenty-four million dollars to, as of today with the Grayson transactions, fifteen thousand. Harding, who had never particularly trusted him for some reason, had ten thousand, though he'd only put in a measly two hundred thousand to begin with. And Marti?

Poor Marti had nothing. Zip. Zero. Zilch. The big goose egg. All her precious Swan inheritance gone to fucking Marguerite Grayson who probably had the SEC on speed dial. Bottom line?

He, his wife and his closest childhood friends were all broke.

Suddenly he was sideswiped by a wave of nausea. Denton scrambled to the gray bathroom where he vomited violently into the rust-stained toilet. His shoulders heaved and his diaphragm flexed uncontrollably as it purged him of every last content in his stomach.

Sweat broke out all over his body and Denton began to shiver, leaning against the stained toilet and wishing he were a little boy again, back in his own clean bathroom of his childhood home, with his mother perched on the edge of their large, porcelain bathtub, rubbing his back and wiping his mouth with a damp, warm washcloth.

But there was no mother in the bathtub. There was only a gigantic roach wriggling upside down on its back, clawing the air and fighting for his life, fighting his tiny destiny of inevitable extermination.

Chapter Twenty-two

The Cleveland Police Department after hours resembled a massive futuristic warehouse uninhabited by humans or even, for that matter, robots. Smooth gray concrete corridors zigzagged like rodent holes to vacant cinderblock rooms marked only by garage doors pulled down to meet countertops. Aside from slips of yellow light peeking underneath, there was no sign of life on the other side.

Marti, Lisa, Boots and Claire clicked down the corridors in their high-heeled Stuart Weitzmans and Tod's and in Lisa's case, fourteen-hundred-dollar Giuseppe Zanotti pythons, the designer of which Marti had been able to squeeze out of Boots on the ride down. They passed prostitutes, ornery drunks, pissed-off drug dealers and their anxious girlfriends and mothers who had been called away from the TV to scrounge up money and make bail. Everyone was on their cell phones. Everyone eyed the Hunting Hills wives.

"This place is so depressing," Marti said, a vague champagne headache spreading from temple to temple. "They should call in Jesus.

He could fix it up. You know, add some windows. Uplift the color scheme."

"It's supposed to be depressing. It's the police department," Lisa said.

"Too bad I couldn't bring my babies. Look at all the places to run." Boots turned the corner to a room marked PROCESSING. Like all the others it was nothing more than a garage door. The women stood mutely, unsure what to do next.

"I think we need to ring the bell." Claire pointed to a buzzer by the garage door under a speaker.

Boots pushed it and after an intolerable two minutes, a woman's voice demanded to know who they were there to see.

"What's her last name, again? I forgot," Claire whispered to Boots.

"Goss," Boots said. "Karen Goss."

"Karen Goss," Claire announced to the box.

"Spell it!"

Claire took a guess. "G-O-S-S."

"Hold on," said the voice.

Boots tugged at the hem of her bright green Turtle Fur pullover.

"It's good Kit didn't come," Marti said to Lisa, "she'd never have been able to handle this place."

The women waited some more.

Maybe this was what Claus von Bulow had had to endure even with his delicate condition and fine European upbringing, Marti thought. Marti knew everything about Claus von Bulow and his former comatose wife, Sunny. She knew that Sunny still got her hair done every day at a private facility in upstate New York. And she knew that Claus's ex-mistress Alexandra never went anywhere without a bee pollen specialist. From January to April of 1982, Marti had been glued to the TV, obsessed with the trial. Aside from the total twenty hours she'd spent in labor for both her girls, they'd been the most painful hours of her life.

Beeep. The women jumped as the alarm buzzed and the door flew open revealing a hidden world beyond, a world filled with bright lights and the click of computer keyboards. A fit black woman in a blue uniform, her hair in a bun, held up a clipboard. "Which one of you is Goss's lawyer?"

"Lawyer?" Marti said. "Why does she need a lawyer?"

"I'm her lawyer," Claire lied. "Claire Stark."

The cop flicked her brown eyes up and down. "I've never seen you before."

"I'm new."

"Uh-huh."

"And I'm her sister," Boots piped up. "Karen called me."

"Right. And I'm Carol Brady."

The cop wasn't buying it, so Claire said, "Of course, we could always call Karen's other lawyer. But I'm guessing you'd rather not have Roy Phelps around."

"That's for sure." She looked over Claire's shoulder to where Lisa and Marti huddled together. "OK, but just you two. Those chickens wait here."

Claire had never been in the Cleveland Police Headquarters and yet she felt like she was on familiar turf. For the first time since she'd touched down from Prague she had a sense of belonging. The ringing telephones and bustle of cops, the cacophonous chatter, the glow of the overhead fluorescents and the smell of burnt coffee in Styrofoam cups. It was heaven.

"Good going," Boots murmured. "You pulled that off like a pro."

"You learn a few tricks being a reporter for twenty years."

"You can't smell the booze on my breath, can you?" Boots exhaled.

"Just the cigarettes."

"Thank god."

They passed a brooding black man whose bloodied head bandages bespoke an unsettled evening. He slouched in his splintered swivel chair and rolled a toothpick in his mouth, staring at their legs.

"Hi!" said Claire.

"Hi!" said Boots.

He cocked his chin. "Wassup?"

Boots was about to stop and explain exactly what was up, but Claire yanked her forward.

"This way, ladies." The police officer led them to a cubicle where they found Karen, white as a corpse, clutching the sides of her molded plastic chair. Her thin legs were crossed so tightly they looked like a twisted cruller. Despite her trauma, whatever that had been, Karen remained fairly put together. Her outfit, a tasteful ensemble of Dolce & Gabbana rust velvet jeans and matching tweed jacket (with fake fur trim) reminded Claire of a silken purebred Irish Setter she'd once come across in a dog pound.

"I thought you'd never get here. It's been a nightmare. Look!" She pointed upward.

Claire, Boots, Karen and the police officer studied the drab acoustical ceiling. "I don't get it," Boots said. "What's wrong?"

"What's wrong?" Karen's eyes went wide with fright. "Fluorescents. Everywhere. I've been underneath them for that whole hour. I don't even want to think what that's done to my brain cells."

The cop made a check on her clipboard. "She's all yours, ladies. The victim witness coordinator says your friend here is free to go just as soon as she speaks with Lucy Aldridge."

"Who's Lucy Aldridge?" Karen asked.

"A lawyer. Kind of like an advocate for you people." The cop winked and wiggled her head as though that Lucy was some piece of work.

Boots said. "You people? What did she mean by 'you people'? Does she mean people from Hunting Hills?"

"Maybe," Karen said, thoughtfully. "It's like what I was talking about the other day. Racial profiling, though only in reverse because we're white and rich instead of black and poor. Then again, it might have something to do with something else." She held up her hands. "Do you think we have time to go to the little girls' room? My hands are filthy. The viruses in this place . . ."

"Don't use the bathroom here," Boots hissed. "It must be crawling with germs. Let's go."

"What about Lucy Aldridge?" Claire asked.

Boots rubbed her arms as if she were freezing. "I don't give a flying fuck. I don't want to spend another minute in this place."

"We were mugged," Karen said, suddenly. "I was in Edgewater Park with Monica, Bob's secretary."

"What were you doing with Monica?"

"Monica and I are friends. We take the same yoga class." Karen shot a glance at the fluorescents. "Anyway, we were in my car, talking, when a bunch of jerks showed up shouting that we were lappers and ruining America and we should die. They bashed in her side view mirror, took my wallet and lots of pictures. If it hadn't been for a bunch of gay guys making out on the park benches they would have killed us."

Boots furrowed her perfectly tweezed brows. "Lappers. What do you mean, lapper?"

Claire swallowed hard. She was getting the distinct impression that not only was Karen *not* a prude, as all the Hunting Hills wives suggested, but that between her outings with the mysterious Monica and her kitchen sill sensi stash, she was probably the most experimental of the bunch.

"Knock, knock. Got a few minutes?" A petite woman in a merry red suit and a file under her arm appeared at the opening of the cubicle.

Thank god, thought Claire, *saved by a bureaucrat.*

"I'm Lucy Aldridge," she said, sticking her hand toward Karen. "I'm so glad we got a chance to talk tonight before you went home." Lucy Aldridge had tidy shoulder-length brown hair and pearls in each ear. Claire pegged her as fresh out of grad school, the ink barely dry on her MSW.

"Excusez-moi," Boots said, apparently under the misimpression that she was addressing the head waiter at *Le Chez*. "Will this take long? We were kind of in the middle of a party when Karen called."

"You were?" asked Karen. "What party?"

Boots bit her lip. For all her stern warnings to keep mum, it would be she who let the cat out of the bag.

"I'm afraid this is much more important than a party. Your friend here," Lucy put her hand on Karen's shoulder, "will become a very controversial figure in the next few days. She'll need all the support you can offer. Take it from someone who's been there, the media can be ruthless."

Boots's fingers gripped the gold chain of her bag ever more tightly. "Media?"

"If all goes well. Look at her. Mrs. Goss is extremely photogenic. She's rich. She's married to a well-known business person. We've been searching for a case like this for years and we couldn't have gotten someone better."

"Who's we?" Boots asked.

"OGLE." Lucy reached in her purse and pulled out a card carrier like the one Eric had given Claire. "The Ohio Gay and Lesbian Endeavor." She handed each of them cards which said, OGLE—Lucy Aldridge, Civil Rights Attorney. "With Karen at the forefront, we're sure to get the Ohio Revised Code changed to have violence against gays and lesbians classified as hate crimes, with the enhanced penalties those entail."

Boots just stared at the card, which her delicate white fingers held stiffly. It was unclear to Claire whether Boots would faint on the spot or if she would simply crumple in shock.

Karen raised her hand. "Pardon me. But what if I don't want to be in the media spotlight?"

"I think after I explain our mission you will." Lucy sat down on a chair and took Karen's hand in hers. "Karen. Tonight you and your lover . . ."

"Lover!" Boots screeched. "Do you mean Monica? She's not a lover. She's a secretary. You are *extremely* confused."

Lucy checked with Karen. "I see. So you're not out of the closet yet?"

"Excuse me?" Boots asked. "What closet?"

"That's an expression," Lucy said, "for being gay."

Claire was desperate to take Lucy aside and quickly introduce her to the funky culture of Hunting Hills. How the women kept—and followed—a rule book that included admonitions against answering the home phone and scheduling pedicures and therapy on the same day. How they didn't make it a practice of discussing their lesbian lovers in public. It just wasn't done.

Boots took Karen's hand. "Come on. This is nonsense. We're going home."

Karen pulled away from Boots and slowly stood. "I think I'd like to have a few minutes alone, if you don't mind."

"Of course," said Claire, only too glad to get the hell out of there.

"I mean with you, Claire."

Lucy and Boots turned to Claire in confusion. Claire, meanwhile, felt her face grow hot. "I . . . I . . . don't know what I can . . ."

"Please." Karen smiled slightly and Claire noticed that she was close to tears.

"We'll be back in five minutes," said Lucy who made the mistake of reaching out to Boots's elbow.

"Let go of me, you freak!" shouted Boots, shaking off her hand.

When they had gone, Karen pointed for Claire to sit in the folding chair. "It's like this," she said, clasping her hands in front of her. "I'm not gay. I'm bi and I'm not sure I'm even that."

Claire wondered why Karen had chosen to tell her this. Was it because Claire was an outsider and Karen needed a shoulder to lean on? Whatever it was, she decided to keep her mouth shut and let Karen vent.

"It's Bob's fault. A few years ago he had a typical midlife crisis and got the bright idea to invite couples in. And not for bridge." Karen smiled. "For sex."

"Ahh," said Claire, trying to act as though this was the kind of thing she heard every day.

"I'm such a space cadet that it took me a while to catch on. Bob would invite over the Markinsons, Tricia and Kyle, they'd pass around the high octane pot and then Kyle and Bob would kind of, you know, put Tricia and me together in the bedroom."

"But Bob wouldn't join in," Claire said.

"God, no. He likes to watch me with other women, not participate. It gets him excited. I only played along to save our marriage."

"And how often does he do this . . . to you?" Claire sensed that Karen wanted to place the blame entirely on her husband.

"It started out once or twice a year, but lately it's been once or twice a month. It's why he sent Chip to Exeter, to get him out of the house even though he knew perfectly well that would kill his chances of getting into Yale. The bastard."

"What about your other son?"

"Birch? He's not stupid. On our so-called 'game nights' Bob makes sure he's staying over at Gunther's house. He thinks Birch doesn't know, but everyone knows. Even Marti and Lisa and Boots, though they pretend they don't."

Which meant they were probably aware of her sensi hash too.

Claire resisted the inclination to call John and ask him if he was aware of this Bob and Karen and Ted and Alice scandal, but Karen read her mind. "Don't tell John. He's too . . . proper. If he found out what we two do he'd never treat Bob the same and that would crush him. Bob really looks up to John."

"Why are you telling me this, Karen?"

"Because I need your help." Karen wiped a tear away with the back of her hand. "I don't mind being fodder for the Hunting Hills rumor mill, but I can't stand the thought of my name being in the papers as someone who was caught in Edgewater Park, with a woman suspected of being her lover. I've got two sons to think of, Claire, and a scandal like that could ruin their lives."

Understandable. "I agree."

"When we met at Holly the other day, you mentioned that you knew the executive editor of the *Cleveland Citizen.* What was his name?"

A sense of dread descended over her like rain flowing over a window. *She wants me to go hat in hand to Eric, goddamn him.* "Eric Schmaltz."

"Eric Schmaltz. That's right. Listen, I know it's not TV, but it is the only paper in town. Maybe you could call him and put a kibosh on this." Tears began rolling down her cheeks. "Otherwise, honestly, I think I might have to kill myself."

"Don't say that." Claire stood and put her arms around Karen's rigid, fat-free body. "Try not to worry, Karen. I'll see what I can do. Eric probably wouldn't be interested in a simple mugging anyway."

"He might be when he finds out the woman who was mugged is the wife of the largest outdoor activities supplier east of the Mississippi and," she buried her face in the shoulder of Claire's coat, "that she's a dyke."

"Not you too!" Boots exclaimed, marching in with Lucy at her heels.

"I'm sorry, Lucy," Claire said, giving Karen's shoulder a firm squeeze, "but as you can see, Karen is very upset. She's too spent to talk about this tonight. She needs to go home."

"Exactly what I've been saying all along," said Boots.

"I don't want to be a hard ass, but I'm prepared to be if I have to." Lucy played with one of her pearls. "This case is now, or will soon be, part of the public record. There were witnesses. The police took statements and there probably will be arrests. This isn't a minor car accident that can be slipped under the rug. This is a veritable hate crime. So, if your friend won't cooperate, then we at OGLE will have no choice but to go to the press without her."

Boots looked like she'd been sucker punched. Karen, on the other hand, seemed clueless.

"If that's what you want, press coverage, then I can help."

Karen looked stricken as Claire fished in her purse and produced the set of business cards Eric had given her.

"What are you doing?" Boots asked.

Claire handed Lucy a *Cleveland Citizen* card. "Some people might argue that I have conflict of interest since I know Karen, but I'd really like to have an exclusive on this story. I can promise you excellent play."

Lucy read the card and Claire was pleased to see how quickly she reacted. "Really? How much play?"

"Try front page Sunday." Claire had never in her life told such a whopper and she was having difficulty looking natural, especially with Boots glaring at her so hard she was burning holes.

"Well . . ." Karen began until Claire ever so slightly stepped on Karen's right foot.

"We're best friends." Claire entwined two fingers. "We're like this."

"So, can I call you at the paper tomorrow morning to set up an interview?" Lucy reached into her file folder and flipped through several pages. "I don't have the proposed hate crime legislation here. It's back in the office. There's also a state-by-state breakdown we have of where gay-bashing has been elevated to hate crime and, oh, our volunteers have been keeping records of violence against gays in Cuyahoga and the contiguous counties. You could run a chart." She jotted a few notes. "This is so exciting. Do you think they'll let you do a series? Because a series would be fantastic. I can find you at least ten other victims."

Claire folded her arms and let Lucy rattle on as Boots silently led Karen out of the cubicle.

This is the easy part, Claire thought. *But what's going to happen when Lucy calls the* Cleveland Citizen *newsroom at 10 a.m. and finds that not only doesn't Claire Stark work there, but that the operators have no idea who she is?*

There was only one option. She would have to confront the one man she'd been going out of her way to avoid. Eric Schmaltz.

She just hoped and prayed that if John ever found out he'd be understanding. That was *if* he found out, though Claire had no intention of letting that *if* come to pass.

"How was the book group?" John murmured as Claire slipped into the warm bed next to him, her cool and naked body spooning into his warm one. He wrapped an arm around her waist and nuzzled his chin into her hair. "Anything exciting happen?"

"Not much. Karen was assaulted by gay-bashers while having a lesbian tryst in the park." She yawned. "And the gay community's going to make her their showpiece for new hate crime legislation. That's all."

John chuckled softly. "Where'd you come up with that one?" Then he rolled over and went to sleep believing, as she wished she could, that it had all been just a dream.

Chapter Twenty-three

What to wear? What to wear? Wasn't that the eternal question? They should invent personal dressers, in addition to personal shoppers, Marti thought. She could make a killing with an idea like that.

It was 8 a.m. and Marti, drenched in sweat from her morning workout with Todd the personal trainer, stood in her closet trying to choose the ideal outfit for her trip to the *Cleveland Citizen.* A light snow dusted the ground outside, a freak early November storm, since the television forecaster promised that temperatures would rise into the high sixties. As she doubted a *CC* editor would give a tinker's dam about how hot her haute, she was reduced to basing her fashion choice on the weather. A very sad state indeed.

She decided on her Elle Tahari cropped pants and—God willing the snow should melt by nine thirty—her Kate Spade open toe suede sandals, which did wonders for her sculpted calves. She threw on her Lida Baday ribbed wool sweater in lentil. It was not a perfect match with the Tahari pants, but the Italian wool sweater did have a low V-neck and above all Marti wanted to look sexy. Like, *duh!*

No one had an inkling of her plan. It was going to be a surprise, one that she'd cooked up all by herself late last night after coming home from the police department and popping two Motrin and then gnashing her teeth over Boots.

Boots had taken over—as Boots always did in every crisis—and pushed Marti and Lisa aside. Then she wouldn't tell them anything except that Claire had been a big help to Karen and that, because of the mess Karen had made, Claire would have to go down to the *Cleveland Citizen* first thing in the morning and prostrate herself before her old boyfriend. Marti was forced to call Karen later that night to find out what happened.

Well, Marti had thought, *if that's the way this game is played, then I'm going to the* Shitizen *too*. And so she was.

It was never a good idea to exclude Marti Denton from any scandal. You'd only end up paying for it later.

Marti examined herself in the dressing room mirror, running through the five checkpoints—hair, makeup, clothes coordination, shoes and ass. All perfect. All except her hair which was in dire need of highlights. That meant a trip to New York City and that got her to thinking about Denton and whether he was still alive or if he had keeled over from his fake heart attack at his room at the Ritz.

While she was in the kitchen brewing a pot of decaf coffee and dipping into the other half of the no-fat strawberry yogurt she had saved from yesterday's breakfast, she dialed Denton on his cell phone. It rang four times and then bounced over to his answering service, which it sometimes did when he was on another call. She left a message, hung up and splurged on a quarter grapefruit, confident that he would return her call immediately.

When he didn't after a half hour and when she got a call from his secretary at Anderson Brothers, asking in a hushed and urgent voice, "Where is he, Marti? Everyone around here is *bullshit,*" Marti called the Ritz.

Big Mistake.

"I'm sorry," said the snooty Ritz desk clerk, "but we do not have a James Denton registered here."

"Then he must have checked out."

"Hmmm, no. I've already run that option and there has been no Denton staying with us this week. Perhaps in another hotel in the city?"

Though Denton wouldn't have even considered staying anywhere else, Marti, feeling foolish, said, "Of course. He must be at the Plaza."

"Yes," said the clerk. "Of course."

Marti snapped her phone shut and dug into the other grapefruit quarter not stopping to think—as her personal nutritionist had reminded her—whether the food she was putting in her mouth was fuel for her body or comfort for her heart.

Finally, after finishing the entire grapefruit and stomping around the kitchen in her Kate Spades so furiously that even Rachel put the TV on mute, Marti called Lisa.

"Denton is having an affair. And I think you know who with."

Lisa said nothing.

"Are you still there?" Marti shook her cell phone. Curse his thing and its limited range. "Lisa?"

"I'm still here," Lisa said. "What do you want from me, Marti?"

It was an absurd question. Marti didn't want anything from her except the truth. "Tell me who it is. I know you know. You know who everyone is sleeping with."

Lisa let out a long sigh. "I don't. Honestly, Marti, the other day when we were driving to Holly I just threw out that he was having an affair. It was only speculation."

"You can tell me, Lisa. It's not like I'm going to go all Clara Harris and run over him with my Benz."

"Who's Clara Harris?"

But Marti wasn't paying attention. (Which wasn't unusual.) "I bet when he didn't meet up with Marguerite Grayson, you know, the grand dame who's gotten him in so much trouble, that he was with her."

"Marguerite?"

"Her. *The* her. It couldn't be his secretary. She was in the office during his breakfast meeting with Marguerite and she's got an ass on her that won't quit. You know how Denton hates big asses."

"Oh, yes," said Lisa.

"You do?"

"From what you've told me."

"It can't be someone from the club because I'd have heard about it." Marti tried to recall every single man-hungry woman she knew. "I'm at a loss. Maybe it's one of his clients."

"Listen, Marti. I have to be honest with you."

"Uh-huh." Marti was flipping through the family Rolodex, searching for names. It would never have occurred to her that Denton's database was on a computer. Marti had nothing to do with computers.

"You have to forget about Denton."

"How can I forget about Denton? He's the father of my two daughters. He's the only man I've ever had sex with. I can't just forget about him."

"For now, I mean. You have to call Mrs. Distal and get on with it. You have to think about what you really want and that is John."

Marti stopped at B—Corinne Berenson, the sister of Denton's brother's wife. Denton didn't get along with his brother, Carl, nor his wife, Dee, who moved to the West Coast the year after they married. Carl was two years younger and had estranged Denton with his anti–Hunting Hills attitude. Denton would not tolerate any disrespect of Cleveland or the Greater Cleveland area.

But Denton had always had a thing for Corinne, a former socialite twice divorced who'd been reduced to selling real estate, albeit through a boutique agency called Etienne Williamson Properties. Corinne wore coral gloss lipstick and called herself an "estate agent." She was also willing to do whatever it took to hook husband number three.

"Corinne," Marti said. "I bet he's involved with Corinne."

"This is exactly why you need Nomadd. You're all over the place. We were talking about John and Mrs. Distal. Boots told me she talked to you about how Mrs. Distal can help and, trust me Marti, I couldn't be without her. I'll call her for you. I have her number right here."

"You do?" A question flitted across Marti's hungover brain. Something having to do with why Lisa would have Mrs. Distal's number at her fingertips. But the question couldn't be formed and Marti found it impossible to pin down, like a snowflake or the price of gift wrapping at Board and Basket.

"Hi, Mom." Lois was in her school uniform, her highlighted brown hair ironed into flat sheets, though it was after nine and she was supposed to be at Holly.

"Oh my god," said Marti, repeating the oft quoted Hunting Hills *au revoir*. "Look at the time, I've got to go." And hung up, turning her attention full blast on Lois. "Why aren't you in school?"

"Test morning," Lois lied, grabbing a Granny Smith apple from the refrigerator. "SAT preparation."

"I thought those were on Saturdays."

"Not during playoffs."

"Oh," said Marti, confused. "Well, then, why aren't you taking tests?"

Lois grabbed her key ring. "Because I'm happy with my score. A 1250's good enough for me. See you later."

Marti watched as her increasingly elusive daughter backed out her Toyota Highlander and pulled down the driveway, not to go to school, but to meet with a far more shady character than herself.

Chapter Twenty-four

Wallaby's Diner was, like the rest of Haywire Falls, out of a bygone era.

The waitresses went by names such as Janine and Dorie, which they proudly displayed on nametags pinned to their bubblegum-pink uniforms. They could balance two cheeseburgers, a hot dog, chicken fried steak and four large chocolate milk shakes, not to mention fries, on a metal platter as they squeezed among the booths of customers.

Lois loved the place, as most children who'd been lucky enough to grow up around Haywire Falls did. Her standard order was a club sandwich and strawberry milk shake despite Marti's nervous encouragement to change the milk shake to an unsweetened herbal tea and make the sandwich on whole wheat bread, no mayo and no bacon while they were at it.

But Lois wasn't meeting Marti at Wallaby's this morning. She was meeting Denton and, as usual, he was late.

"Stool for one, hon?" asked Evelyn who, with a blond beehive hairdo and cracking gum, was straight out of diner waitress central casting.

"Actually, I'm meeting my father so I'd like a booth."

Evelyn regarded the teenage girl skeptically. Booths were scarce, saved only for regulars and big tippers, which was why Lois didn't mention her father's name. Denton was neither. In fact, he was like a tipper in reverse.

"Sure, why not. Breakfast's almost over anyway." She grabbed two long, plastic laminated menus and led Lois to the back, dangerously near the smoking section.

Lois sat down at the blue-gingham-covered table with the yellow plastic rose in its glass vase and, feeling awkward to be by herself, fiddled with a purse in her lap. She opened it twice to check that the twenty-dollar bill was still there. Lois wasn't used to cash. She was a credit card baby.

Lois adored her father because he was impulsive and generous. It was Denton who had sprung the Highlander on her, despite Marti's objections, complete with floor mats and a place to stick her iPod. If Lois so much as grumbled about a teacher's unfair grading or the way a boyfriend hadn't IM'd her, Denton was on top of it, either making a polite phone call to the teacher at home or finding a way to take the inconsiderate lover boy aside, reminding him that Lois was a special girl who would not be disrespected.

But last night when he called looking for her mother, Lois had the distinct impression that, for once, he needed her more than she needed him.

"Hey, Muffincakes," he'd said, trying to be jolly. "How about you skip your morning classes tomorrow and meet up with me at Wallaby's for waffles?"

This was not Denton's standard operating procedure. Sure, he might whisk her down to New York City to see a Broadway play or invite her friends to go waterskiing at their summer place on Lake Michigan, but he never, ever encouraged her to skip school.

"I don't know. We have a pretest in calculus second period."

"But it's not a test, test. It doesn't count toward your final grade."

"No." Though Lois was struggling in calculus and couldn't afford to miss any help.

"All right, then. Nine thirty it is. At Wallaby's. Better not tell your mom. She's a tight ass about cutting class."

Evelyn approached her, holding two pots of coffee, one with an orange rim. "Wanna cup?"

"Not exactly," Lois said, smiling. "Do you have any Diet Coke?"

"You ordering breakfast?"

"Waffles."

"And you still want a Diet Coke?"

Lois wondered if there was something wrong with that. "Is that OK?"

"Whatever flips your switch." Evelyn walked away just as Denton came through the door.

He looked awful. So awful that Lois at first didn't recognize him. He'd lost weight. His skin was pale white and puffy and his lips were the oddest color. Almost brown and red. He was so different from his usual tall, robust demeanor, though she couldn't quite remember when she'd seen him last.

"Sorry I'm late, Muffincakes," he said, stooping to kiss her.

Lois flinched at his cloud of too much aftershave.

Denton slid into the seat opposite her. He kept his camel hair coat on, though he peeled off his black leather driving gloves. "You look terrific. God, you're beautiful. Do you know that?"

Lois rolled her eyes. "You always say that, Daddy."

"That's because I mean it. Every day I see you I'm floored by how much prettier you are than the day before."

"You're just my dad." She played with a lock of hair. "No one else says that."

"That's because all the boys you know are chicken shit. Give them a couple of beers and they'll be gushing. Looks like the waitresses have been ignoring you."

"Not really. I ordered a Diet Coke when you came in."

"Bullshit. That's the way they treat teenagers. Like crap." Denton snapped his fingers for Evelyn, who narrowed her eyes as she finished up with other customers.

Lois prayed that the waitress didn't remember him.

"Can I get a cup of coffee over here?" he asked impatiently. "And my daughter still hasn't gotten her Diet Coke."

Evelyn, who'd seen it all, filled Denton's thick white ceramic cup and handed Lois the Diet Coke, the paper still on the top of the straw. "You two having anything to eat?"

"Lois will have the waffles with extra syrup and whipped cream," he said, sparing his daughter the mortification of ordering like a pig. "And I'll have two eggs over easy. Rye, no butter. Bacon lean but not burnt."

"Please," Lois added.

Evelyn pointed her pencil toward Denton. "Do I know you?"

"I don't think so," Denton said, wide eyed.

"You eaten here before?"

"Many times."

Lois gripped her purse, her gaze flicking anxiously between the two.

"I would have remembered someone so good-looking, if you'd been my waitress before."

Evelyn grinned, as much for Denton's effort as for the bogus compliment. After she left, Denton said, "That one's a total bitch." He sipped his coffee. "So what's up with you?"

Lois wanted to ask, actually, what was up with him and the midweek breakfast meeting. Instead she said, "Mom told me you were in New York."

"She's right. I was." He ran his fingers through his hair. "That's why I look like shit. Woke up late and had to make it to LaGuardia in twenty minutes to catch the Continental express. Right after this I'm going home to take a shower. Then I'm going back to the office."

Lois leaned toward him, her small face girlish and pinched. "Is everything OK, Daddy?"

"Of course everything is OK. Don't be adolescent. I've just got a lot of stress." He gulped some more coffee. "That's why I'm meeting you. There's no one else on this planet who can cheer me up more than you, Muffincakes. You are my sunshine, my only sunshine."

"Shhh. Don't sing. It's embarrassing." Plus, he did not have a very good voice.

"I won't sing if you tell me what you've been up to. How's that Gunther idiot doing?"

"He's OK. I guess." Lois and Denton had an unspoken agreement not to discuss sex. Denton didn't want to hear it and Lois didn't want to tell it, though she was sure he'd heard about how her generation was walking the line that defined intercourse. "I think we're going to break up soon."

"You should get Birch Goss to take you to the Assembly Ball."

"He's a year younger than I am." Lois averted her eyes so Denton couldn't see that it was Chip Goss, away at Exeter, whom she secretly had a crush on. "Anyway, there's other stuff in my life going on besides boys."

"Oh? Like what?" He sounded perplexed by this.

Like finding a world beyond Hunting Hills, she wanted to tell him. A world where people were focused on more than gossip and fashion and who was in and who was out. A world where reading a good book wouldn't make you a "freak." Or where status wasn't based on whose daughter and granddaughter you were. Where girls could grow up to be something other than darling accessories on their husbands' arm. Where men were not valued according to how much money they made.

Lois had never confessed to anyone, not even her closest friends, how much she lived in dread of becoming her mother, though it hadn't always been that way. When she'd been a little girl, she'd tried to emulate Marti in every way. She'd rummage in her dressing table and try on all the makeup. She'd brushed her hair long and flat and tried on Marti's clunky jewelry, her colorful silk scarves and even, once when she was thirteen, her bustier.

Then came high school and instead of making plans to leave Hunting Hills for college, to blow this popsicle stand, her friends were already talking about what they'd do, who they'd marry and where they'd live when they came back. It was during these discussions over the Holly School lunch table or at sleepovers that Lois sensed her soul leave her body.

No way was she going to end up another Marti Denton.

Lois did not want to watch her weight with caliper precision or spend her days shopping and primping and living for her husband. She did not want to have to identify herself as a mother of three settled in Hunting Hills. In fact, the very thought of it gave her nightmares.

What Lois wanted to be was a writer, though she could never have told her parents that. Hunting Hills parents were like vultures, always circling overhead, their keen eyes on the lookout for a child's talent to exploit. When Ava in fourth grade innocently mentioned during dinner that she might like to play the cello, Marti and Denton inundated her with private lessons, a clinic and a weekly stint in the youth orchestra until she was so burnt out she refused to look at the instrument.

The same thing had happened to Chip Goss. He'd made the mistake of writing a fairly well-crafted essay on *A Separate Peace,* which earned him an A from Seymour Simchez, the toughest teacher at Tate. Next thing he knew his parents had packed him off for a month at a Vermont writers' retreat.

"Here you go." Evelyn plunked down the waffles with the melting whipped cream and pool of brown syrup. She handed Denton the eggs and rye, refilled his coffee and asked, "Is there anything else?" in a tone that implied there better not be.

"We're fine, Evelyn." Denton winked.

"I love this place, don't you?" he said, salting his eggs liberally.

"It's OK and Mom had better not see you do that," she said, pointing to the salt with her fork.

"Just think what she'd say if she saw you," he shot back.

Lois shrugged and sipped her Diet Coke.

"So what's this about Wallaby's being just OK. This used to be your favorite diner."

Lois said, "It's not Wallaby's. It's Cleveland. I want out."

Denton was about to bite into his rye, but stopped. Lois predicted he was going to say something like, "Cleveland? But we don't live in Cleveland, we live in Hunting Hills, the greatest place on Earth." Or, the alternative, "How can you say that? Cleveland has everything to offer—a great university, major league baseball, football, a famous orchestra and renowned art museum, not to mention an extensive park system and a Great Lake."

He didn't, though. "Really?" he said. "How come?"

"I don't know. I'm tired of it." She didn't want to insult him by insinuating that the home he'd chosen for her childhood had turned out to be a real drag. "I want to go to England, maybe. Or California. I like the West." Realizing the West might have reminded him of his estranged brother, she added, "Though, it's pretty nice here too."

"No it's not. It's a pit." He dropped his toast and leaned toward her, as though the Cleveland Booster Police might be on the premises. "You want to know a secret?"

"OK."

"I agree with you. I'm sick of Cleveland."

"You?" she said, swallowing the waffle which was gradually making her sick. "But you're always so big on it. Mom says all the time that Ava and I shouldn't dis Cleveland around you."

"Your mother's talking out of her ass. You want to know another secret?"

"OK," though she wasn't too sure.

"We're getting out of here. You and me."

Lois noticed he hadn't included Marti and Ava. "What do you mean?"

"Just you watch." He went back to cutting up his egg. Denton always cut up everything before he ate it. "In the upcoming weeks or maybe even days, big stuff is going to come down. It'll pop your top and then, when the smoke's cleared, you and I are going out West. How does Seattle sound? That's what your generation's into, Seattle, right? Coffee. Punk bands."

Frankly, Lois hadn't a clue, though she said, "Seattle sounds cool." She felt queasy and pushed her plate away.

"What's the matter?" he said.

"Sugar overload." She sipped her Diet Coke and checked her watch. "And I better get back to school."

Denton snapped for Evelyn. "Check please, Evelyn, and make it fast. I've got to get this kid back to class."

"Uh-huh." Evelyn ripped the check off her tablet and placed it on the table. "You done, hon?" she asked, frowning at Lois's half-eaten waffle.

"Hmm-hmm."

"You want me to wrap it up?"

Lois watched as Denton pretended to go through his wallet. "No, thank you."

"Why don't you go while I settle up?" he said. "This could take awhile."

"OK, Daddy." Lois gathered her coat and purse and kissed him on the cheek.

Denton flung an arm around her. "Remember what I always say, Muffincakes. Don't let the shitheads get you down." He squeezed her tightly and let go.

For a second, Lois was stunned. What had *that* been about? Probably some midlife crisis thing. She waved good-bye to Evelyn, who was at the cash register, and went outside to the gray autumn morning. The hard rain the night before had stripped the trees of almost all the leaves and had it been a few degrees colder it might have snowed. The cobblestone streets still glistened with dampness. For some reason, the scene reminded Lois of a book she'd read. *Sherlock Holmes.*

She strolled over to the stone bridge overlooking the gurgling Haywire Falls and felt her nose grow cold. After a few minutes of watching the frigid water tumble over the rocks, she returned to the diner. Denton was gone.

"You forget something?" Evelyn asked.

"Maybe." She set her shoulders. "My father didn't pay the bill, did he?"

Evelyn squinted over the booths. "I don't know. He just stepped outside. He said he left the money on the table." Then, getting concerned, she bustled to where Lois and Denton had been sitting. The bill was still there and on top of it were two quarters.

"That jerk. I thought I recognized him. I bet he's stiffed me before."

"Here." Lois opened her purse and handed Evelyn the twenty. "It's not like he can't pay. He can. It's just a game he plays."

Evelyn pinched the twenty. "You're a nice kid to have such an S.O.B. for a dad."

"He's OK, mostly," Lois said, slipping the strap of her purse over her shoulder. "It's just that he's got his quirks like anyone else. Though, one of these days, those quirks are going to get him in a lot of trouble, I think."

"You better believe it. It's not the big stuff that brings down crooks, it's the little stuff. Like they say, lots of splinters make a tree." Evelyn shoved the twenty in her apron pocket and proceeded to clear the table. "If you've learned that at your age, then consider yourself ahead of the game."

"I will," said Lois, who before that day had never heard the word "crook" associated with her father. Though it dawned on her that of course Evelyn was right. Denton was a crook and it was just a matter of time before everyone, besides Evelyn, knew.

Chapter Twenty-five

Claire parked on 121st Street and took in the windowless fortress before her. The *Cleveland Citizen*. An odd name for a newspaper and yet . . . and yet she liked it. She liked the way the building wasn't a landscaped, sprawling job out in the burbs. It was an ugly concrete hub in the inner city. A Clark Kent type of place where sweethearts connected reporters to rewrite. Where reporters kept whiskey bottles in their bottom drawers and editors loosened their ties on deadline.

Its interior did nothing to dispel the illusion. She drank in the oily smell of ink and the rumbling of presses in the basement. Standing before the double glass doors to the newsroom, Claire feared she just might break into tears. Even though the newsroom was empty, even though it had hardly any windows—lest reporters daydream by looking to Cleveland's dirty industrial skyline—it was a newsroom still. The epicenter of free speech and free assembly. The people's advocate open to all . . .

Except her. The door didn't budge. It was locked.

"Hey, you can't just walk in there." A receptionist in a black and white checked miniskirt and black sweater plunked a cup of coffee on her desk. She was still in her overcoat. "Do you have a pass?"

"Uh, no." Claire stupidly felt in her pockets for a pass, like one would magically appear.

"Then are you meeting someone?" She sat down and booted up her computer. "Because it's awfully early. Most of the reporters aren't in yet."

"I'm meeting Eric Schmaltz." Claire said this definitively so the receptionist wouldn't give her lip. "He's expecting me. Claire Stark. Or, Claire Stark Harding."

"Three names. Impressive." She checked her computer screen. "See now, I don't see even one of those names on my calendar. Not a Claire, a Stark or a Harding. You sure you got the right day? Is this an interview or are you just a reader with a complaint? If it's advertising, that's upstairs."

Claire was losing patience. She was tired from last night and stressed out from the prospect of meeting Eric behind John's back and not in the mood to put up with nitpicking receptionists who treated her like everyone else.

She caught herself. It was happening. She was succumbing to the Hunting Hills curse of superiority. *Stop it,* she told herself. *Nip that in the bud right now, Missy. Keep in mind that you're not that far from Mudville, West Virginia.*

"Hello?" The receptionist was waving her hand. "I said you can go in. See? The buzzer's buzzing. His secretary said it's OK."

Claire apologized and went in.

"Geesh," she heard her say, "that's Schmaltz for you. First they can't wait to get to see him. Then they don't dare."

Eric Schmaltz's office was exactly how Claire had pictured it would be, which is to say, schmaltzy (the word had to come up eventually).

Frames covered the walls from ceiling to floor. Frames containing every award he'd ever won, from a notable Pulitzer Finalist to a forgettable Third Place West Virginia Associated Press Honorable Mention for spot reporting on a twin-engine plane crash that injured a dog named Sparker. His first paycheck was framed, as was his first obituary. First front-page story (about a two-headed snake) and even the announcements of his first two weddings. In each of the yellowing, wrinkled clips the bride was victoriously radiant, while Eric looked as though he'd been dragged down the aisle by his earlobe.

And then she saw it. The framed lead story of their sheriff's series. Claire bent down to inspect the photos the paper had run of her and Eric side by side. Kids. Two naive, eager kids. Eric was handsome; without his gray he was almost endearing. He was also too sure of himself in light of his inexperience, while she was a mere baby. And that hair? A chin-length bob, angled downward. A silk scarf tied at her neck. Who dressed like that? Ever?

"Mary Tyler Moore." Eric walked in, his arms laden with several national papers, a cigar and his coffee. "That's the first thing people say when they see that picture. They say, 'What the hell are you doing with Mary Tyler Moore?' "

Claire straightened the frame and stepped back for perspective. "Whoever said that was dead on. That was exactly who I was trying to be. Mary Tyler Moore. Though I never did find the apartment in the Victorian house or the best friend, Rhoda." That wasn't entirely accurate. She'd had Josie.

Eric dumped the papers on his cluttered desk. "I hated that show. It was stupid. There was no real news. Then again, I hate all TV. It's ruining America, you know."

"I didn't know. Thanks for the FYI." And then, not knowing what to say, she smiled at him like an idiot. Eric must have been completely flabbergasted at her early morning appearance but was too savvy a newspaperman to let his confusion show.

"I suppose you're kind of flipped out that I'm here," she said.

"Flipped out? I never flip out. Have a seat." He clamped the cigar between his teeth and popped open the top of his coffee.

Eric looked fit. He was wearing a navy tie and white shirt under a gray tweed jacket. He was clean shaven and lean and his eyes were twinkling. He wasn't the same old Eric from West Virginia who refused to talk or speak to anyone until his third cup of coffee and a cigarette. He'd changed and then she realized how.

"You're not hungover, are you?" She took the seat closest to the window. "You're actually in a good mood and it's not even noon."

"Stopped drinking long ago, darling, when my editors scratched mini fridges from their budgets. Too cheap to pay for booze myself, dontcha know." He paged through the newspapers, his eyes scanning the headlines in search of anything he had to jump on.

Maturity is a marvel in a man, she thought. "I guess you're wondering why I'm here after I kind of blew you off."

"Blew me off? Let's not play around. You basically told me to go fuck myself. And fuck myself hard." He held up the *New York Times*. "Do you read this every day?"

Ashamed to admit she didn't, she said, "I try to."

"Save your buck fifty. It's crap. I never read the *New York Times* and you know why? Because it's pompous. Pompous papers drive me nuts. So do old girlfriends who have their housekeepers answer the phone so they don't have to talk to their old boyfriends who are trying to give them a break."

This was not going to be easy. Claire had known it wasn't going to be easy, crawling back to Eric and begging for a favor. But did he have to make it this hard?

"The truth was that I felt everyone would be better off if I cut off all contact with you," she said, though as soon as the words passed her lips she knew it was a lie.

Eric leaned forward, the unlit cigar still clamped in his teeth. "It's not like I'm desperate, Cupcake. You wouldn't believe the women I could have if I just whistled." He took out the cigar and pointed it at her. "I'll tell you what the truth was. The truth was that I was trying to help *you,* you poor little rich girl stuffed among the stiffs in Hunting Hills. Instead, I find myself calling up to Rapunzel who sends her housekeeper instead of her hair."

"What?"

He rolled his hand. "It's a metaphor. Go with it. I've been taking writing courses up at Case."

"I don't know what I can do to make up for it, but . . ." Claire detected, with horror, that her pits were becoming soaked. She folded her arms and was about to go on when Andrea, his secretary, buzzed him that a "Mrs. Marti Denton" was there to see him.

Marti Denton? The first question that popped into Claire's mind was whether it could be the same Marti Denton until she asked herself, how many Marti Dentons could there be?

Eric put his secretary on mute. "Anyone who calls herself Mrs. Marti Denton must be a friend of yours. What's up?"

Claire couldn't imagine what Marti was scheming. How had she even known about her meeting with Eric? "I am as mystified as you are. She didn't tell me she was coming down here."

He lifted his finger off the mute button and told Andrea to send her in. "Guess we'll find out. Are there any more from the Hunting Hills coffee clutch on the guest list?"

"Just me." Marti stood at the door dressed to the nines and such a total knockout that the cigar almost fell from Eric's mouth. Her slim pants led to pixie ankles and her sweater was cut low enough to make an imagination run wild. It wasn't often that women came to the *Citizen* dressed ready for hot sex and a good time and Eric, who could handle Cleveland Mafioso hit men and psychotic readers with ease, seemed at a loss as to how to handle this sweet housewife.

"Sure, sure." He stumbled up and promptly bumped into the corner of his desk before nearly tripping over the coffee table to get to her. "I'm

Eric Schmaltz, editor." He held out his hand which Marti shook limply. "That was *executive* editor. I don't know if you caught that."

"Oh, I know. I read your paper."

Which was news to Claire.

With abundant confidence, Marti minced past Eric and sat in the other chair, her adorable pink Fendi purse in her lap. She winked at Claire and crossed her legs. "Thought you could use some support," she whispered.

Claire didn't know whether she should be touched or if Marti *was* touched. This could be disastrous.

"You two know each other, eh?" Eric was back at his desk, unable to take his eyes of this gorgeous creature with the golden brown skin and sexy blond hair.

"Uh-huh. Though it wasn't Claire's idea to show up here. It was mine. I took the initiative."

"How nice. How very, very nice." His grin was so sickeningly sappy, it was giving Claire a toothache. "Though, actually, I have no idea why she's here. Why are you here, Stark?"

In the shadow of the glorious Marti Denton, Claire had been reduced from a cupcake to a Stark.

"Because of Karen Goss," Marti cut in. "We don't want her name in the paper."

"Ah, hah."

"If that's OK with you."

"Of course, anything." Eric turned to Claire. "Who the fuck is Karen Goss?"

There was no keeping Karen's predicament from Marti now that she was here. Claire couldn't very well tell her to go away or take Eric aside. Carefully avoiding eye contact with Marti, Claire explained how their friend had been mistaken for one half of a lesbian couple during a gay-bashing in Edgewater Park. And that in order to put off the lawyer from OGLE, Claire had had to tell a tiny white lie that she was a reporter at the *CC*. OK, not that tiny.

"Oh, ho! So, you're a reporter when it's convenient to be a reporter and not one when you don't want to be, is that it?"

"I had to think on my feet." Claire opened her purse, took out the cards and handed them to him. "There. So you know I won't be pulling that stunt again."

"My ass. You're in deep, deep trouble, Stark, and you know it. Impersonating a reporter is a serious offense." He lit his cigar and puffed on it. "There will be penalties. You can take that to the bank."

Marti wasn't sure if he was joking or not. She glanced nervously at Claire who didn't seem perturbed at all.

Claire said, "I'm surprised you're allowed to smoke in here. Doesn't the *CC* have a no-smoking policy?"

"Let's see." Eric punched a button on his phone. "Andrea? Does this rag have a no-smoking policy?"

"Yup," Andrea replied.

"How long has that been in effect?"

"Ten years."

Eric released the button. "What do you know? Learn something new every day." He tapped an ash and kept on puffing. "All right, Stark, who's your lawyer?"

"Lawyer?" Marti squealed. "You can't sue Claire. It's not her fault. You have to understand Karen's history. Her husband . . ."

"You *know* about that?" asked Claire who'd been under the impression that she was one of the few who'd been let in on the secret.

"Everyone knows about what Bob does to Karen," Marti said. "That doesn't make her a lesbian."

Eric interrupted. "Seems to me she is if she's down at Edgewater Park after hours making out in a car with another woman, that makes her a damn good candidate. Are you telling me that wasn't what she was doing?"

"I'm telling you it's more complicated than that," Marti replied.

"Karen's totally innocent. What's happening to her is a second crime in itself. Victimization of the victim."

"If I could speak to you alone, Eric," Claire said, hoping to cut Marti off, "you might get a better picture."

Marti said, "It's her husband's doing. Bob Goss. He's the one who made Karen kiss all those women and brought in other couples to their bedroom. Bob is the one who should be taking the heat."

"Hold on, Hold on." Eric held his temples like a vise, as though his head might pop off from the news. "This is Bob Goss of Goss Outdoor Outfitters, right? Are you telling me Bob Goss is forcing his wife to have sex with other women?"

Claire groaned as her head swelled in pain. Freely handing Eric this kind of suburban smut would be like handing Hitler the atomic bomb.

"I never thought of it that way, but I guess you're right. Bob did force her. Yes. Isn't that horrible?" Marti asked.

"I don't know about that. Might be kind of tasteful if it's done with the right lighting," Eric said whimsically.

Claire slid in her chair feeling like a deflated soufflé. She wouldn't put it past him to strip the scandal across the front page, thanks to Marti. She could see the series title now: THE HILLS ARE ALIVE WITH THE SOUND OF . . . SWINGING?

"What's wrong with you, Stark? You think I'm going to run with this?"

"I do." She fought the urge to kick him.

"I wouldn't do that. This is a family newspaper, right Mrs., uh, what did you say your name was?"

"Denton. Marti Denton. Of Hunting Hills."

"Yes," he stubbed out his cigar, "that I gathered. Look, Mrs. Denton, I have no intention of running a story about some rich housewife who likes to go over the fence every once in a while."

"Thank you," Marti said, relieved. "Thank you so, so much."

Not so fast, Claire thought, he's not through. Eric was the king of the quid pro quo.

"However, in return I may need your help with a project I've been working on."

"Absolutely. Anything."

"Do you know a sweet old lady in your neighborhood named Diana Plimpton?"

Claire extended her leg under his desk and pressed her foot down on his toe, hard. Eric grimaced, flashed her a dirty look and kicked her foot back.

"Diana Plimpton?" Marti brightened. "I *love* Diana. Her sister too, Daphne. They knit the most incredible sweaters. Fair Isle. Diana used to send them to Holly and we'd sell them for hundreds of dollars. Fantastic fund-raisers. I know because I'm chairwoman of Holly's capital campaign."

"You are aware, of course, that Diana murdered her husband."

"Murder?" Marti said. "All she did was throw a frying pan at his head. I don't think that's murder."

"Yes, well. Details. Anyway, I want Claire to interview Diana. Unfortunately, Mrs. Plimpton until now has declined all my invitations. But it occurs to me that since you and Ms. Plimpton are such good friends, Mrs. Denton, then you might be able to sway her opinion. You know, arrange for her to be interviewed by Claire, here."

"Sure. Diana's a doll. I can easily . . ."

Claire was out of her seat. "No way, Eric . . ."

"What did you say the OGLE lawyer's name was?" Eric clicked his pen and perched it over a piece of paper. "Was it Susan or Lucy Aldridge?"

Beaten, Claire sat down and regarded him sullenly.

"So how about it, Mrs. Denton? You arrange the interview. Claire writes the story and I deep six all news releases of Karen Goss's foray into our great city's seamy underside."

"Sounds good to me." Marti pulled out her cell phone. "I could call Diana right now. Her number's in my address book."

"Excellent." Eric turned to Claire with a triumphant expression. "It's amazing how nice *some* ladies are out in Hunting Hills. Too bad I can't say the same for everyone."

Chapter Twenty-six

Sneaking around was hard work, harder than Claire had expected. She wasn't used to it, aside from the tiny white lies she occasionally told to spare hurt feelings or to encourage an interview, as she had with John in Prague. Lying might have come easier if the person she was deceiving wasn't her beloved husband or if she hadn't fallen physically ill, which she did moments after making the pact with Eric.

Upon leaving the *Citizen,* a piercing damp wind whipped up from Lake Erie and down 121st Street as ominous black clouds rolled overhead. Claire clutched the collar of her unfashionable L.L.Bean stadium coat and headed toward her car, her nose running and throat suddenly sore from either the gust or the stale air from Eric's smoky office.

"Cigarettes." She cursed, starting up the car. "That's what I get for smoking." Her joints ached and her eyes were heavy when she arrived home in a pelting, unforgivable drizzle. Dawn heated up a can of Campbell's soup for her, the salty old-fashioned noodle kind. Claire drank half of it, along with a cup of chamomile tea, and crawled into bed, pulling the covers over her head.

She dozed fitfully, images of Eric blue-penciling her copy and Diana Plimpton hitting her over the head with a frying pan replaying themselves over and over. The phone rang repeatedly downstairs and she heard the *stomp, stomp, stomp* of Dawn's clogs as she rushed to get the calls. Claire had specifically asked that the answering machine be turned off so John wouldn't have to hear Eric's gloating. Dawn, who normally didn't seem to give a hoot, looked sad at this.

She awoke around five, disoriented and sweating. Outside the windows it was dark and the house was hushed except for the faint *zip* of the occasional car on wet pavement. On the end table next to her bed, in Dawn's careful schoolgirl writing, was a list of names and times of the phone calls. Except for one from John and one from Boots, the rest were from Eric.

As it happened, Lucy Aldridge had called the newsroom demanding to speak to a Claire Stark, according to one of Dawn's notes. A fed-up receptionist forwarded the call to Eric who readily lied that Claire was a new hire who hadn't yet introduced herself to the newsroom operators. He also told Lucy that he'd assigned the Karen Goss story to Claire but that, space and advertising being what they were, it might take a few days for the "exclusive" to appear. In the meantime, he reminded Lucy that the rules of exclusivity barred her from going to any other media. If she did, he couldn't assure her the *Citizen* story would be placed prominently.

The note concluded with an ominous warning that Eric must have dictated carefully: "YOU OWE ME, STARK. DON'T RENIG."

Claire crumpled up the message and tossed it in the wastepaper basket, hiding it under a load of used Kleenex.

John came home late and somewhat out of sorts, though he put that all behind him once he saw she was truly ill.

"Don't look at me." She blew her clogged nose into a tissue. "I'm a mess." This was an understatement. She'd seen herself in his mirror. Red nose. Baggy eyes. Never in her marriage had she been so monstrous. "I'm sure none of your fembots ever got sick."

"Shut up and open your mouth." He stuck a thermometer under her tongue and took her pulse. Claire watched dumbly like a sick child watches a mother. In her delirium John in his light blue T-shirt and jeans and ruddy complexion seemed nothing short of godly. Invincible to germs.

He frowned at her temperature. "It's one hundred point two." He kissed her on the forehead. "Guess you won't be going to Marti's party tomorrow."

"I have to go. I'll just slug the NyQuil."

"Brave girl. How about you relax and let me take care of you." Then he rushed off to fetch tea and toast and aspirin.

He would have to be such a saint. A freaking Florence Nightingale, Claire thought, hating herself. *This is what I get for deceiving my husband—torture by the angry bitches of the universe.*

He returned with a plate of fluids, a big bottle of NyQuil and a DVD of *My Big Fat Greek Wedding,* a movie she adored but that he so despised she once found him using it as a coaster for his beer. He ran her a bubble bath and brought her more tea and when she came out, warm and pink, powdered and hydrated, she found he'd changed the sheets on the bed.

"Scooch over." He fluffed up her pillows. "I'll watch it with you."

He put his arm around her and Claire rested her head on his chest, sniffling uncontrollably. He didn't nag or tell her to "quit that." He simply brushed back her hair and handed her new tissues. He laughed when the Portokalos family tried to push lamb on vegetarian Ian Miller and didn't even complain when, so caught up in Nia Vardalos finally making it with sexy John Corbett, Claire accidentally blew her nose in his T-shirt.

"What were you doing today that you got a cold?" he asked when the movie was over.

Claire coughed. "I went downtown. That wind off Lake Erie cuts right through you."

"It does. You should have been here when the old stadium was still standing. You practically froze to death in the dawg pound."

"Hmmm."

"So what were you doing downtown? You could have stopped by and said hello."

"I didn't want to bother you."

"Don't be silly." He kissed her forehead. "I'm glad you like the city, Claire. In a way, Cleveland's a gem of a town. Next time you have an urge to come down, stop by or I'll start wondering if you've got another man on the side."

"Not me."

"At least you weren't downtown reporting for duty at the *Citizen*. You'd be sicker than you are now, working for them, especially with Schmaltz trying to buy your soul. No good thing ever came out of that paper. Every person associated with it sooner or later becomes a slimeball. I probably shouldn't say this, but if you started writing for them, I don't think I could ever respect you the same way."

She burrowed her head under her pillow. She hadn't officially lied so far. Hadn't made a clean breast of it, either, but hadn't out and out fibbed about not seeing Eric Schmaltz. Perhaps she should just tell him the whole story about Karen and Bob's secretary and Lucy Aldridge and how she got roped in to writing for Eric. He would be mad at first, a bit annoyed, but surely he would understand.

"Listen, John . . ."

"I know it's been difficult for you, giving up the one thing you truly love, journalism. Everyone who hears what you've done says the same thing; she must be some woman. It's a wonderful thing, Claire, the way you support me. I owe you. . . ." And then, so choked up he was unable to go on, he kissed her and tucked her in, leaving Claire to invent new expletives to hurl at Eric until the NyQuil finally kicked in.

Chapter Twenty-seven

Marti was dressed in a butter soft Armani padded leather jacket and high-heeled Cole Haan embossed burgundy lizard boots when she set off to pick up last minute items for John and Claire's Late Blooming Love party on the cloudy November morning. Having bypassed the notion of white tissue bells and matchbooks engraved with the couple's name and anniversary, Marti had decided on a more tasteful theme of an intimate fall gathering charmed by the Olde English colors for passion—royal purple and crimson. She had read all about them in *Gourmet* magazine.

The linen napkins in brass rings were a deep plum to match the tablecloths, and the candles were red in antique candelabras. Already the dozens of flowers had arrived—black magic roses, dark red hypericum berries, purple statice and yellow sunflowers—vases of them filling the Denton household. Money was no object.

Last on her list was a trip to Board and Basket so she could sign off on the wine she had ordered and pick up a few jars of hot pepper jelly. Only three jars left! This was OK by her. She didn't mind the routine chores or the hassle because for the first time since Lois had been born, Marti was floating on a cloud.

Something miraculous had happened to her and, for once, it had nothing to do with Barry. Marti was electric, surging with power, all because she was carrying a secret that set her apart—and maybe slightly above—those around her. It was the secret of Karen's lesbian tryst, a scandal to rock all Hunting Hills scandals, and only Marti and a select group of Hunting Hills wives were aware of it (the cops and OGLE and the *CC* not counting for much).

It wasn't merely this *arcanum arcanorum* that had her so charged. It was her performance at the *Citizen*. Thanks to her, and her alone, her friend had been saved. Not Boots, not Claire—her. Ditzy, blond, spacey, boy-crazy, eternally helpless Marti Denton.

And, oh, it had been so scary to walk into that newsroom with those gruff reporters staring at her and then, with cool, professional Claire probably taking her for a fool, facing down Eric Schmaltz. Scary, yes, but empowering too when he conceded to her request and promised not to put Karen's name in the paper.

She pulled down four hot pepper jars and caught an imaginary whiff of Eric's sweet cigar smoke. No, it wasn't the smoke, it was the tweed. She was a sucker for tweed and men who looked like men instead of Denton, who had puffy baby-soft hands and who whimpered at the slightest bruise. Eric was world wise and, she speculated, relentless in bed. She dreamily added one more jar, so caught up in her Eric Schmaltz musings that she was forgetting that the whole point of the party had been to seduce John.

Helmudt, Board and Basket's owner, had already put aside the case of wine, packed away in the rear of his Volkswagen, which he used for those special deliveries. Marti handed him the basket of hot pepper jellies to wrap and Helena, Helmudt's pseudo-German wife, cleared her throat.

"The total is $743.56 and how would you like to pay that today?" Helena folded her arms, her lipless mouth set firm.

Marti was debating whether to toss in the most adorable jar of blueberry preserves tied with a gingham bow and assumed Helena must have been speaking to someone else. No one talked totals in Board and Basket. Certainly not to her.

"Excuse me, Mrs. Denton," Helena said again.

Marti put down the preserves. Helmudt, sensing trouble, waddled to Helena's side. "We had a bit of a problem with your last order." He lowered his voice so the other customers wouldn't hear. "When you were in the other day with Mrs. Harding and you bought that Turkish . . ."

"Yes, yes, yes." Marti wanted him to cut to the chase. She didn't have a minute to spare. "What's this all about?"

"The order," Helmudt said again. "The payment of it. It . . . failed to go through."

"I'm sorry?" Marti was momentarily distracted by the most outrageous display of peacock feathers. Perfect for the space over the guest room fireplace. "I'm not following."

"I mean," Helmudt wiped away a trickle of sweat that had popped out on his florid temple, "that there were insufficient funds. In your account. At least that's what came back."

Helena sniffed.

Why were they bothering her with these petty problems? She had a party to get underway and yet there were Helena and Helmudt, standing there like big white doughy spaetzle. Didn't they see she was in a rush?

Behind her a woman in a gray cloth coat cleared her throat. In her hands were paltry items, a cookbook and garlic press, nothing compared to the hundreds of dollars Marti had just purchased in wine. Helena rushed to serve her as if she were her more important than Marti. Inconceivable!

"We put it through twice," Helmudt continued tediously. "I assumed there must have been a mistake. The Denton account is always good. I never have to think about it."

"Of course."

"And I thought maybe an account might have been closed."

"I don't think so."

"Then I checked with the bank and they said the account was still open. Now normally I charge five percent for a return, but not in your case, Mrs. Denton. If you can straighten this out perhaps . . ."

Clearly he wanted her to do something even though this situation, whatever it was, was totally out of her control. There was only one thing to do.

"Let me call Denton. Maybe he knows what this is about." Marti rummaged through her purse for her cell phone.

"I'd appreciate that."

Denton, to her shock, answered on the second ring. "Hey, babe."

"You're alive. You didn't have a heart attack after all." It didn't matter that Helmudt was in earshot. Clerks, even owners of Board and Basket, were members of the invisible class.

"I'm fine. Busy as all hell. What's up?"

"I'm here at Board and Basket and Helmudt's just informed me there's been a problem with our account."

"What kind of problem?"

"I don't know. Something about insufficient funds."

"Shit. Fucking bank. Charlton screwed me over." Denton slapped his desk. "Is Helmudt there? Put him on."

She handed the phone to Helmudt, relieved that the matter had been passed off and also slightly concerned since the party was to start in four hours and she needed to pick up Lois from the dermatologist's, where all the Hunting Hills girls hung out. Then she needed to take a quick nap and a shower and have her hair blown out. Who did everyone think she was? Superwoman?

Helmudt was going "Uh-huh," and "I see. I see. All right, then."

Marti flashed Helena a triumphant glare but Helena, like all Germans Marti had ever met, refused to be defeated.

Helmudt handed her the phone, already hung up. "It's taken care of," he muttered, without the general conviviality Marti had come to expect from the Board and Basket. "Wrap 'em up, Helena."

Helena grabbed a jar and twirled it sloppily in the purple tissue paper while Helmudt stomped toward the storeroom.

Marti tried Denton again, but all she got was his voice mail. He'd hung up before telling her whether he was coming to his own party.

Chapter Twenty-eight

The last time Claire had seen Diana Plimpton was fifteen years before in the Harkin County courtroom, her shackled hand lifted in victory to a crowd of sympathetic spectators. She'd been fifty-five then, a petite woman who wore her graying blond hair cut in a modest pageboy, a small bow clipped over her right ear like Rose Marie of the *Dick Van Dyke Show*. She was fond of tweed skirts and simple crewneck sweaters over white button-down collars. Her happiest year, she'd confided to Claire before her trial for murder, had been the one she'd spent in Wellesley's Drama Club putting on *Much Ado About Nothing,* where she had starred as Hero.

Her batterer of a husband, the esteemed and revered Kendrick Plimpton, correction, *Doctor* Kendrick Plimpton, had not been particularly handsome or charming though, as head of Baylor Preparatory School for Boys, he'd been venerated in his small West Virginia community for his schooling and self-help publishing. He'd written five books on how to raise boys into strong men, all of them touting the unsung benefits of extreme corporal punishment.

Apparently, he'd tested most of his theories on poor Diana, whom he would not allow out of the house for more than forty-five minutes in one spell. He used to tape a stopwatch to her car dashboard and set it himself to make sure she didn't run over her allotment.

If she did—or if she burned the rice or shrank one of his shirts or committed any one of the many infractions he'd deemed unpardonable—he would at first dress her down verbally and then proceed to inflict whatever corporal punishment he felt appropriate. Cigarette burning was his favorite because it could be done in the back of the knee or on the sole of the foot, secret places Baylor's Ivy-educated benefactors would not think of looking.

That was until Diana defended herself with a frying pan and Kendrick, much to her surprise, keeled over dead. Then everybody saw the fresh wounds and the old scars because her defense attorney had them photographed and enlarged on a movie screen for all the jury to see. Still, Kendrick Plimpton's mystique could not be conquered and the good people of Harkin County sentenced Mrs. Plimpton to a sentence of no less than fifteen years to life.

Now, sitting next to the baby grand piano in the antique-filled living room of the house Diana shared with her spinster sister, Daphne, Claire felt an odd sort of excitement beneath the chest cold and NyQuil that were coating her thoughts. It was the same anticipation a person experiences running into a faint acquaintance from college, more a mixture of curiosity and nostalgia than a desire to really spend time with the person.

"Diana will be right out," said Daphne, an almost translucent woman with snow white hair in a bun. "She's finishing lunch."

Claire relaxed in a colonial-era maple rocker, studying the birds outside the Darcys' plateglass window. Whoever had set out the feeders had done their research. Red cardinals. Goldfinches. Chickadees, even a Baltimore oriole or two (who should have been much further south this late in the season) flocked to the feeders. Claire spotted a cedar waxwing, several sparrows and, her favorite, a tufted titmouse.

Of course, one didn't need a degree in psychology to understand the relationship that might have existed between fragile Diana Plimpton and birds. Flight. Cages. Freedom. Claire was fascinated.

"That's it. I'm done. Now, how about you?"

She turned from her bird-watching to see, in horror, tiny Diana Plimpton looming over her, a large iron skillet raised in her hand. It was the same Diana, the same tweed skirt and wool sweater, though every feature on her body seemed smaller, more elfin. Except for the deadly frying pan.

"Oh!" Claire gripped the arms of the wooden rocker, her mind sifting through a zillion possibilities. Diana had gone insane. Diana didn't recognize her. Maybe thought she was an intruder. A snooping reporter. Claire wanted to move, but she couldn't. Diana was blocking the way and, manslaughter conviction or no, she was a little old lady and Claire had not been raised to push little old ladies to the floor.

Snort! Diana's wrinkled little face scrunched into a spasm. She lifted her hand to hide her face.

Snort!

Was she laughing or did she have some sort of condition? Claire carefully rose, the box of Kleenex falling off her lap.

"Diana. Please," she pleaded.

"God, do I love doing that." Diana collapsed on the piano bench, bending over in laughter. "And it's so rare I get to these days. Daphne won't let me tease the neighbors and no one else around here understands."

Claire discovered her knees were shaking as she fell into the rocker and picked up the tissues. "You scared the . . ."

"Shit out of you, didn't I?" Diana snorted again. "It's true. I saw it on your face. You were frozen. Frozen in the face of a five-foot-two, seventy-year-old woman. If I had . . ."

"Diana!" Daphne raced in, a dish towel over her arm. "I told you not to do that."

"And I told you to take a picture. Where were you?"

Daphne muttered apologies to Claire and offered to make tea before returning to the kitchen, swearing a blue streak under her breath and carrying the iron skillet under her arm.

When she was safely around the corner, Diana lowered her voice and said, "Marti Denton told me why you wanted the interview, though I told her that I wouldn't have talked to any other reporter but you. You were the only reporter who treated me fairly back in West Virginia."

Something Diana said caused Claire to back track. "Wait. Marti told you . . . everything?"

"You bet. Don't look so alarmed. I've known about Bob and Karen Goss for years from Carol Weaver, who used to visit me in Mercerville. That's the penitentiary."

"I know." Claire responded in a whisper, though she didn't know why.

"But Daphne has no idea." Diana waved her away. "Such a virgin. I haven't been able to watch anything more racy than a PG-13 since I've been here. I am soooo tired of *Harry Potter*."

Claire was amused. "You're very open about everything, Diana."

"Why shouldn't I be? I'm seventy. I spent fifteen years in the slammer for a crime that I'd commit again in a minute. Do you know that every night I heard lockdown in Mercerville, I breathed a sigh of relief, knowing he couldn't hurt me anymore. I'm free, Claire. At an awful price. But really, truly free."

Claire glanced at the birds flittering around a tube feeder. She was itching to scribble down what Diana was saying, but that would have meant producing notes. Notes that could land in Eric Schmaltz's possession, which was the last thing Claire wanted.

"Aren't you going to write what I said?" asked Diana gesturing to Claire's notebook. "I sat up all night putting that line together. I thought it packed a punch. I've got more, if you want them. I was almost a movie of the week on *Lifetime,* you know. One producer called my saga a three-hanky mini-drama."

"Some other day." Claire rested her elbows on her knees, choosing her phrasing carefully. "You don't like the *Cleveland Citizen,* do you?"

"Me?" Diana put her hand to her chest. "No. I think it's a sensationalist scandal sheet. I can't believe you're working for them, Claire. I remember you as a much more *ethical* reporter."

"But I'm not working for them. Not really."

"That's true," said Diana, thinking about it. "Marti said you were doing this as a favor to Karen and that the article might actually cause problems because of your husband's history with the paper."

"He doesn't like the *Citizen* because of the lies they printed about his father," Claire explained.

"I can understand that, all too well, though I was in Mercerville when all the gobbledygook over Hugh Harding surfaced." She clucked her tongue. "He really was a pillar in Hunting Hills, Hugh. Very supportive of Holly, even though he didn't have children there. I remember John as such a cute boy too. So serious. Always had a book under his arm."

Another Hunting Hills moment, Claire thought, amazed that a woman she'd interviewed on a homicide story years ago in a different state had known her husband longer than she had.

"What I have in mind, Diana, is using you, if you don't mind, to play a trick on the executive editor, Eric Schmaltz."

"Trick?" Diana cocked her head. "I'm not following. Are you saying that you're not going to write a story on me?"

"I'm going to write a story all right." Claire stood to help Daphne, who was carrying a heavy tray loaded with teacups and a teapot. "Just not the story he has in mind."

Diana raised a salt and pepper eyebrow as Claire set the tea tray next to her on the bench.

She's no dummy, Claire thought. *She'll get it.*

"You mean, not about my . . ."

"That's right." Claire nodded, glad that the solution had come to her at last. "I knew you'd understand."

"I more than understand," Diana said, helping herself to a cookie. "I definitely approve. OK, now tell me what you have in mind."

Chapter Twenty-nine

A strange car awaited Marti when she arrived at her four-car garage. Strange because it was so nondescript. It was a shiny black sedan with a blue handicap waiver dangling from the rearview. Odd.

Inside, Rachel was dusting the den, her favorite dusting spot due to the TV, which was on mute so she could read the closed captioning while listening to music. The den was spotless thanks to *The Price Is Right.*

"Who's here?" Marti asked, plunking down her bag of hot pepper jelly.

Rachel pulled off her headphones. "Some woman. She's upstairs waiting for you. I think she's in your bedroom."

Some woman. Could it be *the* woman? Denton's woman? But Corinne Berenson didn't drive a nondescript black sedan. She drove a Volvo. And what kind of mistress would park her car in the third bay of her lover's four-bay garage and then help herself to his wife's bedroom? What kind of mistress would have a handicap waiver?

Marti took the steps two at a time, filled with questions. She turned the corner into her plush carpeted bedroom suite and heard the sound of hangers sliding over the wooden rods in her closet where a rather large woman in a black and white houndstooth camel hair jacket stood assessing Marti's wardrobe.

Not Denton's type one least little bit. Talk about a fat ass!

The strange woman said, "You must be Marti."

"What are you doing?" Marti rushed into the closet and grabbed the coat hangers. "Just what do you think you're doing?"

She quit rustling and stood back, chewing on the end of her sunglasses and analyzing Marti's miniskirt and boots with scientific scrutiny. "I see from your outfit that the affair has already started. Am I, perhaps, too late?"

It took Marti a while—as most hard thoughts did—but she eventually caught on. "You're that woman. That personal shopper. Mrs. . . ?"

"Distal. Anna Distal. Your friend Lisa called me. She kept insisting that you had to have a new dress by tonight. I'm sorry if I was presumptuous but she was hysterical that I survey your attire right away."

Nomadd. Lisa must have upped her dosage. "Thank you. I'm so sorry for being rude." Marti put the hangers on a rod and fixed her mini. "I've been under tremendous stress lately. You can't believe."

"Oh, I can." Mrs. Distal's soft hand slipped into hers. "Sit down, dear. The start of an affair is exhilarating, yes, but it can be horribly anxiety ridden. That's what I'm here for. To handle the niggling details so you can concentrate on having fun."

And before Marti could say "prenuptial agreement," she was on her dressing room settee and Mrs. Distal was handing her a blue Motrin and a glass of water.

"You must have read my mind." Marti drank the water in one gulp. "It's been a brutal forty-eight hours. My daughter had the gall to tell me that 1250s on her SATs were fine. I think my husband's having an affair and I had to go all the way downtown to the *Citizen* to help a friend of mine who got herself in a pickle." She took a breath. "Then Helmudt at Board and Basket was extremely annoying about my account even though he knew perfectly well that I have twenty-four people coming over tonight for an informal dinner party."

"I see. That's why your friend was so desperate to get me over here. The party."

"Yes. The party."

Mrs. Distal perched herself on the edge of the settee. She smelled of rosewater and old wool. "Why don't you tell me, dear, about this wonderful man you're having the affair with. You are having an affair, aren't you? Or is it still in the planning stages because I rarely execute a contract unless the affair is underway. I've found over the years that I waste too much time on mere fantasies."

"It's underway, all right," said Marti, who truly believed this. "We have an understanding."

"An understanding. That's quaint."

"Though we haven't . . . consummated it yet."

"Ahh. That's too bad." Mrs. Distal tapped a cane that Marti hadn't noticed before. "Technically, extramarital sex defines the start of an affair. Maybe I should come back when you have . . . you know?"

Marti bit her lip. Boots and Lisa had so talked up Mrs. Distal that she was afraid of losing her. "That would be a mistake if you're concerned about wasting time. Tonight John . . ."

Mrs. Distal held up her hand. "Please. No names."

"Tonight he and I are slipping away from the party. There'll be plenty of drinks and food and when everyone is preoccupied, John . . . He and I will be alone."

"Hmmm." Mrs. Distal nodded, accepting the idea. "I take it he is married as well?"

"Yes, though not long. About six weeks. He met her in Prague and got married very fast. In fact, this party's for them."

"Daring," said Mrs. Distal, grinning. "Ingenious."

"Thank you."

"But, considering that he's a newlywed, aren't you afraid that your advances will be rebuffed?"

Marti bristled at the word. "Rebuffed? Me? No. He loves me. Last summer, at my friend's pool party, he told he me he'd been searching all his life for the perfect woman only to realize she was right in front of him. But I was so stupid." Marti slapped her temple. "I didn't respond as I should have. Then he went off and, brokenhearted, married impulsively."

"And how long have you known him?"

"All my life." Marti thought back to when she first noticed John Harding doing a perfect pike from the high dive at the Garfield Country Club pool. He was thirteen and she was twelve and though they'd known each other as little kids, she'd never actually *seen* him before that moment. His body was brown as a nut, not an ounce of fat, and he could do amazing, breathtaking feats in the air. "Our friends always said we were meant to be a couple but because of one thing or another, we never were. Also, between you and me, I thought he was boring until he remarried."

"Not an uncommon phenomenon in Hunting Hills." Mrs. Distal got up and looked out the window of Marti's closet, which was bare because it faced the patch of woods beyond the backyard. "If he has known you forever and you have known him forever and then he spontaneously marries a stranger, have you ever considered that perhaps things are in reverse?"

Marti was baffled. "I don't get what you're saying."

Mrs. Distal turned so that she was silhouetted in the fall light. "I'm saying that perhaps this new wife, she is the affair. And you, you are more like the wife who is trying to hold onto her husband."

This was supposed to be taken as a profound statement, Marti suspected, but she was tired and the Motrin hadn't kicked in. She wished Mrs. Distal would put aside some clothes for her, assure her John would be hers for ever and ever and be gone.

"What he needs, and what he apparently found in Prague, was what we all want. The spice. The magic. The spark that makes us aspire to be more than the loathsome individuals we know we are."

"I see," said Marti, who didn't.

"That is what makes an extramarital affair appealing, don't you think? Just when you fear that the days will go on interminably, that the stirrings of passion and romance and wanting have died, someone enters your life who sets your world ablaze. Surely you've seen that in your friends who've . . . gone off."

Marti plunked her chin on her fist and thought about the men and women she'd grown up with who'd had affairs. "Honestly, I have to say that all the people I know who've had affairs have had them with people they've known since they were kids. My parents, even. And the only passion stirred in them was one for golf."

"That's Hunting Hills for you. There is no other community that fears change more." Mrs. Distal chewed the end of her glasses again. "Then again there's this point about Prague."

The way Mrs. Distal said "Prague" gave Marti hope. "What do you mean, *'Prague'*?"

"I mean 'Prague.' "

"So?"

"So, marrying in a foreign country has lots of," Mrs. Distal tapped the glasses against her teeth, "legal issues. I once handled a case, almost the opposite of yours, where a couple of so-so artists got quickie divorces and then eloped to Paris. However, their marriage wasn't valid because they hadn't filed some affidavit with the U.S. Embassy, which was stupid because it was right near the Louvre where they took their vows."

Things began to click in Marti's brain, which in recent years had been virtually click free. If John and Claire got married in Prague and they didn't file the necessary paperwork then, "They might not be married!"

"It's a possibility to investigate."

"You're a goddess. No. Wait." Marti hopped up. "You're like my fairy godmother."

"Don't get ahead of yourself, dear. Every wise mistress checks her facts before leaping to conclusions. Is there a lawyer you can trust? Someone who can make a few phone calls for you?" She glanced at her watch. "I assume all public offices are closed for the weekend over there. Might as well wait until Monday."

"Absolutely! But what do I do about tonight?"

"Hmmm." Mrs. Distal was back to surveying Marti's wardrobe. "This black dress is nice. It's safe and what men expect women who are having affairs to be wearing. Of course, you could always put on what you wore the night of that party last summer when he told you that you were the perfect woman. It might rekindle fond memories."

Marti had been hot, hot, hot that night. There was no disputing that. Young and leggy and free. Mrs. Distal was worth whatever it was one paid her. "That's an excellent idea. An absolutely excellent idea. You are wonderful. You're as wonderful as Boots and Lisa said you were."

"Oh, please," Mrs. Distal said, adding quickly, "That'll be six thosuand dollars for the retainer."

Marti ran to the top drawer of her armoire. Opening it, she pulled out a slim checkbook. "Most of my trust is tied up in stock, but there are still some cash reserves. My husband handles it, though."

"Then we'll have to take precautions. Make out the withdrawal slip to my charity. That way you can get a tax break too. Husbands are much less scrutinizing when it comes to tax breaks."

"And that charity is?"

"The Lower Chardon Cavalier King Charles Spaniel Rescue Society."

Marti hesitated.

"Trust me. Your accountant will know better than to ask."

Mrs. Distal took the check and, folding it, stuck it in her bosom. She gave Marti a card where she could be reached at the Lower Chardon

Cavalier King Charles Spaniel Rescue Society and kissed Marti on the cheek before hobbling down the stairs.

She hadn't even reached the kitchen before Marti was on the phone to the legendary lawyer Roy Phelps asking him to, as discreetly as possible, contact the necessary authorities in Prague.

Chapter Thirty

Showtime!

Denton washed his hands in the Anderson Brothers executive bathroom and checked his watch. Seven fifteen. Marti's party was underway and by the time he strolled in, a half hour later, everyone should be sufficiently shnockered to accept him jovially without too many nosy questions. Shit. Hadn't he put up with enough of those all day?

After leaving Wallaby's Diner and taking a shower at home (only Rachel was there), Denton had spent most of the day driving to the various Mail Boxes Etc.s. Trash Day, as he called it.

When he finally made it back to Anderson it was after six and most of the firm had left for the weekend. Only a few secretaries remained, including his, and he had actually wanted her to see him. The shocked look on her face when he strolled by whistling, "I'm Just a Girl Who Can't Say No" was priceless.

Denton *loved* that. This was what lying was all about. He pitied all his classmates from Tate who'd obeyed the motto of "Fidelity, Integrity and Trust." They were missing out on the best life had to offer.

Unfortunately, there was no way to avoid going home and showing up at one of Marti's dreadful parties. It was OK, though. It was going to be good. Because he needed to go home. He needed to reconnect with the people who had put him over the top—Ty Renfrew, Bob Goss and, to a lesser extent, John Harding. Solid men all three. Men who would back you when the chips were down—and the chips were definitely down. Heck, they were off the table. All the more reason to slip into the schmooze groove.

Next to lying, Denton considered schmoozing to be his special forte, like a concert pianist's ability to play Beethoven or a physicist's grasp of neutrinos. Denton wasn't merely his clients' stockbroker, he was their golf partner, their drinking buddy, fishing pal. Godfather to their kids. Once, even, an emergency babysitter to a screaming baby.

People, especially really rich people, didn't invest 20 percent of their wealth with a broker without expecting the personal touch in return. Denton was there with the personal touch . . . and then some. It was this over-the-top service, and not his lying, that justified his two-million-dollar annual bonus. In his mind at least. Really, the inflated statements had been incidental. Props at best.

Denton removed his jacket and rolled up his sleeves, stuck his finger in the knot of his tie and wriggled it askew. There. Hard day at the office.

Showtime!

Chapter Thirty-one

Until Claire met Bob Goss at Marti's party, she hadn't thought it possible for one human being to be so boring.

There were clues, looking back, that should have forewarned her to steer clear. The white T-shirt under his classic Peruvian flannel shirt in Stewart black plaid. The cell phone clip on his belt and the handy flosser in his shirt pocket. But the reporter in her couldn't resist chatting up the Outdoor Outfitter King who, in all seriousness, wore a helmet when walking in the woods, lest he trip on a root and suffer a massive head injury.

That is when he wasn't arranging kinky sex scenarios for his wife.

"I can't get enough of this stuff, can you?" Bob said, bypassing the smoked baby octopus and the mouthwatering oyster and artichoke cornmeal fritters for the hunk of cream cheese drenched in hot pepper jelly. "I don't know how they make it but it's out of this world."

"They pour a jar of hot pepper jelly over cream cheese," Claire said.

"You're kidding me." He plunked another teaspoonful on a Ritz.

"I am not." Claire was still suffering from her cold, despite a double-dose of medicine, so the sentence came out as, "I ham not."

Bob backed away in alarm.

"You're not contagious, are you?"

She dabbed at her red, raw nose. "Not unless we get the sudden urge to make out."

Bob pursed his lips. "Oh. I don't foresee that happening."

That this geek was the creative driving force behind Goss Outdoor Outfitters was unbelievable. That he was worth millions of dollars and owned a private jet and yacht, not possible.

That he was a voyeuristic sexaholic and stoned . . . forget it.

For he was stoned, Claire was sure. There were his eyes—red rimmed and glassy—and his appetite (the maid had to open another jar of pepper jelly before the first cocktails were drunk) and the syrupy B.O. smell. That was OK. It was only that she didn't usually associate potheads with white socks and endless dissertations on the brilliance behind the L.L.Bean periwinkle color choice.

"Ten years ago it was Dartmouth green. That was the must-have color for outerwear. You know the green I'm talking about? Not quite hunter, not quite evergreen. Consumers were mad for it. Had to have their down vests in it, their tents, their canoes. Geesh, even their fucking thermals. Evoked both an appreciation for nature and an Ivy League intellectual standard. You got it?"

"Uh-huh," said Claire, now on her second martini and contemplating the European-looking man by the fireplace in the navy blue blazer with the longish jet black hair. *Why couldn't he be the one organizing neighborhood orgies?*

"Then slam, out of left field comes L.L.Bean with periwinkle. Instant hit. Market completely taken by surprise."

"Really."

"Brilliant move. Here we are—by 'we' I mean us and Orvis, the majors—with our Dartmouth Green and Sahara Sand and Chestnut

Brown and Wood Smoke Gray and Montana Midnight and wham, periwinkle. Evokes purple British heathered moors as well as Nantucket snails. Perfect. Well, you can imagine the reverberations."

"Absolutely." It was as though Bob were on the other side of a thick piece of Plexiglas. Plexiglas made up of NyQuil.

"It hasn't been the same since, has it? Oh, sure, Land's End has its lilac, but you know they were bought by Sears so right there you're losing your upper-crust clientele. *Those* people want lilac. They don't even know what periwinkle is. Hell, they'd snap up a purple."

They were thankfully interrupted by Marti who, for some reason Claire hadn't quite figured out, was prancing around in white shorts, floral sandals and a pale green top despite the occasional flurries falling outside the window.

"Has anyone seen Denton?" She called out. "He was supposed to be here by now. He called from 271. He's coming back from Dayton."

"Again?" observed Lisa who *was* on her third martini.

Marti shot her a look.

"I mean, it seems like you're always saying that Denton's on the freeway coming back from Dayton."

"That's because he is," said Marti, her attention now turned toward John, who had gone into the library to check out the latest in her book collection. Quietly she snatched a glass of white wine off the maid's tray and slinked after him.

Claire was too groggy on cold medicine to make sense of it.

"Denton's a super guy," Bob said.

"Haven't met him either." She debated if it would be too obvious if she excused herself to go to the bathroom, to check on John, anything to get away from Bob.

"You haven't met Denton? Geesh. Let me fill you in on a little secret." Bob was about to put his hand on her shoulder but, remembering her germs, opted not. "I wouldn't be half as wealthy as I am now if it hadn't been for Denton. I'm telling you. You listen to me. Are you listening?"

"I'm listening," said Claire, lying.

"You have any money at all. You put it with Denton. You know how crappy this market it is, right?"

Claire wasn't sure if responding with "I don't give a flying fig" might have been offensive.

"Investors are getting 6 percent, if that. Worse, most are losing value." He checked over her shoulder. "Between you, me and the cream cheese, I'm getting 20 percent on my returns."

"No!" Though she had no idea what that meant.

"So's Ty." He nodded toward Lisa's husband, Ty, a rotund balding man with glasses, a full head shorter than his much younger wife.

"So's John. Though he could be getting more if he put more money in." Bob poked her in the chest. "You tell him to do that, OK?"

"OK." Then, hoping to change the subject, she said, "Boy. You guys are lucky to have such a smart stockbroker as a friend."

"Not luck." He tapped his temple. "Brains. That's what we've got. Ty. John. All of us know plenty of stockbrokers. Went to school with them and there's not a day that goes by that my phone doesn't ring and it's a college buddy on the line asking me how life is and, sure enough, he's a broker looking to drum up business. What makes us different is we know how to pick 'em."

"Hmm." Claire strained to look around the corner to see what John and Marti were doing.

"Spending money is easy. Making it is hard. My old man used to change his own oil and tip 15 percent, though he was a self-made millionaire. He wasn't throwing around bills and wearing this so-called bling bling like you see the up and coming generation doing. And you know what?"

"What?"

"That's *why* he was a self-made millionaire. He was smart about money. Careful." Bob hungrily eyed the refreshed platter of cream cheese and hot pepper jelly the maid was just placing on the table.

"That's what separates us from the youth. We appreciate the value of a dollar. We don't take it for granted."

"I think you're wanted in the kitchen," said a low voice in her ear.

It was the European man. He inclined his head kitchenwise. "Sorry, Bob, it's an emergency."

But Bob was focused on the cream cheese and he was perfectly glad to have Typhoid Mary leave the room.

"I can see why his wife prefers women."

"Pardon?" asked the European, who was following her to the kitchen.

Claire shook her head. "I was just talking to myself."

"Yes. Why not?"

Marti's tastefully done kitchen was the exact replica of the cover of *Country Home*. Either that or it *was* on the cover of *Country Home*. Claire remembered standing in line at Heinen's, looking at the cover and thinking, *Who actually has a kitchen that coordinated and spotless?* And the answer was, Marti!

The theme was colonial. George Washington level colonial. There was a massive brick hearth in one corner and distressed wide pine floors throughout. Only the stainless steel of the eight-burner Wolf stove (that looked hardly used) and the side-by-side twin Fisher & Paykel stainless refrigerators gave away its modernity. Otherwise the thick butcher-block counters were authentic, as were the Amish handcrafted pine cupboards and deep soapstone farm sink. Even the bricks must have been reclaimed from an eighteenth-century historical treasure.

Claire felt the distinct prickles of jealousy. She now loathed Boots's sterile plastic kitchen with its peppy yellow walls and stainproof Corian. This! This was what she'd been looking for but in a million years could never have devised so expertly. She felt so inadequate, like she was missing a vital housewife chromosome that could sense the need for knick-knacks.

A wave of dizziness passed over her and Claire sat on a stool. "Isn't there some emergency I'm supposed to be tending to?" she asked the European.

"Yes. You're in desperate need of another drink." He swiped the glass from her hand and helped himself to Marti's bar. "I don't know how you stood it as long as you did."

"NyQuil. NyQuil and martinis. You could live through a nuclear war and not even notice the explosion if you're on NyQuil and martinis."

He laughed and his black, black eyes twinkled as he blithely poured vodka and vermouth into a steel shaker.

"That looks very dangerous," Claire said. "I don't think I should trust it. Or you."

"Me? I'm innocent." He had a lovely accent. Italian or Spanish. "It's those other men out there who are dangerous. They look respectable with their suits and ties and their Swiss watches, but you'd be surprised what goes on in their nice secluded homes."

"You're talking about Bob Goss."

"Am I?" He poured the drink into two glasses.

"And I bet you're Val. Kit's husband. The guy I'm supposed to watch out for."

He laughed again, a lustful Mediterranean laugh. He handed her the martini. "Drink up. Incoherency is just an olive away."

"Where's John?" She'd vaguely remembered him slipping into the library with Marti.

"He's with Marti."

"Still?"

"Yes. But don't worry about them. This night, I see, has been a long time coming." He sat next to her, so close that the cuff of his blue blazer was brushing against her wrist. "For us, perhaps, it is just beginning."

Chapter Thirty-two

Marti closed her eyes, placed her hand on the doorknob and prayed for divine guidance before opening the library door. John, who was renowned for hating parties, had secluded himself there, and when Marti entered she found him perusing one of the big, thick books Denton frequently ordered off Amazon but never actually read.

In this case it was Roy Jenkins' *Churchill: A Biography,* one thousand pages. Denton liked to buy his books by weight and show them off on his shelves. The thicker the spine, the more intelligent he appeared, the more comfortable clients would feel turning over huge sums of money to him. Which in the end was all that Denton really cared about.

John put down the book and took the glass she held out to him. A fire crackled in the gas-lit fireplace and in its golden light his features seemed so much more noble than her husband's. She wanted to fling her arms around his gray cashmere V-neck sweater and caress his strong neck, kiss the sharp angle of his jawbone. But Barry had suggested she first lay a foundation of "love speak" which would open the gates to free flowing communication. Verbal and otherwise.

"It's nice to see you looking so summery," John said, sipping the cabernet and leaning against the mantel. "I think your getup is great. Why give into winter? That's the spirit."

"Do you remember?" She twirled slowly. "I wore it at Lisa's pool party."

"That would make sense."

"No." She put down her glass and walked closer to him, so close that it would have been easy for her to run her well moisturized hands up his broad chest. "You don't understand. I wore it for you." Her fingers brushed his neck.

"How thoughtful." John flinched and pulled away.

Marti's touch had shocked him and not in the way he would have hoped. He considered himself married and, more importantly, very much in love. And yet seeing her so bewitching he had to admit that she stirred feelings in him. Old feelings that he thought he had buried forever in a chapel back in Prague. Feelings that a newlywed husband should not have.

Stay the course, Harding. Think of Claire. Think of your vows.

Marti sized him up, the way an owl regards a field mouse. He was thinking about her. Wrestling with himself. Good. The ball was in his court.

He fumbled it. "I see Denton's reading *Churchill*. I didn't know he was interested in that period."

"Denton's not interested in anything except money. Period." Marti licked her upper lip. She knew how to bide her time.

John flipped through the heavy Churchill book. "I trust that doesn't mean he's still doing his disappearing act."

"Do you see him here tonight?" She swept her toned arm dramatically.

"I'm sure he's just tied up in work. Denton's very dedicated."

God, he was gorgeous, Marti thought, studying John's every move. The way his long fingers flipped through the pages or how that muscle in his jaw flinched. The slight bulge of the Adams Apple at his neck. She couldn't wait to pull off his sweater and slowly unbutton his shirt, to see the unbridled desire in his gaze as they moved closer and closer toward making love.

"John," she began, newly fortified. "You know, don't you, that I threw this party for a reason."

"For Claire and me. Yes. It was very sweet of you, Marti. Thank you."

"No." She took a step closer. "That was just a ruse."

"Pardon?" He put the book down. It was so big that it almost fell off the table.

"I know it's silly, John, the way you and I have known each other for years."

"You're right. Geesh. It's got to be more than thirty. Maybe, even, thirty-five." *Love and honor and forsake all others.*

"But something's changed."

"I'd say a lot has changed in that time, Marti. For one thing, we're old now."

She pouted. *Why is he making it so hard on me? Doesn't he realize I'm granting his most cherished wish?*

"Don't be a nincompoop, John. You and I both know what I'm referring to."

"Do I? I'm not sure that I do."

She twirled again. "Last summer? By the pool? Why do you think I'm wearing this?"

His face was blank. Totally and completely blank. Little did she know how hard he was working to remain that impassive.

Not so girlish now, Marti clarified so his meathead would get a clue. "I think your exact words were, 'All my life I've been looking for the perfect woman and I realize that she's been here in front of me all along.' "

"I see. Hmmm." He shoved his hands in his pockets and examined his shoes.

Marti had no idea how to read that. Barry had instructed her to follow the cues from his body. But what kind of cue was this? Are my cuffs too long? Is that a spot on the carpet? Maybe I should switch shoe polish?

"Listen, Marti, if you're going where I think you're going. . . ."

"We have so much in common. The same friends, the same background. Even our parents hung out together, John."

"Still. . . ."

"I mean we can walk into the Garfield and everyone knows who we are. No one knows Claire. She doesn't even like the place."

John had no idea what to say to that.

"Think of the pajama parties we've been to. I bet you can recall exactly what I wore each year. I sure as hell know what you wore. Do I dare mention the MacLeod tartan boxers from 1983?"

He had to smile. Betsy and Doug Klein's 1983 pajama party was the closest he and Marti had ever come to seriously making out.

"Aha!" she wagged a finger. "Now you know where I'm going."

John tried to choose his words carefully. "I admit that I've always had feelings for you, Marti. . . ."

"See! I knew it!" She impulsively threw her arms around him. "Yes. That's exactly where I'm going. And this is why I wanted to be alone with you tonight. Why I've wanted to be alone with you ever since you returned from Prague. I've been dying to tell you that you don't have to be heartbroken anymore. I've decided that I love you. Really, truly love you, John, and that I'm yours."

On a wild impulse she fulfilled the fantasies that had tormented her since she first heard Boots say the word "married," and planted her collagen-filled lips squarely on his, anticipating the ardor he'd return amidst the enthralling danger that at any moment someone could open the unlocked library doors and they'd be caught.

John closed his eyes and drank in her warm, flowery scent, the sensation of her body pressing against his, her soft lips that tasted of sweet grapes. Six months before, a moment like this would have been a dream come true, Denton be damned. Denton didn't deserve a passionate, loving woman like Marti. He was a pig. Possibly a fraud. And Marti was desperately in need of love, love which John would have been all too glad to give her. Over and over and over again.

Forsake all others and to thine only be true.

Marti was in heaven now that she'd shared her secret. His body felt good against hers. Right. Firm and strong. Not a thing like Denton's. As John's hands moved to her bare shoulders, the concept that *it was actually happening* sent ripples of arousal up and down her legs.

Until his firm and strong hands slowly, gently pushed her away. "I'm sorry, Marti."

She was befuddled. Horribly befuddled. Her first thought was that John, being so damn ethical, was thinking of Claire out of duty. "I understand," she whispered, searching his face. "You don't want to hurt Claire. And I don't want to hurt Denton or Ava and Lois. But, John, we're not getting any younger. We can't postpone joy. It's not being fair to ourselves."

John picked up the glass and slugged the rest of the wine in one gulp. "Jesus, Marti. Where did you get that crap?"

"Barry."

"Who the hell is Barry?"

"My life coach."

"Well, send him back to the minors." He put down the glass and sighed. "Marti, actually you don't understand how I . . ."

"That's what I'm trying to say. I *do* understand. You love Claire. At least you *think* you love Claire. But you know and I know, John, that we belong together. It was my fault we didn't become a couple sooner, but now I've seen the light. Is it ethical of us to put obligation before love? Is it right for us to deny the joy we deserve simply because of bad timing?"

John didn't know what to say to this. He, too, had always been of the opinion that he and Marti had suffered from being out of sync. Yet, after meeting Claire, he figured that his feelings for Marti were nonsense. Now though . . .

He berated himself. There were many mistakes he'd made in his life, many flaws to his character, but adultery wasn't one of them.

"I have to go." He went to the door that led to the patio.

"Why?"

"Because I can't do this, Marti. You are a beautiful woman and God knows there have been times that I've thought I've loved you, too. Including as recently as last summer, even though that was wrong since you're married."

"Hardly." Her chest tightened. She couldn't let him walk out that door.

"It's not only that I love Claire or that we took vows in a church before God . . ."

"God understands. He knows what's in our hearts. That's what Barry says."

John rolled his eyes at the mention of Barry. "I don't care about Barry or God. I care about Claire. To be disloyal to her would be the ultimate sin. Do you realize what she's done for me out of loyalty? She's followed me to Hunting Hills. She's done nothing short of sacrificing her career, her very identity as a journalist."

Marti was tempted to say that wasn't true. That, actually, Claire was writing a piece for her old boyfriend at the *Citizen,* but fear of revealing Karen's scandal prevented her from saying so out loud.

"Claire's unquestioning support of me is the closest I've ever come to grace. She has laid the foundation of trust, trust like I've never known before. And I am bound by that trust, Marti. Claire knows that I'd never do anything to hurt her and I trust that she'll never hurt me. She's proved it already."

"I see." Marti brushed off her bare arms with clear annoyance. "I guess I look pretty silly in this outfit now. I sure as hell feel silly."

"Shit, Marti. Don't. You're unbelievable." He strode toward her, kissing her platonically on the cheek. "But now I really do have to get some air before I do something stupid and lose my resolve."

Marti was so close to what she wanted; however, she was not willing to give up that easily. Once again she slinked her arms around his neck and gently brought his face to hers. Her lips were so full, so inviting that John could sense himself giving in despite his convictions, his vows and love for his new wife.

"Marti!" It was Denton, calling for her from the mudroom. "Where are you, babe?"

"Oh my god!" She backed away from her object of desire as though he'd abruptly caught on fire. "Denton's here. He's actually here!"

John was speechless, relief pouring over him.

"I can't believe it!" She let out a high-pitched squeal of delight and clapped her hands.

John thought that this must have been how Odysseus felt as he passed the sirens, strapped to the mast, pining with desire. It was wrong. He knew his feelings for Marti were wrong and dangerous and deadly. And yet . . .

He needed to be outside in the cool night air to clear his head. Without saying a word, he opened the back door and stepped onto the patio.

Marti didn't even notice him leave, however. She was already out of the library, her Manolo Blahnik floral thongs clicking against the hard, gray slate as she rushed to meet the center of her world. The man who was responsible for all her wealth and happiness and job satisfaction.

Her husband.

Chapter Thirty-three

"Who the hell threw a party and didn't invite me?" Jim Denton's voice boomed throughout the kitchen as he slammed his briefcase on a table and threw off his topcoat.

"Denton's here!" Lisa squealed from the family room where she and Kip Hopkins had been flirting about what board games are ideal for playing naked in bed. "Come on, everybody. Denton."

"Do you know Denton?" Val murmured to Claire as the partygoers raced in to greet the conquering hero.

"Nope." In her over-the-counter martini and NyQuil haze, Claire decided this Denton fellow resembled the Good Witch of the North from the *Wizard of Oz.* Pinky and fluffy and benevolent to the Munchkins gathering around him.

"You're lucky. He's a crook. You grow up in Sicily like I did, you can tell these things."

"Though you have no problem drinking his liquor."

"Why not? He has no problem taking my wife's money." Val leaned back, his slim body with the open white shirt and navy Italian jacket so out of place in this Midwestern atmosphere.

Denton was gulping down the cream cheese on Ritz Lisa was feeding him while her husband fixed him an Absolut over ice with a lemon twist.

"How'd the market go today?" Bob Goss asked and then, glancing around to the privileged crew, "How did *our* market go today?"

They laughed.

"Up, I hope?" Ty said, winking.

Denton held them all in suspense as he stirred the Absolut with a beefy finger, took a sip and said, "I think you'll be pleased. Unless eight percent is a disappointment."

"Yeah!" they cheered and applauded.

"Where's my wife?"

The clapping stopped as Ty eyed Lisa nervously.

"She's with John," Val said with a slight taunt. "In the library."

"No, I'm not." There was the *click, click, slide* of sandals on the wide pine board kitchen floor as Marti rushed in and threw her arms around her husband's neck in the same way that, minutes before, she'd hugged John. They exchanged a big kiss—to which everyone went *aww*—and then Marti asked him how Dayton was.

"You mean New York," Ty said. "That's where I thought you said you were, Denton, New York. At least, that's what I told Dick Anderson."

"When did you run into Dick Anderson?" Denton leaned against the butcher block, trying to appear casual.

"I didn't." Ty cleared his throat. "He called me. At work." He scratched behind his ear. "We don't have to talk about it now."

"No. No." Denton flashed a grin. "I'm interested. Dick's been calling around for me?"

"He called here too, Denton," Marti bubbled. "I told him I had no idea where you were and he seemed fine with that."

"It's the office. That's how disorganized it is." Denton completely loosened the knot on his purple and white striped tie and ripped it off. "I left my calendar. They could always reach me on my cell."

It fascinated Claire that no one had introduced her to Denton even though she, along with John, were supposedly the guests of honor. Denton had made eye contact with her once or twice, but, having seen that she wasn't loaded down in diamonds and gold, showed no interest in finding out who she was. She considered Val's slam and figured he probably was right. The guy was a crook. Perhaps that's why John didn't invest much money with him.

As for John. Where was he?

"Maybe you need a new secretary. You could take mine," Bob Goss offered. He turned to Karen, who stood as still as a wax statue in her white fall pants suit, a New Age smile pasted on her face. "She even works overtime on weekends for Karen, if I pay her enough, though whatever enough is, is beyond me. Monica keeps asking for raises, the greedy wench. You couldn't believe what it costs me to have Monica entertain Karen, eh honey?" He gave Karen's rigid frame a possessive squeeze.

Lisa had heard it and so had Marti and Claire. They regarded each other hastily. *Bob paid Monica to be with his wife!*

Denton, clueless, finished his drink. "Maybe I should be running Anderson instead of being office manager. I'm the only one making money in that bunch."

"What's wrong, hon?" Bob said as tears rolled down Karen's cheeks. "I was only joking. I don't really pay her *that* much overtime."

But it was too late. What was done was done. Karen was out the door and in Bob's Land Rover, speeding as fast away from Hunting Hills as she could.

Chapter Thirty-four

"No one's seen her all weekend." Lisa briskly yanked a black snow-burnt tomato from her garden. "Bob said she hasn't even been home to get her things. Not her contact case or her makeup. Though I guess that makes sense since what do lesbians need with makeup?"

Claire let this slur slide. "Does Bob know what happened in the park?"

"Apparently not." Lisa tossed two wooden stakes over the fence edge. "He's clueless about what he said at the party that Karen would find so offensive she'd have to run off. When I pointed out that all us wives have known all along about his so-called *game nights* and that he let the cat out of the bag by implying that he paid his secretary to make out with her, he went into deep denial. Claimed I'd been gossiping too much with the book group and he didn't know what I was talking about."

Claire hugged her stadium coat as a frigid wind enveloped them in cold damp air. She was not eager to relapse into the flu for the sake of a bunch of tomato stakes, but Lisa insisted that she accompany her to the garden—her "passion." Lisa was wearing kid gloves and high-heeled boots to winterize her tomato patch.

Claire thought, only in Hunting Hills.

Around nine thirty a Mercedes SUV pulled into Lisa's driveway. Lisa was in the shed putting away the stakes and Claire was shoveling manure on the cold, black overturned soil. It was Bob Goss in Karen's car.

Claire couldn't tell if he had come with news about Karen or if he'd come to go duck hunting. He was wearing thick khakis stuffed into Wellington boots and his hands were shoved into a pristine Barbour-like coat. He trudged toward them and when he saw Claire, he signaled with hand signs to determine if she was still contagious.

"All clear," she yelled.

He nodded and approached. "Where's Lisa?" he asked, without saying hello.

"Hello," Claire said. "Fine day, isn't it?"

Bob—Swinging Bob, as Claire liked to think of him—said nothing. He stared at her with bloodshot eyes. Stoner eyes.

"She's in the shed." Claire pointed to the shed where Lisa emerged, her lip gloss somehow miraculously refreshed.

"Hey, you hear from Karen?" she asked, running over. "Is she OK?"

Bob shrugged. "She called last night and wanted to talk to Birch. He could barely stay on the phone with her and I don't blame him. She's abandoned us."

"Hmm," both women murmured in unison.

"I told her that if her leaving us gets back to Yale and it screws up Chip's admissions chances, she's going to have a mighty price to pay. It's the most self-centered thing she's ever done."

Claire could feel Lisa tense and she lightly touched the sleeve of her coat to keep her in check.

"Do you have any idea where Karen is?" Claire asked.

"That's what I came to get out of you two." His glare switched between them, his red eyes zigzagging faster than the needle on a polygraph. "I know you know where she is."

"Don't be weird." Lisa pulled off her gloves.

"This is some sister solidarity thing you wives have going. That's what it is." He nodded, it all becoming evident to him. "OK. I'll let you play it that way."

He went back to his car, stopped and turned. "Oh, yeah. I got a call from a Lucy Aldridge this morning, looking for Karen. When I asked her who she was, do you know what she said?"

"Can't imagine," Claire said.

"She said she was from the Ohio Gay and Lesbian Endeavor, that's what." Bob punctuated this with a *humph.*

The two women remained mute.

"I thought so. I thought so. You know exactly what's going on. Well, by this afternoon so will I. This Aldridge woman suggested I call the Cleveland Police Department and as soon as a certain detective gets in, we're gonna have a chat. Then I'm calling Roy Phelps."

They watched as Bob got in Karen's Mercedes and backed out.

"Goss Outdoor Outfitters designs the most ugly clothes," Lisa said. "Their Barbour is such a poor imitation. Do you know that it's not even waxed?"

Chapter Thirty-five

Marti lazed naked in bed Monday morning thinking about God, *the* God, and her own personal lesser god. Denton's side of the bed was unusually rumpled and warm and she was certain he'd slept there all night. His snoring had awakened her twice.

Yes. The tide had turned.

She rolled over and admired the gray dawn breaking through her window, a metaphor, she hoped, for the rest of her life. New adventures awaited her and Friday night's faux pas with John seemed like ages ago. It had been bad enough that no one had tasted the baby octopus and that hundreds of dollars worth of sushi hadn't been touched or that three jars of pepper jelly hadn't, thanks to Bob Goss, been enough. Those were mini tragedies, nothing to have a nervous breakdown about.

Nothing compared to what Marti liked to think of as The Awakening.

It took place after the guests left, after Karen had fled in the Land Rover and Lisa and Claire went to look for her. Denton and Marti, alone and frosty, had stood opposite one another in the kitchen. Marti hadn't been sure what to say. The night would have been exhausting on its own without Denton suddenly making his grand appearance and John his dramatic "Claire's-so-loyal" speech.

"There's something I have to tell you, Marti." Denton was eating Skittles from a bowl she kept stocked, a kind of leave-the-light-on-for-you gesture that Denton, the Skittleholic, found touching.

"Whatever, Denton," Marti had said. "The night's already ruined. There's not much more damage you can do."

"I'm sorry. That's all I wanted to say. That I'm very, very sorry."

His words hung over them like the yellow and white striped awning that adorned Garfield Club patio.

"What did you say?"

"I said I'm sorry. I'm sorry for everything."

In all the years she'd known him, from the pre-society sixth grade dance class at the Greek Orthodox Church, where he had stepped on her toes during the box step, to his awkward teenage fumbling during the Fourth of July fireworks display on the Hunting Hills community polo fields to his constant hanging up on her—never, ever had Denton uttered those magic words.

"Oh, Denton." Marti went to him and rested her head on his big and tall chest. "That's OK."

"Thank you," he whispered, his sticky tropical sour fruit lips kissing her hair. "I shouldn't be forgiven for what I've done."

"You haven't done anything wrong. You weren't around because you were so busy at work, that's all. That's what happens when you're the breadwinner."

He sighed. Tired from stress and the bad mattress at the Empress, Denton didn't have it in him to tell her the rest. How she was broke. How *they* were broke. How he was drafting plans every hour of every day now. Tonight he just didn't have the courage. Hell. He wasn't man enough. Isn't that what his father had always told him?

"Everything's fine now that you're home to stay." Marti broke away and looked up at him. "Not to be one of those bossy boots, but you are home to stay, aren't you?"

"I don't know what you're talking about. I never went away." He smiled down at her.

"I didn't think so." She returned to resting her head.

Denton begged off having sex that night and Saturday night too. On Sunday, he suggested they drive up to Michigan with Lois and take Ava out to lunch. It turned out to be a wonderful day. Lois spent most of the drive sulking about Gunther (who'd beaten her to the breakup), but was encouraged at the sight of cute guys wandering around Michigan State's campus. They put pay to dumb old Gunther's listless attitude and Ava said Lois would draw them like bees to honey if she upped the highlights in her hair and dropped a few pounds.

They lunched at a college hangout in East Lansing, a place called the Rock and Bowl. Denton dismissed Marti's warnings about E. Coli and ordered a huge hamburger cooked raw with a side of fries which she and the girls picked at while they discussed the Assembly Ball.

Marti had found the perfect off-the-shoulder dress for Ava. It had been pricey. (She whispered the exact amount in Ava's ear as Denton pretended to groan and be upset even though he loved it when Marti splurged.) If Ava thought it was OK, they could get it fitted over Thanksgiving break. Afterward, the nuclear family went shopping and bought stuff for Ava's dorm room—a wall hanging, a few pillows, a funky light and some new clothes. Material acquisition was one of the few activities that brought the Denton family together.

That night Marti was sure Denton would want sex. A Hunting Hills wife should always be ready for sex. This included blow jobs and hand jobs, both of which should be performed with ingenious twists, turns and tickles, altered periodically to add a touch of variety. A wife needed to remember that if she didn't do it right, someone else would.

But Denton didn't want sex. He said he had too much stress. Marti made the mistake of delicately mentioned Viagra, to which Denton reacted as if she'd suggested he explode his dick or something. Said he was plenty man enough to get it up on his own and that Viagra was a hot marketing ploy aimed at middle-aged men with extra cash who were sold the myth of declining testosterone.

"Chill out," she said. "It was only a thought. Ty Renfrew uses it . . ."

"Exactly." Denton pulled the cover over his shoulder. "Just give me time, Marti. I'll come around. Let me get past the financial statements for the third quarter." He kissed her with a peck and went to sleep.

Marti lay awake and thought of John. It was funny that she hadn't thought of him all weekend. Not once. She took this as a good sign. This and Denton's return. Maybe, just maybe, her life was returning to normal. Denton would be home more. Ava was doing well in school. Lois had stopped holing up in her bedroom. Barry had been right about worry. It was stupid. Positive thoughts could cure everything.

But she hadn't counted on Roy Phelps calling her the first thing Monday morning. He'd gotten through to Prague and with some persistence, along with a credit card transaction of five hundred dollars, he'd found proof that, indeed, John Harding's marriage was a sham.

Chapter Thirty-six

Denton was having a super day!

He'd managed to win a new account. Herb Mackinaw, the owner of the Empress Hotel as well as the China Dawn local Chinese food franchise and the Tip Top Motel chain in Northeastern Ohio, had met Denton during his "retreat" at the Empress and had been so impressed by the overworked stockbroker's dedication to his clients that he swore three million dollars to Anderson Brothers. This made returning to the firm so much easier.

The secretaries, his boss, even his green-eyed fellow stockbrokers, were genuinely eager to see him, though Tim Watson, a congenital "poor performer," sniped that "wouldn't it be nice if all of us could take a mental health week."

Fuck Watson. Dick Anderson was top dog and Denton, who prioritized constantly, cared about no one except the one on top.

Toward the day's end, the top dog quietly entered Denton's office and shut the door, as if they were going to chat about last Sunday's round on the links or what he should buy his overweight wife for her birthday.

"Good to have you back, Denton." Anderson perched himself, one thigh over the corner, on Denton's desk. He was in his traditional black undertaker suit with the gray and white striped tie. His graying hair and jowls epitomized the face of financial security. Legend was that Dick Anderson had been born with such a trustworthy demeanor, a bank officer had approved a loan for him when he was only eighteen.

"I won't ask where you've been or what you've been up to. We've all been there. Me too."

"Thank you for understanding." Denton pushed back his chair, showing that he had nothing to hide.

"Had a nice chat with Marti the other day. She was busy, as usual."

"Aren't they all?" Denton chuckled. "The wives."

"Gosh. I can recall when little Marti Swan used to come over and play at our house with Delia."

(Delia was one of those Hunting Hills natives who had fled west to California right out of high school. She, like Denton's brother, wouldn't return even for holidays, believing that Hunting Hills and Cleveland possessed hidden tar pits that trapped the unaware.)

"She loved our dog, Max." Anderson shook his head. "Crazy Max who used to eat golf balls. She just had twins, you know."

"Max?"

"No. Delia. Max is long dead."

"I'm sorry."

"Don't be. Delia's over the moon. Took years of in vitro fertilization which, if you don't mind me saying, cost twice her college education."

"What's money for?"

"Yes. What's money for." Anderson frowned. "Do you know that Marti had no idea where you were?"

Denton arched his eyebrows. "That so?"

"Hadn't heard anything about Marguerite Grayson either."

"I try not to bring my problems home from the office."

"What are we going to do about Marguerite Grayson, Denton?"

Denton's tie suddenly felt tight around his throat. "I have no idea." He thought back to when he was a kid and how his parents had dragged him every year to Marguerite Grayson's Christmas open house in her rambling mansion. He remembered sipping nonalcoholic eggnog and sitting on her stiff couch and wishing desperately that Marguerite had kids his age or *Gilligan's Island* reruns on TV. Or any TV, for that matter.

"Luckily, I've managed to open a few channels of communication with her and her lawyer and the prospects of a return are looking positive."

This was indeed good news. Denton beamed, thinking of the sixty million dollars he could absorb and spread around his various accounts. Happy times were here again!

"Except she insists that I be her broker, which is only sensible as I'm sure you agree."

"Absolutely." Denton's hopes deflated.

"And I think it's best, in light of the office turmoil during your unexplained absence, that I unburden you of the duties of office manager. Watson's not lighting the world on fire, but he is a solid, dependable overseer. He's been doing a bang up job while you were out. Already he's spotted some . . . irregularities." Anderson smiled a rack of dentures. "Though I'm sure you can explain those easily."

Denton thought he might pee in his pants. He panicked, unsure if he had brought a bag of Skittles to work. "Absolutely." He forced himself to act nonchalant. "Get in any duck hunting while I was out? You know you always have a standing invitation to our getaway in Michigan."

"Thanks, but I like the one I have already. Watson will be in this afternoon with the computer records. The guy's such a geek he insisted on going through everyone's databank." Then he rapped his knuckles on Denton's desk and left.

Denton was too frozen with shock to begin planning the next Big Lie. He was scatterbrained, unable to focus on what he had left on his office computer and what had been strictly relegated to home.

Sheila. He picked up his phone and pressed the button for his secretary.

"I'm halfway out the door. I have to leave early for a dentist appointment," snapped the lazy loaf of a woman.

"This won't take a minute. I need to know what computer files Watson downloaded from my system." Denton was already at his screen, scrolling through, not knowing exactly what he was looking for except, perhaps, a sign.

"A minute!" Sheila shrieked. "That'll take more than a minute. Watson was in there all Friday."

Denton hung up. Skittles. What he needed right now, immediately, was a bag of Skittles. Preferably sour.

The phone rang. Once. Twice. Sheila was at the dentist's so she couldn't pick it up and, not eager to turn away more clients, he had to answer for her.

"Denton here."

Silence. And then a muffled sound. Denton couldn't frame it until he heard the voice.

"Hey there, old buddy." It was Bob Goss, issuing the standard Hunting Hills greeting except not with the standard Hunting Hills bon vivant. "How's it hanging?"

"Fast and loose and out of use." The words rolled off Denton's lips.

"Say, uhm, I wonder if I might ask you for a bit of a favor."

"What's up, Bob?"

"Seems I'm going down a road I hadn't anticipated and I'll be needing to change my cash flow."

Denton tensed. "Divesting?"

"Divorcing."

"What?" Karen and Bob Goss had been together since college. Sure

Karen had run out on the party Friday night but that was Karen for you. Flighty and oversensitive. "You two? That's impossible."

"Apparently it's quite possible." Bob paused to guffaw. "I was late getting off to work this morning, what with Karen taking a little TLC on the OTT, when who should appear at my door but two plainclothes from the Cleveland PD."

It was happening. Bob Goss was pulling out all his money because he'd been tipped off that Denton had been doing some creative financial management. The cops were finally on to him. Fuck Marguerite Grayson. Denton opened drawers searching madly for Skittles.

"I'd called them and they'd been nice enough to come to my house. I didn't think the police did that any more, did you, Dent?"

"Uh, no."

"The news is not good, old fellow."

Denton went down on his knees. Thanks to his "free-hands" headset he was able to clasp his hands in prayer and throw himself at the mercy of the Almighty. *Please, God. If you will give me this one break I will stop. I will stop forever. I will make good with my family and my friends.*

"Turns out that they were there looking for Karen. She and my secretary were attacked at Edgewater Park a few nights ago. She never told me."

"Was she hurt?"

"How the hell do I know? I have no idea where she is. I do know, however, that she's not coming back to this place. This is no longer her home. She is not fit to step inside." Bob was becoming uncharacteristically angry.

Something was up. Denton tried to pay more attention because maybe, just maybe, this "situation" had nothing to do with him. "What the hell's going on, Bob?"

"My wife." Bob's voice became muddled. "She's a goddamn lapper."

"Lapper?" What the hell was a lapper?

"The cops came to tell me they found the suspects. They were arrested today for smashing my secretary's SUV in Edgewater Park and they're making no bones about what they saw. They saw my wife . . . doing it. Doing it with another woman, Denton, on her own! She did it for herself. Not for me. For her!"

Denton got off his knees and sat on his chair, brightening. God had granted his prayer. The cops hadn't come to Bob Goss's to talk about his Anderson Brothers money. They'd come to talk about Karen. Karen the lesbian. It was a miracle. A blessing!

"Gee. I'm sorry about that, Bob. What can I say?"

"You can say, 'Let's get your money out, Bob, and overseas before Karen gets her hands on it.' That's what you can say."

Denton went to his door and locked it. "You don't want to do that, Bob."

"Yeah. I do. I've talked to Phelps. Get the money out now and in a protected account where Karen can't get her sick fingers on it."

"It doesn't work. Trust me on this. Keep your money where it is." Denton was close to tears. He tried to remain cool but he was losing it. If Bob Goss pulled out all his money, it could be the end. Scratch that. It *would* be the end. He'd be looking at an SEC investigation. He'd be looking at jail.

"I haven't got your third quarter statement yet, but I'm looking at my second quarter right now," Bob said. "I've got a little over twenty-four million sunk with you, Denton, and I need it all. I know it's a blow, buddy, but I'm sure you understand."

Beads of sweat popped up on Denton's forehead. He could stall him. He would have to find a way to stall him. Maybe there was some more cash he could scrape up from somewhere . . .

Knock, knock, knock. "Hey, Denton. Got a few minutes?"

Watson! Watson was at the door. The varmint couldn't wait to rummage through the garbage can of his life like some flea infested rat. He put the phone on mute. "On the phone, Tank. Give me five."

"I'll come back in five."

The clock said 3:45. He went back to Bob. "That's my office . . ." He caught himself. "That's Anderson. I've got to go. We'll talk about . . ."

"I'm coming over right now and getting my money before you close. There's something up, isn't there, Denton?"

In his pocket, Denton found a few old Skittles. Even though they were covered in lint and dust, he popped them into his mouth. Raspberry and electric lime. "Come on, Bob. You've got to back off."

"I wondered. I wondered what was up when you started disappearing. Gone for a whole week and didn't tell anyone. Anderson told Renfrew that there'd been some irregularities the office was investigating. Wanted to know if we'd seen them in our statements."

Denton mustered a chuckle. "Jesus Christ. This is nuts. You know me. You *know* me. I'm Birch's godfather."

"Renfrew started doing his homework. Started checking. He turned over copies of all his quarterly statements to Anderson on Friday. Did you know that, Denton?"

Knock, knock, knock. "I need to speak with you, Denton. It's important." Watson again. The doorknob jiggled. "Open up."

Denton pictured the scene outside his door. The secretaries wringing their hands, their headsets still on as they turned to each other with curious expressions. The green-eyed, envious junior brokers talking among themselves, shaking their heads and exchanging loathsome stories about him.

Knew it all along. Impossible to produce returns of 20 percent in this market. Guy couldn't make it on his own talent so he had to cheat. Lazy. Shifty. Jailbait. Daddy got him the job, you know.

Denton put on his best Tate voice. "Come on over, Bob. See for yourself. I'll have the check ready based on today's closing figures." He hung up and opened his briefcase to pack away his favorite items. A photo of Marti, Ava and Lois under a tiki hut in Maui. A picture of his dearly departed mother. A pack of mint-flavored dental floss and Altoids. His Palm Pilot and, from his bottom right drawer, locked, his father's .38 caliber Remington.

Then he calmly opened the window behind him and jumped.

Chapter Thirty-seven

John hadn't been able to push Marti out of his mind since Friday. The encounter had left him with an unsettled feeling.

It was guilt.

He put down his Cross pen and swiveled in his chair to regard the evening as it descended on Cleveland's cityscape. This was his favorite time of day to be in the city, when lights lit up the Terminal Tower and the Flats came to life. He was glad he hadn't joined the trend of moving his business to the burbs, land of the box stores and overdesigned industrial parks with names like Renaissance and Enterprise. Venture Park. As though a name hinting ambition could transform a former cornfield into a bastion of capitalism.

But the burbs didn't have black people or crime, both of which white businessmen found unsettling. You could park your Lexus in a lot and find it still there in the evening. Your commute was shorter—impersonal, but shorter. The train, which John chose to ride every day from the Shaker Heights Park 'n Ride to the Terminal Center, wasn't even an option in the burbs. At the end of the day, everyone wanted to shuttle in their hermetically sealed SUVs from the Enterprise Centre to their residential development with its own dorky name. The Windsor Estates of Hunting Woods.

He couldn't wait for Ingrid to graduate so he and Claire could get out of this town. And, he hated to admit, away from the temptation of Marti Denton.

His secretary buzzed. Ty Renfrew was on the phone. It was an emergency.

"What the fuck is going on?" Ty Renfrew bypassed the common list of Cleveland business-boy formalities.

Unsure of what Ty was getting at, John said, "I don't know. What's this about?"

"You really don't know?"

"I don't think so." A vague question as to whether Marti was spreading rumors about Friday night crossed his mind.

"Jim Denton's gone AWOL."

"What do you mean Denton's gone AWOL?"

Ty Renfrew related the call he'd received the week before from Dick Anderson and how, in reviewing his statements, Ty had noted that his stocks had been sold and resold in perfect accordance with upswings in the market. "I always figured Denton had the touch. You know what I mean by the touch."

John knew, which was exactly why he'd invested $200,000 with Denton. Enough to preserve a friendship, not too much as to cause serious financial ruin in case the stocks tanked. Which apparently they had.

"It's bullshit. Bogus. I don't know how he did it but . . ." Ty Renfrew took a deep breath. "Shit. I don't know why I'm saying this. I feel like such a goddamn sucker."

"I'm sure it's not as bad as you're thinking right now."

"I just got off the phone with Anderson. They've sorted out what they can of my account. You're not going to believe it."

John sat back.

"Twenty-two thousand. That's how much money's in my account. Twenty-two fucking thousand. Though you wouldn't know that from my statements. My statements tell an entirely different story. I'm a fucking bazillionaire in those."

John didn't have to ask how much Ty had invested with Denton. He was familiar enough with Renfrew's wealth to know it must have been in the multimillions.

"Where's Denton now?" he asked.

"Beats me. He's split. Crawled out the window of his office. Dick told me they had to break down the door."

This was unbelievable. It was like watching a movie. How could so close of a friend, a guy with whom they'd bunked at summer camp for five summers in a row, who'd been to all their weddings and bachelor parties and every major holiday . . . How could he lie to all of them?

"You won't believe how it came out," Renfrew said. "Karen Goss. She's come out of the closet. Did you know that? That's why she left the party Friday, to be with her girlfriend. Apparently there was some incident at Edgewater Park Wednesday night and the police were involved."

Claire's words floated back to him. She'd made a joke of it, that Karen had been caught in a lesbian love tryst and he'd passed it off as a dream. Had Claire known? If so, he wanted Renfrew to get off the phone so he could call her right away.

Renfrew was rambling now. He'd been talking about Bob wanting his money and not getting it from Denton. "I don't know how Bob's taking it. He's lost more than any of us. Lost a wife and his retirement fund in one day."

The hold button beeped red. "Gotta go, Ty. I'll get back to you." He took the other call, hoping it was Claire. He was dying to tell her.

"John?" The voice was barely recognizable it sounded so far away and frail.

"Marti?"

"He's left me, John. A message on my answering machine. That's all I got after twenty years of marriage." She was crying so that he couldn't make out what she was saying. "I'm going to end up like Patty Cox."

"Who's she?"

"The hostess of the Garfield Club," and with this she let loose a torrent of fresh sobs.

"Where are you?"

"Home. Boots picked up Lois. I didn't want her to see me having a nervous breakdown."

"I'll be right there."

"Will you?"

"Give me a half hour." For the first time it annoyed him that he worked downtown. He'd have to take a cab to Shaker.

"Thank you," she whispered. "I am so afraid of being alone. I think I'm about to go crazy."

He hesitated, his instincts kicking in, warning him that he was walking into a trap. And then he dismissed that. Marti Denton, even in a crisis, was no match for his self-control. He was a man, not a robot programmed to do whatever his master—or mistress—desired. He was responding like a gentleman, not a lover.

"For you, Marti, anything."

Chapter Thirty-eight

Heads were going to roll if someone on Eric Schmaltz's staff didn't produce a halfway interesting story for page one besides Claire's exclusive interview with the infamous Diana Plimpton. That baby he had budgeted for a box in the upper right corner. He couldn't wait to read it.

So far in the Monday night edit meeting his pathetic excuses for news editors had suggested a piece on a zoning study that might call into question the need for expanded parking at Jacobs Field. A sob story about a Lakewood amputee who knit five hats a day for the Good Samaritan shelter in the Flats. And a half-assed piece from the sports department on renewed hope for the Cleveland Browns in the Super Bowl. Again.

"How many stories have we run on renewed hope for the Browns in the Super Bowl?" Eric asked his sports editor, Duncan Brezowski, who was finishing a paper basket of French fries.

"I dunno." Duncan patted a spot of ketchup on his Hooters T-shirt. "The way I look at it, you can't have too many."

"You would." Eric pointed to the Minister of Culture, a local celebrity whose hair was longer than it legally ought to be for a man in his fifties. "What's up with the Rock and Roll Hall of Fame? I heard that you were writing up a piece about a donation of . . . What was it?"

"Famous smashed guitars. Pete Townshend's, Kurt Cobain's, Jimi Hendrix's, though his were kind of like more incinerated." The Minister of Culture twirled a dreadlock. "Yeah, about that piece. I didn't get it done."

Eric rolled his hand. "Because . . ."

"I had stuff to do."

If the newspaper guild weren't in cahoots with the Teamsters, he'd have fired that prima donna on the spot, Eric thought. But as he liked the convenience of two working kneecaps, he let the minister keep his job.

As a last ditch hope, Eric turned to his metro editor, Daryl Jenkins. Daryl was a nice enough guy, father to six, poor schmo, and on the short list for a major myocardial infarction since he slaved twelve hours a day. But he was incapable of knowing a blockbuster when it was dangled in his face.

"Daryl?"

"Let's see." Daryl put on his half glasses and read off his story list, which was scribbled on a yellow lined tablet. "Well, we have that zoning study I suggested and there's a preview to tomorrow night's city council meeting, though I'm not sure that's front page."

"It's not." Eric rested his head on his hand and dreamed of a real newspaper with a staff that actually left the newsroom in search of scoops.

"Marialisa's working on a cute little . . ."

"I don't want cute. I want above the fold top left."

Daryl pushed up his glasses. "That's all I got except for what came in late this afternoon. OGLE's making a big deal about this gay-bashing down in Edgewater Park."

Eric lifted his head. "Gay-bashing?"

"Aww, shit," said Duncan. "Not another homo story. That's all we've been running lately are homo stories. Gay marriages. Gay adoptions. I'm sick of it."

"For the record," said the Minister of Culture, "I want to object to what Brezowski said. It's homophobic."

"Fuck you," said Duncan. "Cut your hair."

"Just because I have long hair doesn't mean I'm gay, not that there would be anything wrong with that if I were."

"Shut up, both of you." Eric got up and rounded the table to read off Daryl's legal pad. "Who's doing the story?"

"Sanchez. He's interviewing OGLE's lawyer when she gets out of Channel 3. I guess that would be around six fifteen."

"Channel 3?"

"She's going on all the local TV. They're hot for it, though, if you ask me Eric, I think we should play it down. The story smacks of sensationalism."

"Exactly." Eric threw open the door of the conference room and jogged down the hallway to the newsroom. Sanchez was off the phone, typing and eating Doritos. Eric liked Sanchez. He was a ruthless little bastard who made secretaries cry and threatened legal action wherever he went. But he was the *Citizen*'s ruthless little bastard.

"What have you got on this Edgewater story?"

Sanchez looked up. "Some rich bitch was making it with her girlfriend Wednesday night when a couple of toughs from the Heights came in and beat the crap out the car. Cops arrested them today, Justin Marquay and Jorge Sariglano, both nineteen. Nuevo Nazis and avowed homosexual haters. OGLE's touting the case as evidence for enhanced hate crime penalties though they have a problem as their cause celeb ain't so keen on it."

"And she is?"

Sanchez checked his notes. "Karen Goss. A source of mine in the PD says she's married to some guy who owns a sporting goods chain."

"Bob Goss. He owns Goss Outdoor Outfitters and it's more like L.L. Bean." Eric tapped the top of Sanchez's computer monitor. Lucy Aldridge must have run out of patience and figured that Claire was not going to get around to the exclusive. Fine by him.

"You reach Goss yet?" he asked Sanchez.

"I put in a couple of calls to a bunch of Gosses around town."

"Hunting Hills. She's in Hunting Hills."

"Should have figured." Sanchez wrote a note. "Probably her number's unlisted."

"I can get it."

"You know her?"

"Sort of." A familiar flash of auburn hair caught his eye. She was talking to the receptionist. What a stroke of luck. Claire Stark in the newsroom right on cue.

"Keeping working on it. I got it penciled for page one, top left."

"About time." Sanchez flipped open the phone book as Eric hustled off to catch Claire, who already was headed toward the elevator.

"Wait a minute. Wait a minute." He hooked her arm as she was about to step in. "Not so fast. You didn't even stop by to say hello."

Claire spun around, her green eyes flashing and her highlighted hair shimmering in the lobby lights. Eric had to admit Hunting Hills had been good to her.

"I intentionally came down here at five so you'd be at an editorial meeting." She did not seem at all pleased to see him. "Your story is done. It's on a CD I gave to your secretary. Now if you don't mind I'd like to go. It's a wretched night."

At that point, Eric decided Hunting Hills had been better to her luscious friend Marti Denton. "Where's your pal? The sexy one with the collagen lips."

"You mean Marti?"

"That's her. She's adorable. I could eat her up in one bite." He smoothly led Claire back to his office. "You're adorable too, don't get me wrong. But you're more Appalachian adorable. That Marti, she's a class apart. I mean, I took one look at those legs and I was in love. She's . . ."

"Out of your league and, may I add, extremely married."

Eric opened his office door and pushed her in, locking it behind him. "Married? Who cares about married in Hunting Hills? Aren't they all having affairs over there? Isn't that what they *do*?"

Realizing that she'd been suckered back into Eric's office, Claire threw down her purse and said, "OK, Eric, what's up? I know you're supposed to be in an edit meeting because I passed right by it. Whatever's going on has to be big, seeing as how I'm no longer the object of your affections, so you must need me for some other reason."

He checked the door handle. "Say, uhm, there isn't anything about Karen Goss in the piece you filed today, is there?"

Claire folded her arms, her eyes narrowed in suspicion. "No. Why?"

"Because remember that incident in Edgewater Park?"

"Shit." Her face went white.

"It's going to be all over the TV news. They caught the guys, Claire." He pulled out a chair for her and shoved her into it. He didn't want any fainting going on. Not with deadline a mere three hours away. "Seems the bashers are out-and-out homophobes and OGLE's having a field day. Your nemesis Lucy Aldridge is going to be interviewed by my bulldog Sanchez in an hour. So much for your exclusive, eh?"

"We had a deal."

"Under certain conditions. Now that the cops have made the arrests public my hands are tied. You've been a reporter long enough to know that."

Claire chewed on her bottom lip as she mulled options, of which there were mighty few. He was right, goddamn him. There was no way Eric could hold the story now that it was on the evening news. It was blessed luck that Karen was God Knows Where because she'd be beating off a flood of reporters scrambling over the Hunting Hills white picket fence if she were home.

"You're not saying anything." Eric peered at her anxiously.

"I'm thinking."

"Don't do that. I don't like when women think. It usually costs me money."

She took his hand. "Isn't there anyway you can soften the blow? Put the Edgewater story on the back page, maybe?"

"Yeah, right. How long were you a reporter, Claire? Get real."

"Or at least," she thought fast, "let me line up some friends for Sanchez to talk to. Karen's on a toot, don't ask me why or where, she's just unavailable. What if I get two women who know her well to say that Karen's straight, a mother of two, blah, blah, blah?"

"Would these friends be lying to protect their friend's reputation, perhaps?"

"Do you care? They're quotes from flesh and blood people. Rich people at that."

"Good point."

Claire pulled out her Palm Pilot, rattling off Boots's name and number and then Marti's.

"I love that Marti," he said, writing it down. "Really, I do. She's the kind of woman I'd like to marry for keeps. She's the kind of woman a hardworking man like me would enjoy coming home to, watching her make me a drink, serve me dinner . . ." He paused to savor the image. "I'm so tired of you hard-ass career women. What I need is a bunny cake like her."

"You have to promise to use those numbers only for professional purposes."

He crossed his chest. "I swear. I would never call her up and ask her what she's wearing."

"Eric! She's a friend of mine."

"My bad. I completely forgot about your feelings. What are *you* wearing?"

Claire got up and took her purse. "Tell Sanchez to wait until he talks to Lucy Aldridge before calling Karen's friends. I'd like to give them some pointers before you sic your dog on 'em."

"Aye, aye."

"And if we're lucky, this is the last we'll see of each other and then the *Citizen* will be out of my life forever." It was meant to be a dramatic exit but Claire was thwarted by the lock on the door. "What's wrong with this?"

"It's what's civilized people call a lock." Eric folded his arms, doing absolutely nothing to help her.

Chapter Thirty-nine

Marti inspected her husband's suits lined neatly in a row, his shirts, his pants pockets and even the inside of his shoes. She inventoried his sweaters and underwear. Carefully pawed through his sock drawers and the locked box where he kept his birth certificate. The most interesting things she found were two stubs to an Indians game, an old pocket watch of his grandfather's, a matchbook from Le Grille and a complimentary hotel sewing kit. Everything was as it should be. There was no evidence of another woman.

Why? Why did he leave her?

The phone rang and Marti, who was wearing nothing but a towel around her head, stared at it dully. She was not going to answer it with the expectation that Denton would be on the line, begging forgiveness. She'd made that stupid mistake several times already only to hear the no-fun voice of Dick Anderson or his triple-no-fun minion Tim Watson or Bob or Ty or any of the numerous angry clients who were looking for Denton.

"Pick up, Marti. It's me." There was a pause. "Karen."

"Karen?"

Marti snatched her white silk robe off the hook and tied it, since talking on the phone naked—especially to a woman whose sexuality was kind of iffy—seemed somehow obscene. "I'm here," she said hurriedly. "Where are you?"

"At a friend's house."

That didn't make any sense. Marti and Karen had the same friends and no one had mentioned taking in Karen.

"I can't talk long, I just wanted to say that I heard about Denton and I'm so very sorry. It sucks, Marti, doesn't it? Bad news sucks."

Karen started to cry and Marti, who somehow couldn't cry, found herself comforting her even though, according to the Hunting Hills wives rules, She Who Calls, Comforts.

"It'll all work out, Karen, you'll see."

"Maybe for you. Not for me. My situation is so complicated. Denton might have run away from his job, but at least he didn't run away from you."

"Pardon?" Marti listened for the crunch of tires outside. She went to her closet window where only days before Mrs. Distal had been silhouetted, calmly discussing how Marti might best seduce John at her cocktail party. What a far, far, far away world that was. "What are you talking about, that Denton ran away from his job?"

"Bob called and said that we're broke, all of us including you, that Denton took all our money and pissed it away."

"Bullshit." Karen was hurt and trying to make Marti feel worse than she did. If there was one thing of which Marti was certain, it was that Denton would never ever screw over his clients. "Denton didn't leave his job. He left me. That's all."

"What are *you* talking about?"

"Denton left a message on my answering machine," Marti said, resigned that she'd probably have to retell this story a zillion times. "He said it was over between us. That the first ten years had been great. That the last ten years had gone steadily downhill and he didn't want to be married to me for ten years more. He said he'd be by next week to pick up the rest of his clothes and Skittles but for now he had to get away. He ended with how he hoped that breaking it to the girls wouldn't be too hard on me."

That was almost it, verbatim. Marti had replayed it over and over, the last line hurting more than the rest of his good-bye.

"Oh my god. I had no idea."

A door slammed downstairs and there were footsteps. "John's here, I have to . . ."

"One last thing. Could you thank Claire for me? I understand she really extended herself to keep the story out of the papers. Too bad because they caught the guys. It's all over, Marti."

Marti didn't like that "it's all over" part. It sounded suicidal. "Don't do anything stupid, Karen."

"That's the last thing on my mind and do you know why?"

"Why?"

"Because for the first time in my life I truly know what it's like to be in love."

"And I assume it's not with Bob."

"That's right."

"Or with Brad Pitt."

"Nope."

"More like Ellen DeGeneres."

"In fact, she looks a lot like Ellen DeGeneres. I'll be in touch, Marti. Take care of yourself."

Marti held the phone in her hand, vacantly staring at it and wondering what it would be like to share a life with another woman, if Karen would get a buzz cut and paint her house various shades of purple. Own big dogs and ride motorcycles, go braless and wear Levis.

She shuddered and ripped the towel off her head. Her wavy blond hair fell loose and sexy.

It was an established Hunting Hills wife rule that a wise wife diversifies in case the breadwinner goes out of commission. Therefore, she always has another potential husband on the ropes. This was the penultimate and most secret of all the rules. And yet, for survival's sake, perhaps the most vital.

There was a corollary to that, though not necessarily a Hunting Hills wives rule. If at first you don't succeed, try, try again.

Marti fluffed up her hair and loosened her robe before going downstairs to tell John the news, that his romantic wedding in Prague had been a fraud. And that if he wanted her, there was nothing holding him back.

Chapter Forty

Marti was right, Denton decided. Lisa Renfrew was truly the Uber Bitch.

Here he'd gone to her expecting calming assurances that all would be well or, at the very least, her Lexus SUV for the taking, and how had she reacted? Like a bitch. An Uber Bitch.

"You what?" She screamed so loudly that her kid rushed into the kitchen from the TV room, his or her face a mask of panic, as though Lisa had been burned or raped or something. She threw him or her or it, whatever, a cookie and sent him back to the TV room only to round on Denton for a follow-up blow.

"You lost *all* our money?"

"Not all," Denton said, acting insulted. "You still have close to twenty-two thousand dollars."

Lisa brought her hand to her chest and fell backward onto the flower upholstered breakfast nook. She was ashen and, Denton observed, kind of green around the gills. "Twenty . . . twenty . . ."

"I'm sure Ty has other accounts with other brokers. Most people do."

"We don't."

"Gee. That's a shame." Denton rocked on his heels, biding time until he could get what he came for.

"What about college? Our retirement? Private school tuition? We'll have to sell the house. Ty will have to rebuild from the ground up." Already she was back to scheming, planning. "Or we could sue your ass. Sue you for every penny you're worth."

"No can do. I don't have any more pennies. I'm broke too. So's Marti. She's what we call, in the business, shit out of luck."

"Jesus. No wonder you couldn't get it up." Lisa's hand fell on the thick oak table where lay the remains of her kid's after-school snacks, the mail, a copy of the *Cleveland Citizen* and her keys to the Lexus.

"Hey, can I have those?" he asked, reaching in his pocket for a handful of Skittles.

"You want more? We gave you all our money, what the hell else do you need?"

"The keys to your car, to be exact. I expect the police will be looking for mine and I really don't want them on my tail."

"Where are you going?"

"To see an old friend. A college roommate in Akron." Denton held out his sticky Skittle hand. "So how about it?"

"I wouldn't give you a piece of my mind, you worthless sack of shit. Go fuck yourself."

"No thanks. By the way, if you don't give me the keys to your Lexus, I'll let it slip about our three-month affair, as you call it, and Ty will toss your ass on the sidewalk. Which might not have been so bad when he was a multimillionaire and you could get a decent alimony, but now that he has piss all, it means that you'll be back in Glendale collecting food stamps."

Lisa's flashing eyes betrayed a hatred so virulent that Denton wondered if she were capable of murder. Like that Diana Plimpton woman down the street.

"Take them." She hurled the keys with such force that they hit the Sub Zero stainless steel refrigerator and made a dent.

Denton picked them up. He assumed there'd be more of this kind of hysterical behavior for a while. That was until the hullabaloo died down and people saw that he'd only had their best interests in mind. Then they'd come around. Then they'd appreciate what a great guy he really was, how he'd been trying to cushion the blow from the Recession, instead of thinking of him as the schmuck they'd been erroneously led to believe.

Chapter Forty-one

Claire had lots to celebrate. She had beaten Eric Schmaltz at his own game and had saved her marriage in the process. Her only regret was that she wouldn't be in the *Citizen* newsroom to witness his stunned expression when he read her Plimpton interview. Or, better yet, when it dawned on him that no way could he run as his page one, lead, boxed exclusive, twenty inches on Diana Plimpton's vast knowledge of Ohio birds and their habitat.

He'd demanded an interview. But he'd never said what the interview had to be about.

Claire grinned like an idiot as she pushed a cart through Heinen's produce aisle. Tonight she planned on making John dinner herself. She was thinking of a tenderloin quickly seared with green peppercorns, thinly sliced red baby potatoes tossed quickly in garlic butter, a crisp romaine salad and a rich Cabernet Sauvignon to celebrate. Maybe they could squeeze in a round of tennis beforehand or rent a romantic movie. *Philadelphia Story.*

She examined the potatoes and called Boots, praying that Sanchez hadn't contacted her already.

"I was about to return his call and tell him no comment," said Boots. "I assumed it was about Denton."

"Denton? Marti's Denton?" The big red pomegranates were in. She would make a salad of pomegranate and arugula instead. "What's up with Denton that the *Citizen* would be interested?" Some stupid Chamber of Commerce award, probably. People outside the paper had no perspective on how insignificant these community honors were.

"I'm not sure what's up with Denton. I hear the SEC might get involved."

"The SEC?"

"Let's hope not. Dick Anderson's trying to avoid it, though I don't think he has much choice."

Claire stopped by the gourmet cheeses. Whatever was going on, it was not a Chamber of Commerce good citizen award. "Does Marti know?"

"That's another kettle of fish. After he escaped from his office this afternoon, Denton left a message on her cell phone telling her that their marriage was over and he's leaving. Isn't that outrageous? Twenty years of marriage and she's dumped via her cell phone." As though the cell phone was significant.

"That's awful. Where's Lois?"

"With us. Marti didn't want to see her have a nervous breakdown. Truthfully, I'm very concerned about her. When I picked up Lois today, Marti really did look like she was falling apart."

Claire asked the butcher for two filets of tenderloin. "I'll stop by on my way home and see how she's doing."

Boots was silent for a few seconds. "I'm not sure that's a good idea."

"She doesn't want anyone else to know about Denton?"

"No. She doesn't care about that, though she seems to be having difficulty grasping the fact that not only did he leave her, but that he left his job and he left a bunch of people, including her, broke."

"Shit." Claire thought of John. She knew he didn't have much money invested with Denton and she was glad, as well as a little proud, that he hadn't been suckered in by the Denton mystique.

"It's really no problem. Marti lives just around the corner. I don't mind . . ."

"Claire." Boots's voice turned serious. "It would not be a good idea for you to show up at Marti's house."

"Why?"

"Because." In the background a Pembroke Welsh corgi started yipping madly. "Because she told me John was coming over."

"OK. So . . . the more the merrier."

"You don't get it, do you? Don't you understand how it is between them?"

"How *what* is?" Claire was getting annoyed by Boots's deliberate vagueness. It was high-schoolish. Cliquish. The worst characteristics of women friends.

"I really don't like being in this position since I'm John's ex-wife, but as nothing else is getting through to you it might as well be me. It always is." She sighed. "Listen, Claire, there's something you have to understand about John. He's a great guy. A prince. The best of the bunch. And I have no doubt you two will be married to a ripe old age."

"I sense a 'but' coming on."

"But . . . when it comes to long-term relationships, John has a time limit before he gets bored. I was an exception because, well, because John and I have known each other since childhood. All you have to do is look at the string of girlfriends he's had over the past twenty years and you'll see a pattern. John falls madly in love for two months and, after that, he starts wandering."

"Come on, Boots. Not John."

"No? Tell me. How long did you know each other before you got married?"

Claire wheeled her cart into the coffee aisle and lowered her voice by the teas. "Twenty-eight days. A full lunar cycle."

"Let me ask you something, Claire, what man in his mid-forties marries a stranger in a foreign country after twenty-eight days? A man who has a reputation, a *history,* for loving them and leaving them back at home, which is exactly John's reputation in Hunting Hills."

"You're crazy."

"Am I? Plenty of my girlfriends adore John, but they wouldn't for a millisecond be married to him because they know that that's exactly how long he'd be faithful. And not a millisecond more."

Claire felt overheated, as though the Heinen's heater was on full blast. There was a sneaky element to what Boots was saying that she could not deny. John *had* had a string of girlfriends. She often teased him about it, though Claire had assumed he'd put that philandering in his past. Yet, what was his past? She didn't really know.

Boots did. And Marti and Karen and Ty and Denton and just about everyone else in Hunting Hills. All except her. His wife.

Claire fought back tears. "Then all the more reason for me to go to her house. If John and Marti are doing something then . . ."

"That's not what Hunting Hills wives do. Confrontation is not our style."

"Then what do they do?"

"When your husband cheats, you shop. Combat shop. Miu Miu. Roberto Cavalli. Prada. Dolce & Gabbana. Spend as much of the S.O.B.'s money as you can and if he wants to stay married and wants to keep his family together, he'll shut up and pay the bills without making a sound."

"And that's the way it is."

"That's the way it is."

"Oh my god." Claire winced as the Starbucks coffee grounder roared in full blast.

"You're sad now, but eventually you'll get used to it. Think of tonight as your initiation. Congratulations, Claire, you're officially one of us."

Chapter Forty-two

"Man, oh man, am I in the mood for a thick, juicy steak." Denton took a sip of his Absolut on ice and picked out the lime with his stubby fingers. "I am so glad I ran into you, Dr. Henkin."

Dr. Michael Henkin smiled weakly. If truth be told, the last thing he wanted to do on a Monday night was go out to dinner with Jim Denton at the Outback Steakhouse. He'd much rather have gone home and watched the game, done his laundry and eaten leftover lasagna his girlfriend had made him on Saturday night. He would have too, if Denton hadn't shown up in his office at six thirty, right when he was finishing the third rear molar of Doris DeBartolo.

"Hankie!" Denton had yelled. "Guess who's in town for the night, ole buddy." And then, much to Henkin's chagrin and to Mrs. DeBartolo's surprise, Denton had started chanting, first slowly, then faster, "D . . . U . . . D . . . U . . . D . . . U"

"Denton was my roommate at Tufts," Henkin had explained, handing his receptionist the DeBartolo file and making a note for Mrs. DeBartolo to return to have her bottom right bicuspid drilled.

"Tufts Dental?" Mrs. DeBartolo asked.

"D.U." Denton cut in. "Delta Upsilon. The finest fraternity in America. If it hadn't been for Hankie here I'd have never have passed rocks for jocks. Can you believe that these days I'm a broker knee-deep in numbers?"

He couldn't. Jim Denton was the stupidest man he'd ever met. Lazy. Drunken. Just a total waste-case. Back at Tufts, Denton's attitude had been that grades didn't matter since a cushy financial sector job awaited him in Cleveland.

Then a scholarship student and a graduate of the increasingly plagued Firestone High School in Akron, Henkin had unfortunately known exactly what Denton was talking about and predicted that after graduation Denton wouldn't so much as shake his hand if he ran into him at a Cavaliers game.

His speculation panned out. Denton never called or never sent him a Christmas card, though Henkin's ex-wife Judy insisted on doing so out of perverse curiosity. And once Henkin did run into Denton in the bathroom of Gund Arena and Denton's only response had been to flash him a quick thumbs-up.

Then, some twenty-plus years later, Denton suddenly appears in his dental office on a Monday night, claiming to be The Best Friend from College. And now they were at the Outback Steakhouse.

"So how are the kids?"

"Kid," Henkin said. "A boy. Sean."

"Got a photo?"

Henkin reached into his jacket which was hanging on a hook by their booth and pulled out his wallet. He flipped it open to show his hero, his pride, the love of his life. "Sean turned ten last month. He's a real boy. Skateboards. BB guns. The whole shebang."

"I bet the whole shebang." Denton nudged Henkin's arm. "Look at how many *she's* his father banged."

Henkin put away the photo. God, Denton was disgusting.

"Where's John tonight?"

"It's Sean. With Judy. He lives with her."

"And Judy is . . . ?"

"His mother. My ex wife. She used to send you Christmas cards."

"Ah." Henkin sucked lime juice off his thumb, which was stained red and green. "To ex-wives. I have one waiting at home too." He toasted and then excused himself to go to the bathroom.

Henkin checked his watch. It was seven thirty. By nine, he told himself, the ordeal would be over. All he had to do was hang in until nine. It might even be fun if they got to reminiscing.

When Denton returned, there were patches of green and blue at the corner of his mouth. "Seems like you're doing pretty well for yourself, Hankie. Temo's and you must have quite a deal going." He was referring to Temo's Chocolate Company, a beloved candy store in Akron.

"Yes," said Henkin, who, like all local dentists, had heard the jab many times before.

"I trust you've invested wisely. We're not getting any younger, Hankie, and there are plenty of opportunities even in today's bearish market for middle-aged investors to retire as millionaires."

So this was what this drop-in was about, thought Henkin, Denton's rounding up business. "I'm fine."

Denton leaned toward him. "*Are* you?"

"Yes, I am." He was relieved when the familiar buzzing at his waistline signaled an incoming page. He checked his beeper. It was his answering service. *Bless them. May it be an emergency extraction.*

"I better take this outside." Henkin held up the beeper.

"By all means. Mind if I order another round?"

"No. Go right ahead." Henkin bet they'd split the bill in half, even though Denton had ordered Absolut and rib eye while he had ordered plain water and a salad.

The answering service relayed the number, which turned out to be a pay phone outside a twenty-four-hour gas station in Twinsburg. No one there had made a call. Might have come from a customer. They shouted around and waited for the bathrooms to clear. Henkin patiently shifted from foot to foot. It was freezing. He would have worn his coat if he knew it was going to take this long. They checked the people pumping gas and in the cars parked nearby. Nope. No one had called a dentist. No one with a toothache.

Henkin clicked the beeper back on his belt and returned to the warm restaurant. The food was waiting for him.

Denton was not.

"Your friend had to go," said the waitress. "He said he's awfully sorry. He just remembered an appointment. He left you this." On the table was a ten spot. Enough to pay for one and a half Absoluts. "You want me to wrap up your dinner? He took his with him."

"Sure," Henkin said, taking out his wallet and handing her his Visa. "All I wanted was to be at home anyway, watching the game and doing my laundry."

Chapter Forty-three

Morning fog rose from Haywire Falls and shrouded the Starbucks over which Barry's brick office was located. Marti had never been to Barry's so early. Usually she worked out with Todd from six to eight, cardio and weights or yoga and abs. This morning was different. This morning she had to see Barry; it was a matter of utmost importance.

She kept the engine running with the heater on, waiting for someone to open Starbucks so she could go upstairs to his office. She didn't have an appointment but she didn't need one. Marti was Barry's most extra special client. He'd assured her of this over and over. And he'd want to hear what had happened to her. He was vested.

It was comforting to picture how he would take care of her. He'd arrive in one of his bright yellow or green silk shirts, holding an herbal tea. He'd spread his arms wide, welcoming. It was Barry who'd given her permission to be young again, to let out the adolescent girl within her. Ever since she'd been graced with this advice she had felt young and free of worry. She owed Barry nothing less than her womanhood.

They'd spent many hours discussing her sex life, how Marti and Denton had never had the chemistry required for total fulfillment. Marti didn't even know what an orgasm was, not really, until Barry gave her a vibrator and a book. She tried it and had been shocked. Literally. At first she'd assumed that the battery-operated device was sending out sparks until Lisa explained that that was how an orgasm was. Electrifying.

It was soooo different from sex with Denton.

"I wonder," she'd told Barry the summer before, when John was in Prague and still unmarried, "if that's what sex with someone like John Harding would be like." They were sitting barefoot on his famous embroidered cushions, their legs tucked underneath them, cupping jasmine tea in their hands. On the brick walls hung Native American art and lots of feathers.

Barry had stroked his fine gray goatee. "There's only one way to find out, girlfriend."

"You mean I should have sex with him?"

"What you must do, darling, is become the vaginal lacuna."

"The what?"

"Allow me to explain. A lacuna is an opening and the vagina, well, you know what that is, no?"

"Yes," Marti had said shyly. "I've had two daughters."

"Exactly my point. Think of yourself as the vagina of your family. Through you two wonderful spirits have been brought to the earthly plane. Through you, your husband derives spiritual and physical sustenance. The more you open yourself to other people, the more life you bring forth and you sustain. That is why I say to you, *be* the vaginal lacuna. Open the best part of yourself."

"Be the vaginal lacuna," Marti repeated, vowing never to say those words in public. "But what does that have to do with John? If I have sex with him, wouldn't that be adultery?"

"Adultery is such a negative Western concept. I say to you that intimacies with another human are merely life-sustaining acts. That is," and he had held up a finger, "if you engage in them as the vaginal lacuna."

"So I should sleep with him?" Marti was looking for a "yes" or a "no" here.

"As you will." Barry's pudgy hands had opened, blessing her.

But Barry hadn't counted on one glitch. Marti had no more of an idea what was her will than what was his will or Denton's will or John's will or her mother's will. She had found it completely impossible to distill her will from the wills of those around her.

There he was! In her daydreaming, Marti had almost missed Barry and his assistant Rico unlocking the door to his office. She turned off the engine, yanked the key out of the ignition and got out.

"Barry!" she shouted, waving her pashmina shawl.

She could have sworn that Rico had seen her, but that he closed the door behind him anyway. Something must be wrong. Why hadn't they waited for her?

"Barry?" Marti opened the door that led to a narrow stairway. She ran up it calling his name. "Barry?"

Rico met her at the top of the stairs. He was wearing a white and navy sailor striped shirt and his cropped blond hair was newly dyed. The diamond in his right earlobe glinted. "Barry can't see you." He folded his arms. "You don't have an appointment."

Marti was taken aback. Barry's closing line every week for sixty-three weeks been, "Anytime you need me, just come over. I'm always here for you, Marti my darling."

"He's always here for me." Marti tried to peer around Rico, but he blocked her view of Barry's office. "It's an emergency."

"I am sorry, Mrs. Denton, but Barry can no longer see you."

"Today?"

"Ever."

"What?" *Was he on drugs?* "This is impossible. I've never needed Barry more. He has to see me. He'll want to hear the update on my life."

"His schedule is very full and he won't be accepting new clients now or in the future. Please be careful going down the stairs. They're very steep."

"Hold on." She clutched the wooden banister, not putting it past Rico to push her himself. "Just tell me what I did wrong. Did I call too much? Did I overstay my time? Did my feet smell? Help me, please."

Rico checked behind him before answering. "I shouldn't be telling you this but it's really very simple, Mrs. Denton. You haven't paid your bill. And according to your husband, you never will."

Marti reeled. It had never occurred to her how Barry was paid. She came. She sat. She cried. She blew. She dabbed. She left. Denton had always handled the money end and now this Rico person was telling her that Denton had cut her off.

"Why?"

Rico shrugged, looking every inch the French sailor. "Who knows? From what I hear around town you don't have any more money. I think you are broke."

Broke. Broke. People had been using that word around her lately. First Helmudt at Board and Basket had said that icky stuff about insufficient funds, then Mrs. Distal had called to say she wouldn't be providing her services because the six-thousand-dollar retainer check had bounced. Then there were Karen and Boots claiming that Denton had blown everyone's money and all those angry clients and the people from Anderson Brothers.

And now Barry wouldn't even see her because Denton hadn't paid.

Her eyes were watering. This was so unfair. All those nasty phone calls and then Denton dropping her for no reason and then . . . John. "What should I do?"

"Do, Mrs. Denton?"

"That's what I said."

"Well, for starters I suggest you go out and look for a job."

A job? Rico might as well have suggested that she mate with farm animals. "I don't know how to get a job. I'm not qualified."

"Everybody's qualified to do something. Teenagers flip burgers at McDonalds. Welfare mothers change bedpans in nursing homes. Surely you have some skill."

Marti was horrified.

"The classified ads. Start there." Rico smiled. "That's probably the most valuable advice you've received from this office all year."

Marti stumbled down the stairs into the emerging dawn outside. Haywire Falls looked so odd, not anything like its quaint New England facade she was used to. None of the pretty people were out, yet. No mothers with NASA-engineered baby strollers. No smiling shopkeepers or old ladies in their purple and lace. Not even an early-morning runner in high-end Spandex.

It was as if she'd found herself behind the scenes of a movie set. Garbage haulers dumped yesterday's trash. Delivery men hauled in boxes to Board and Basket and crates of coffee to Starbucks. Litter blew down the sidewalk and bystanders slouched on the wrought iron benches reading the morning paper and . . . smoking!

Worse, they were staring at her, and not in a good way. The garbage workers, the delivery men and the cabbie who was in the front seat of his cab reading the *Citizen* kept shooting glances at her. She squinted at the *CC* headlines.

SOCIALITE VICTIM IN GAY BEATING: OGLE VOWS JUSTICE

It couldn't be. She stepped closer to the cab and knocked on his window. "Excuse me," she said sweetly, "may I see the front page?"

He looked her up and down. "Get out of here, you freak. Buy your own."

"I'm not a freak." Where did he get off speaking her that way?

"You're walking around in your jammies. You sure look like a freak to me."

Marti looked down. On her feet was her favorite pair of pink fuzzy slippers and on her legs her pink silk pajamas under her pashmina shawl.

Clearly, something had to change.

Chapter Forty-four

Claire woke to a *thud* and John standing over her in his navy cashmere coat and Burberry scarf, appearing very well rested and healthy, which Claire definitely was not.

It had been a difficult night. For an hour on the phone with Josie, Claire had tackled what to do with John as she tackled most of a bottle of Chardonnay. The two friends discussed whether Claire should give up and drive to West Virginia so she could lick her wounds at Josie's house or if it would be better for Claire to show up at Marti's naked in a raincoat, so luscious that John would have to come home.

Josie suggested that Claire don an ugly chenille robe, put her hair in curlers, turn on all the lights and wait for John with a flashlight in her lap, you know, making light of it, but Claire wasn't sure there was anything to laugh about. Josie said yes there was, as what smart, secure man in his forties would even think of cheating on a woman as great as her.

Finally Claire did what most women in her situation do—ate pizza, watched TV, finished off a quart of ice cream, took a bath and went to bed. Only Claire couldn't sleep in that big bed alone, so she slept on the couch, hoping to hear her husband when he got in.

The couch part she forgot until John woke her up and she rolled over and onto the floor.

"Oww." She rubbed her back.

John looked very, very disappointed. He was also holding the *Citizen*. This, she knew, was a bad combination.

"Why, Claire? Why didn't you tell me?" He tossed her the paper's front section.

It took her eyes a while to report for duty and her brain to remember its job description, but slowly the words came into focus and something leaden fell into Claire's stomach.

SOCIALITE VICTIM IN GAY BEATING: OGLE VOWS JUSTICE.

By Enrico Sanchez

Citizen Staff Writer.

"Karen," was all she said.

"I know. Go to the end of the article."

Claire followed the jump to page A11. At the bottom of the column, in italics, was the tagline to end all taglines. *Freelance Writer Claire Stark contributed to this story.*

"I did not!" She sat back on the couch. "That is a total lie."

"Then why would they have put that there?"

"Probably Eric's idea of a prank. He might have intended for it to end up on the paste-up floor and somehow it got through."

Though Claire suspected otherwise. Clearly, this was Eric's revenge for her Diana Plimpton trick. The lead front article was a boring piece about rezoning, which meant he must have wanted to slit her throat for turning in twenty inches on tufted titmice. She didn't care. It'd been worth it.

"That's a relief. I knew you wouldn't go behind my back." John shrugged off his coat. "I had to read that tagline over five times, Claire.

You know, if you wanted to write for the *Citizen* I wouldn't have been thrilled, but I wouldn't have stood in your way."

"Uh-huh." She scanned the article, which was filled with dozens of juicy tidbits about Karen and Bob's secretary, witness accounts of them lip-locked in the SUV and how a group of gay men ended up defending the women from assault and battery. Bob Goss was going to have a fit. Karen better not come home if she had any sense.

John went into the kitchen to make coffee. "I suppose what really bothered me was the idea that you were hiding something. I know you would have told me if you'd met up with Eric Schmaltz."

"I met up with Eric Schmaltz." Claire folded the paper and lay it aside. "There. I told you."

"What?" John came out of the kitchen holding the coffee scoop.

"Twice. I met with him twice. Once at the Starbucks to tell him that I didn't want to write for the *Citizen,* though, since you were there, we went to Joseph Beth instead."

"I was at Starbucks?"

"And then last week because . . ."

"Hold on. You met with him twice and you didn't tell me?"

"I am allowed to have a life outside of you, am I not? Or am I supposed to be another Hunting Hills wife. Satellite to her man." Claire stood and folded her arms, wishing she were not in a pair of flannel Pj's covered with poodles.

"What's that mean?"

"Don't play dumb. You've lived here forty-five years longer than I have. Hunting Hills wives have rules. Lots of rules. Most having to do with how to both please and manipulate one's husband. And one of the rules, it seems, is never to confront your husband about his affairs. You're supposed to just accept it and combat shop instead."

John tossed the scoop against the wall. "Are you accusing me of having an affair?"

"You have a reputation, John. Woman after woman after woman. If

I'd known you better before we were married, I'd have figured out that you have a loyalty span of about two months."

"That sounds like something Boots would say. Did Boots tell you that?"

"Can you deny your many girlfriends? By the way, that midnight blue bra is still hanging on the back of the bathroom door. I'd suggest you return it, but I'm afraid of the consequences." Claire passed him and went into the kitchen, flipped on the faucet and took a drink of water—kid style.

"This is nuts." John pounded a door frame with his fist.

"I'll say it's nuts. We've been married all of six weeks and already you're roaming."

"What did I do that brought this on?"

Claire opened the refrigerator and took out a carton of orange juice. "Gee. I don't know. How about spend the night with another woman, for starters?"

"Marti? Marti's a friend. An old friend going through a crisis. And I left you four messages on the answering machine telling you exactly what I was up to."

"And then turned off your cell. How convenient." Claire drank straight from the box, all delicacy going out the window. "Funny, how among Marti's vast circle of friends you were the only one she called to spend the night."

John put up his hands. "You know what? This is bullshit. I don't deserve this." He grabbed his coat off the couch and headed out. "I especially don't need this from a woman who thinks it's more important to be loyal to some scum journalist named Eric Schmaltz, of all people, than to her husband who loves—make that *loved*—her."

He went to the door. Claire gripped the kitchen counter, so confused and devastated and hungover that she feared she might vomit.

"Where are you going?" she asked, immediately regretting the question because it was so clichéd.

"To work."

"And then?"

"I don't know. Maybe to hang out with Ingrid. She's the only person who matters to me right now." He slammed the French doors and left in the gray dawn.

Claire made her way back to the couch and lay down. How had it all gone so wrong? Just last night she'd been planning a celebration. She'd been floating on air, free and in love. And now . . . and now her marriage was kaput.

There was a knock at the French doors. Claire looked up to see an oddly pink figure on the other side of the glass.

"May I come in?"

Great. It was Marti Denton, the absolute last person on Earth she wanted to see. Claire lay back. "Suit yourself."

Marti shuffled in, a large black bag over her shoulder. Black mascara was smeared under her eyes and her hair was a tangled mess.

If she feels miserable for messing up my marriage, then let her, Claire thought, stuffing her fists under arm.

"Uh oh." Marti stood at the foot of the couch. "This is not good."

"Looking for John?"

"Actually, yes. I found Denton's laptop. I thought maybe he could help me."

"Why, of course! That's what John lives for. To help you." Claire hid her face in a pillow.

"Hey, are you crying? Did you and John have a fight?"

Claire didn't say anything. She just wanted Marti to leave so she could be alone. Alone in her misery.

Marti perched herself by Claire's feet. "If this is about John spending the night last night . . ."

"Please. Don't even try to cover. I know there must be some Hunting Hills rule for that too. Rule 111: never admit to a fellow wife that you just slept with her husband."

"Close. That's fifteen. But I didn't. Sleep with John, that is, and I'm not playing by the rules."

Claire closed her eyes.

"He turned me down, if you want to know the truth. Not that I wanted to hurt you or anything. It's just that . . . I guess I was having a bit of a nervous breakdown. I haven't been thinking straight, *duh*! I ended up wandering around Haywire Falls this morning in my pj's."

Claire cocked open an eye and took in Marti. "You went to Haywire Falls like that?"

"Fuzzy pink slippers and all."

"You're kidding. Why?"

"I went to meet Barry, my so-called life coach, though it turns out Barry's concern lasts about as far as one's credit limit. He dropped me too. Dropped me for nonpayment."

Claire lifted herself on her elbows. "You really didn't sleep with John?"

"Not even a kiss good night. To add insult to injury, I had to listen to a half hour dissertation on why you were the greatest thing since sliced bread. So smart. So pretty. So worldly. So trustworthy. On and on and on. If you ask me, John could have exhibited a bit more sensitivity. I mean, my husband had just left me."

"Ohhhh." Claire lay back down and tossed the pillow over her head.

"So are we friends or enemies?" Marti asked.

Claire thought about that. "Frenemies."

"Frenemy? What's a frenemy?"

"Well, call it what you will. Whatever we are, I need your help."

Chapter Forty-five

Claire took a long, hot shower and dressed in a pair of black pants and a green sweater, John's favorite, a Paolo something recommended by a personal shopper from Haywire Falls. She took care to apply her makeup and blow-dry her hair because looking good made her feel good. She'd learned that lesson, living in Hunting Hills, and she had to hand it to the wives for their good sense. Designer clothes, a quality haircut and fresh food could be transformative.

It was one of their better rules.

Because she did not want to go home to face angry clients or SEC agents, Marti rummaged through a drawer Ingrid kept in the guest bedroom and proudly squeezed into a pair of Seven jeans and a Gucci shirt. This was also a "thing" among the Hunting Hills wives, swapping outfits with their teenage daughters. It was like instant validation that they were still hip.

"Actually, I think these jeans are a bit baggy on me." Marti frowned in the full-view mirror as she slid a thumb around the skin-tight waistband.

"Those jeans wouldn't be baggy on Kate Moss," Claire said.

"In real life she's not that skinny. Rather big boned, I've read."

Claire reminded her that they had more important problems than Kate Moss's skeletal structure, a statement that Marti found oddly puzzling.

Downstairs, Claire drew the drapes and booted up Denton's computer. She'd given Dawn the day off so they could snoop through his files without witnesses. Claire suspected that what they were about to do might be considered extremely illegal.

"I'm sure we're breaking all sorts of federal laws," she said, squinting at the nonsensical columns of numbers and quarterly reports.

Marti sat next to her on the couch with a large cup of English Breakfast. "I understand federal prisons are very nice. Tennis courts and swimming pools."

"Drug dealers," Claire said.

"Martha Stewart."

"No personal shoppers or manicures or even catalog shopping."

"Oh." Marti got up and checked the drapes, to make sure they were secure.

Bit by bit they were able to sort out Denton's mess of names, dollar amounts and what Claire assumed were post-office box numbers. Marti could identify many of the clients and where they lived, which made his system all the more confusing. Why would all of them have their Anderson Brothers statements sent to post-office boxes? Moreover, why would they have two addresses—one to a post-office box and another to a street?

"I know for a fact that Donald Sizemore would not have his statements sent to a post-office box in Euclid," Marti said.

"Why not?"

"Because he's my father's golf partner. Donald Sizemore lives on Johns Island in Florida. He's never been to Ohio."

"But look." Claire ran her finger down the S column. "Denton has your own father's statements going to a post-office box in Cuyahoga Falls too."

"Cuyahoga Falls? Couldn't he have picked Haywire or at least Shaker?"

"You're missing the point, Marti. We're not talking about realty status. We're talking about fraud. My theory is that Denton informed Anderson Brothers that his clients' statements should be sent to various post-office boxes. Then he probably retrieved the statements and redid them to falsely indicate that the accounts were making money when they weren't. Each month, he mailed the bogus statements to their real addresses."

To back up her claim, Claire pulled down the official Anderson Brothers stationery on which Denton meticulously reproduced twenty-five statements a month. "He did a hell of a lot of extra work."

"No wonder he was never home. *This* is what he was doing. And all along I thought he was having an affair."

"Who with?" Claire asked.

"Corinne Berenson. Though, really, it wasn't my business."

There were some aspects of Hunting Hills Claire would never get used to.

"I want to find him," Marti announced. "I want to show him what we, I mean you, have found and make him explain."

"I think it's pretty clear what he did. Now we should let the authorities take over," said Claire, who was more eager to turn over the computer to the feds and get it out of her house.

But Marti was adamant. "First I want him to face me and Lois. I want him to look us in the eyes and tell us whether he is guilty or innocent. He might lie to me, but he won't lie to Lois. He loves her more than me. Probably more than Ava or, come to think of it, more than himself."

Claire closed the laptop and carefully slid it back into its case. There was a tone in Marti's voice that made it clear she would not compromise on this point. The sooner they found Denton, the sooner they could go to the authorities so Claire decided she had better well get on the stick. "OK, where do we start?"

"Boots and Lisa." Marti flipped open her cell. "They must have heard something by now."

Indeed, they had. Lisa claimed that Denton had showed up at her home and threatened to shoot her if she did not give him the Lexus. This was according to Boots who said she'd spoken with Lisa an hour after Denton left and urged her to contact the Hunting Hills police, who, being the Hunting Hills police, were at a loss as to how to track him down.

"Lisa's daughter had to be sedated. She gave a statement to the cops saying that a bad man came into the house and started yelling at her mother. My god, she's what? Nine years old. How could Denton do that in front of a child?"

"Denton?" Marti said. "He can be boisterous, but he's never violent."

"Well, that's what Lisa said. Anyway, where have you been?" Boots asked. "Lisa and I have been calling you every hour on the hour."

"I turned off my phone. All of my phones. They were giving me headaches with their incessant ring."

"I let Lois stay at my house instead of going to Holly. I hope that's OK."

"Right now, everything's fine by me. Do you have any idea where Denton went?" Marti asked.

"He told Lisa he went to see an old college roommate down in Akron. The police want to know who it is. They've been looking for you, Marti."

"They'll have to look a little longer. As for now I am incommunicado." Marti shut the phone and turned to Claire. "Michael Henkin. That's where he went. He's a dentist in Akron."

"How do you know him?"

"His wife used to send me Christmas cards each year. And each year I would think, what could be worse than being a dentist's wife down in Akron?

"Now I know."

Chapter Forty-six

Dr. Henkin's practice was in a modest two-story brick building across the street from the Akron Medical Center. The waiting room was empty and Claire had the sense that Henkin was not a fabulously popular dentist, if, indeed, such an animal existed.

"What do we do, now?" Marti whispered. "We can't just go up and ask to see him."

"Why not?" Claire was halfway to the receptionist's window when Marti pulled her back.

"We don't even have an appointment."

This was the problem with growing up in Hunting Hills, Claire thought. Marti might serve a super fast tennis ball and ski double-black diamonds, but she was at a loss when it came to the very necessary skill of being bold.

"Don't worry." Claire approached the receptionist and matter of factly asked to speak with Dr. Henkin.

"You need an appointment," said the receptionist, "unless you're from a pharmaceutical company."

"That's OK. We were just wondering if a guy named Jim Denton stopped by yesterday. This is his wife." She gestured toward Marti who gave a little wave. "She's looking for him. He skipped town."

"He ran away?" The receptionist squinted at Marti.

"With millions of stolen dollars. You'll probably be seeing it on the evening news."

"Really? Do you think they'll be coming down here with cameras and put us on TV?"

"If Denton was here, you can take it to the bank."

"He was here all right. I told Dr. Henkin to watch out for him." She buzzed her boss and said low to Claire, "I feel sorry for his wife."

"You and me both."

Five minutes later, they were in Henkin's office, a one-windowed room that looked out to the parking lot of another medical center. Claire had to agree with Marti, except she wouldn't mind being the dentist's wife. She'd mind being the dentist. A dentist in Akron with a window to a parking lot.

"I am so sorry to disturb you during the work day," Marti gushed when Dr. Henkin walked in wearing a stark white lab coat. "I'm sure this is a horrible inconvenience."

Henkin, a short man with curly dark hair and glasses, assured her it was fine. It didn't hurt that Marti was the Cleveland equivalent of Christie Brinkley. "I don't have another patient for twenty minutes. It's my pleasure."

Claire said, "Without going into too much detail, you should know that your friend Denton is in a lot of trouble."

"I got that sense and he's not my friend. He was a guy I knew in college back in the eighties who suddenly showed up and stiffed me for a forty-eight-dollar dinner bill."

"Cheap," said Marti. "It must not have been a very nice restaurant."

"Outback Steakhouse."

"That's Denton for you. He loves those. He's like a closet steakhouse addict. That's the first place he goes when I'm not around. He knows I'd throw a fit with all that fat and cholesterol. Beef. I mean who eats beef these days? Steroids. Antibiotics. Yuck."

Claire waited for her to finish. "Are you done, Marti?"

"Uh-huh."

"How did Denton stiff you for forty-eight dollars?" Claire asked Henkin.

"I stepped outside to answer a page and when I came back he was gone. All he'd left was a ten on the table."

"How does a page work?"

Marti made a face. "You know how a page works. You can't be that much of a hick."

"I might be. Please tell me, Doctor." The "doctor" was a throw-away, the standard reporter trick of playing up to the medical profession's ego.

"In this case, my beeper went off. I had it on manner mode so it vibrated. I called my answering service and they gave me the number, but when I called back it turned out the call had been made from a pay phone at an all-night gas station in Twinsburg. Either the patient was frustrated that I wasn't around or maybe they bought some Anbesol. I don't know."

"But they weren't there, waiting for your call," Claire clarified.

"That's right. Then I went back in and Denton was gone."

"And your wallet?"

Henkin was bewildered. "It was there."

"Where?"

"In my coat pocket."

"Which you were wearing outside when you took the page."

"No. I'd left it on the hook by our booth and I regretted doing that as it was very cold last night."

"Did Denton by any chance know your wallet was in your coat?"

Henkin straightened his white coat nervously. "Well, uhm, I had just taken it out to show him a photo of Sean."

"Who's Sean?"

"My son."

"I see." Claire cracked her knuckles, a habit she'd forsaken long ago. "I wish we could find out if there's been a credit check done on a person in the last twenty-four hours."

"We can ask Linda," Marti said.

"Who's Linda?"

"My personal shopper. Before she takes on a job she always runs a credit check. She has outrageous connections."

"Let's try it."

While Marti was on her cell calling Linda, Henkin paced like a caged rat. "You don't think he stole my credit card numbers, do you?"

"Not just your numbers," Claire said. "You."

Within an hour Linda the personal shopper had tapped her sources and confirmed Claire's suspicions. It seemed that Dr. Henkin had been running up quite a bill while he supposedly had been spending the morning drilling teeth and checking caps. In fact, somehow he'd been able to drive out to Lorain, Ohio and buy a brand new automobile at Shaw's Ford.

"Lisa's going to crucify him. I bet he traded in her brand new Lexus for a Ford," Marti said, as they left Henkin's office. "Oh my god. She'll never live it down. A Ford. It's like the lowest."

Chapter Forty-seven

"It's over there," said Jack Shaw, owner of Shaw's Ford /Jeep in Lorain, Ohio. Claire and Marti trudged in the drizzle past a fleet of new and "preowned" cars, following the gray-haired Shaw, whose blue nylon SHAW'S FORD windbreaker fluttered in the biting breeze. "So you're a friend of Dr. Henkin's and you want to buy his car? That's a new one."

"When I heard he traded in that beautiful Lexus, I had to buy it, even if my husband called me crazy," Claire said. "Right, Marti?"

"Absolutely." Marti tugged at her coat. She did not like being in Lorain with its auto plants and shipping industry. It was so *industrial.*

"I asked the doctor why he would want to trade in a Lexus LX 470 with five thousand miles on it for a Jeep. I mean, that's a seventy-thousand-dollar car." Shaw stopped at a line of silver SUVs, unsure if he was at the right row.

"And what did he tell you?" Claire asked.

"Said his new wife was too much of a nincompoop to drive it. He'd rather she have something that he wouldn't mind getting dinged." Shaw found the Lexus and depressed the automatic unlock, its front lights flickering in acknowledgment. "I told him a Jeep Grand Limited is nothing I'd let my wife ding. You got your 5.7-liter HEMI and your Quadra all-wheel . . ."

"He said that about me? That I was a nincompoop?" Marti asked.

"You?" Jack Shaw stopped in puzzlement. "No. About his wife."

"Mrs. Henkin. *Remember*?" Claire gave her a meaningful look.

"Oh, yeah."

"I got the paperwork right here." Jack Shaw reached into his royal blue windbreaker and pulled out a pink carbon which almost flew out of his hands. "The title belonged to a Lisa Renfrew of Hunting Hills, Ohio. Dr. Henkin said that was before they moved to Akron last month." Shaw looked up. "That's his wife, isn't it?"

"That's her," Claire said. "You're right. She is a nincompoop."

Marti giggled.

Shaw shook his head. "Those doctors. They keep the first wife long enough to get them to help pay the loans and then they're off with some tootsie who's almost half their age."

"Just like Ben Cox," Marti said, as though even Jack Shaw had gotten wind of the Patty Cox hostess scandal.

"Ben who?"

"Skip it," Claire said.

Jack Shaw insisted they sit in the Lexus and listen to him describe the buttery leather seats, the bird's-eye maple steering wheel, the voice-activated navigation system, the famous Lexus "night view" and the built-in DVD. It went without saying that Claire wasn't paying attention, her thoughts were so wrapped up in Denton.

He must have assumed that Lisa would call the cops. Therefore, he needed to dump the vehicle as fast as possible. But where had he gone?

"What's this?" Marti asked, opening the glove compartment.

"That's the glove compartment. Seen one, seen them all."

"Not all." Marti pulled out a large ring dangling with small keys.

Mailbox keys, Claire thought, trying to contain herself.

"Sorry about that. Just got the car in this morning and haven't had a chance to go through it completely. Of course, when you take it off the lot it'll be thoroughly inspected and detailed with our guaranteed ten-point system."

"No problem. I'll run these up to Lisa. She must be looking for them." Marti winked. "Guess it's a good thing we stopped by."

"Yes," said Shaw. "Now what do I have to do to put you in this car today?"

They ended up placing a five-thosuand-dollar deposit on the Lexus so no one else could buy it. Marti was able to elicit from Jack a description of the car Denton had purchased plus the number on the temporary plates. In one afternoon, they had analyzed Denton's Ponzi scheme, located the man whose identity he'd stolen, apprehended the keys to his mailboxes and even pegged his getaway car.

"We should get jobs with the FBI," Marti said.

"Speaking of which, are you going to call the cops?" Claire asked as they pulled out of Shaw's.

"Hell no. I'm going to call Lisa and Boots. They'll spread the word so fast Denton will be caught in no time. Then we'll be getting somewhere."

Claire was filled with new admiration for Marti who, until that day, she'd written off as a superficial socialite. In their conversations on the long drive to Akron and then Lorain, Marti confided to Claire about the state of her marriage to Denton, how he'd started disappearing, only to leave Post-it notes by the Krups telling her what shirts to take in, what coffee to buy and even how to raise the kids.

"How did you stand it?" Claire asked, after Marti told her the story of the time Denton locked her in the attic during the Super Bowl.

"It's amazing what you can stand when you have two kids. Every time I thought of leaving him or thought of telling him to move out, I'd picture the look on Ava and Lois's faces, how crushed they'd be. And I'd say to myself, Marti Denton, there are a lot of women worse off than you. Suck it up."

Claire gripped the wheel as they passed through the nicer homes on Avon Lake on their way back home from Jack Shaw's Ford. Darkness fell early and already cars had their headlights on, even though it was only four thirty. She hadn't spoken to John all day. Nor had he called.

"How about you?" Marti asked, as if reading her mind. "You haven't said one word about John and I've noticed he hasn't been calling you either."

"I don't know. I think I've totally destroyed our marriage." Claire told her about the morning's fight—even though it had, ostensibly, been about Marti.

"It wasn't about me. It never is. It's all about trust and confidence. Before Barry dumped me, he used to say that 99.9 percent of the problems could be solved with positive thinking. You know, if you can talk yourself into believing you're a good tennis player, you will be. Or, in the case of marriage, if you have confidence that your husband loves you then he will. Look at all those happy fat women."

"Excuse me?" Claire had to concentrate on the road. Marti had almost caused her to swerve into the passing lane.

"The way I see it, there are two types of fat women. There's the type who abuse their bodies and wear sloppy clothes and have no men in their lives. Then there are the pretty fat women. You know, they're in Lane Bryant but they're great accessorizors. Always with a scarf or a big brooch—like Madeleine Albright."

Claire was impressed.

"Don't look so shocked. I happened to have been an international relations major in college. Anyway, *those* women have satisfied relationships and do you know why? Confidence. Sure, they're fat. But they concentrate on the positive."

"Madeleine Albright?" Claire said, unsure if this was Marti's discreet way of calling her fat.

"Barry used Madeleine Albright as an example all the time."

"Why couldn't you tell Barry that you were confident the bill would be paid?"

"I should have tried that."

"Anyway, my fight with John has less to do with confidence and more to do with Eric Schmaltz. He snuck in a tagline on the Karen Goss article this morning."

"Yeah, I read that in the paper." Marti turned to her. "*Did* you contribute to the story?"

"No. In fact he specifically asked me yesterday if there was any quote in the Diana Plimpton piece that had to do with Karen. I told him no. And that was the last we discussed it."

"Whatever happened to that Diana Plimpton interview, anyway?"

"I assumed Eric trashed it. To screw with him, I wrote twenty inches on Diana's knowledge of indigenous birds. The deal was that I had to do an interview with her. Nothing in deal specified what I had to interview her about."

"I would have liked reading that. Diana knows a lot about birds. Probably would have been the only useful piece in the paper."

Chapter Forty-eight

It was the daily miracle. That's what they called it. Eric Schmaltz removed the red grease pencil from behind his ear and circled a copyediting mistake on page B3.

"Elyria didn't vote to *raise* a building. They voted to *raze* a building, you moron," he exclaimed. "Idiots. That's who I have writing for me. Idiots."

His buzzer buzzed. He'd asked Andrea to hold his calls, which he often did when it got close to the five-thirty budget meeting. But Andrea was persistent.

Buzz. Buzz.

"Jesus Christ." He pressed the button. "What the hell is it?"

"I have a call for you on line one."

"So? It's five twenty-five. It can wait."

"Not this one. It's that Mrs. Denton. She was in here last week."

"Yesss," hissed Eric, recalling Marti's luscious golden skin and adorable body.

"I thought you'd want to take it. I'll patch her through."

"Mr. Schmaltz?" Marti asked.

Eric leaned back and stuck the pencil behind his ear. "Please. Call me Eric." God, he loved bored housewives. What would they discuss tonight? And could they discuss it over drinks, preferably at someplace dark like Night Town?

"I could call you a lot worse," Marti snapped.

Sass. Eric liked that. "What can I do you for, Mrs. Denton?"

"For starters, you can do the right thing and explain to Claire's husband that she had nothing to do with that piece of shit you ran on Karen Goss."

My, my. What a pistol. He sat up. "I suppose you're referring to the tagline."

"It was a total lie."

"Not exactly." Eric had been prepared for this call. He pulled out the A section and pointed to the lines he had underlined in the tenth paragraph. "Hunting Hills is a wealthy community of approximately two thousand people with a median income of $500,000. Ironically, there are no hills in Hunting Hills, nor is the discharging of firearms permitted."

Marti said nothing.

"You see," Eric said, "that was lifted directly from Claire's piece on Diana Plimpton. Therefore, according to guild bylaws, I had to give her credit. Otherwise the Teamsters would break my pinkie."

"That's directly from the Hunting Hills annual village report, you scum. Anyone could have written it. You weren't obligated to give Claire credit. You put in that tagline because you wanted to stick it to her."

Eric was intrigued to find that the luscious and lovely Mrs. Denton was also surprisingly quick on the draw. "And why not? She stuck it to me. I assumed the interview with Diana Plimpton would be about the murder of her husband. Not a murder of crows."

"Cute," Marti said. "I watch *Jeopardy* too."

Damn she was good.

"I'll make another deal with you, Mr. Schmaltz. Are you game?"

"Sure." He smiled. This was going to be fun.

"OK. Take out your notebook and get a fresh pen because I talk fast."

It'd been a long time since he'd been this titillated. Eric clicked his pen.

"Yesterday, my husband, a powerful stockbroker at Anderson Brothers, left a message on my cell phone saying that after twenty years of marriage he was leaving me."

Excellent! Eric jotted this down, though he didn't know why.

"And later that night I found out, along with a lot of other people in this community, that he also left most of us broke. We don't have the figures yet, but according to his boss at Anderson, it appears that my husband may be responsible for squandering, spending, I don't know, close to $750 million. Currently my husband is on the lam, though there's a statewide APB out for him."

Suddenly, this wasn't so funny. Eric stopped writing. "Are you serious?"

"Never more so in my life. I don't usually read the business section, but I have a hunch that as far as business stories go this one is going to go down in Cleveland history."

Eric rubbed his forehead. If Mrs. Denton wasn't doped up or drunk or whatever it was those bored housewives did, then this, indeed, was a blockbuster. He wondered if the *Wall Street Journal* was on top of it. He needed to call in his best reporters, the only ones who could write a damn: Ted Wendling over at the federal courthouse. Steve Luttner in business. Was it possible to get a blurb in by tonight? They'd need SEC confirmation, of course, and . . .

"Did you just hear what I said?"

Andrea opened the door to remind him about the five-thirty meeting. He waved her away. "I'm sorry. My secretary just distracted me."

"I said that by the end of the week I expect to be flooded by media and there's only one person I'll talk to and that's you."

He threw down his pen. He was in love. God, was he in love. And, obviously, the feeling was mutual.

"*If,*" she stressed, "that is *if* you come up to my house right now and apologize to Claire in front of John."

There was no way he could do that. He had to marshal the forces on this stockbroker story. And then there was the meeting. "But . . ."

"In addition. I want you to explain how Claire had no intention of ever writing for your fish wrapper. How you tricked and blackmailed her into doing it and then how you nastily pasted on that tagline."

Eric was trapped. The greatest story of the year was his if he could stoop to doing the one thing he truly loathed. Apologizing. God, did he hate apologizing. It's what had broken up his two marriages. His wives' stupid, stupid insistence that once in a blue moon he might say he was sorry—and mean it.

"OK," he said. "But only if you're there."

"Oh, I'll be there. I wouldn't miss this for the world."

Chapter Forty-nine

Claire rummaged through Marti's refrigerator, looking for something, anything, they could turn into a dinner. It was a hopeless case. Yogurt. Celery. Tons of bottled water. Apples. Didn't these people eat?

Marti came downstairs in her own clothes, which were identical to Ingrid's clothes. A sexy white T-shirt and jeans. Her hair was brushed, her lips were glossed and she looked extremely composed. Claire had no idea how Marti was keeping it so together. Her husband had left her and she was broke. Claire would have expected her to fall apart long ago.

"You're an inspiration," Claire said, closing the freezer.

"No, I'm not."

"Yes, you are. Look how calm you're being."

"I've got to be. Lois is on her way home from Ingrid's. When she walks through that door, I want her to look upon me as the rock she can lean on. I have the feeling this is just the beginning of a very rough spell."

Claire nodded. "Is Lois coming alone?" she ventured.

"No. John's bringing her." Marti cocked an eyebrow. "Does that make you glad or sad?"

"I don't know." Claire reached for an apple and washed it in the deep sink.

"It should make you glad. And if it doesn't, I have another surprise."

"What?"

"I called Eric Schmaltz. He's on his way too, to apologize and explain to John how he stuck it to you. It was the least I could do to repay you for the tremendous support you've shown me today, Claire. I can see, now, why John thinks you're so terrific."

Flattery made Claire squeamish. She didn't know how to respond except to point out that no way would Eric drive from Cleveland all the way to Hunting Hills to apologize.

"That's what he said he'd do," Marti said. "He swore on it."

"I don't think you understand, Marti. Eric doesn't apologize. He *never* apologizes. If he's coming here straight away, probably blowing off an edit board meeting, then he definitely has an ulterior motive."

"He has an ulterior motive. I promised him an interview when Denton's story broke. He couldn't say yes fast enough."

This truly floored her. "You did that . . . for me?"

"Why not? You broke all sorts of federal laws for me. And, besides, you wouldn't have had that fight with John if I hadn't been so messed up, thinking he was my solution to Denton." Marti blinked back tears. "Oh, boy, have I been messed up."

Claire put her arms around her as she collapsed in heaping sobs. "It's so awful."

"It's going to be OK, Marti."

"Not for a long, long time," she mumbled into Claire's shoulder.

"Sooner than you think. Bit by bit it will get better. Three steps forward, two steps backward."

They stood that way in the kitchen, Claire soothing her, until headlights came up the driveway.

"I think Lois is here." Claire wrung out a wet dish towel from the sink to wipe the mascara from under Marti's eye.

"Maybe it's Eric."

"Either way, I'm not going to stick around." Claire had planned on stepping into the library or outside. She wasn't ready to meet John. Not quite yet. Besides, Lois and Marti needed their privacy.

"I wish you wouldn't leave," Marti said.

"I'm just going into the library."

"No, I mean." She dropped Visine in each eye and batted her lashes. "I mean, John said last night that he wanted to take you out of here, back to Prague maybe. Please don't do that."

"Why?"

"Because Hunting Hills needs a person like you, Claire. A flesh and blood woman with some guts. And honestly? Because I need you too."

Claire was touched. Truly and deeply touched. "Thanks."

The door from the garage flung open. "Mom! Mom. I'm home."

Claire put her finger to her lips, grabbed her coat and tiptoed down the hallway to the small library. She closed the door gently behind her. Even so she could hear the mother and child reunion, could hear Lois crying and Marti repeating the same hushed words Claire had whispered minutes before.

It'll be OK, you'll see. We'll get through this. You, me and Ava. Three steps forward, two steps backward.

"I need air." Claire slipped into her coat and stepped through the library door to the patio.

It was brisk outside and damp. The leaves in the woods rustled in the wind as clouds passed over a nearly full moon. But it was also silent and beautiful.

Hunting Hills wasn't so bad, Claire thought, as far as places to settle down go. And, besides, first appearances were always deceiving. When she arrived here, she'd taken one look at the pristine lawns and fine homes and assumed—how very wrongly—that this was a community built on perfection. The wives were fit. The husbands worked hard. The children were high achievers with straight white teeth and perfect SATs.

Yet, what was the truth? The women were flawed like anyone else. They smoked and drank and did a little dope. They read erotica and cheated on their husbands—or thought about it. They worried about their kids, who, like teenagers everywhere, mouthed off, screwed up and fumbled their way to adulthood. They managed their awkward, confused, and occasionally angry husbands and they usually helped each other.

Most importantly, the wives broke the rules. *All the time* they broke the rules. Whether it was being perky or putting their husbands in the best light or not calling him at work or spending too much money. It was as though they'd invented the rules just to have something to violate in this artificially created white bread world.

Claire smiled. Yes, Hunting Hills wasn't so bad.

"Marti?"

She peered into the woods. "John?"

Silence.

"Marti!"

"John?" She stepped off the patio and crossed the damp lawn. "Where are you? It's Claire."

"So that's your name."

Suddenly Claire felt something sharp in her spine and she let out a startled scream.

"Shhh." A hand clapped over her mouth and it was clear that the thing pressing into her spine was the barrel of a gun. "Shut up. You're coming with me."

Chapter Fifty

Like hell, Claire thought. She'd been in tough situations before, including an attempted rape in the Bosnian refugee camp, and she was more skilled than panty-waisted Jim Denton had ever been. Moreover, she doubted he'd be the type to pull the trigger or even load it with bullets—that is, if he knew how.

She simultaneously bit down as hard as she could on the palm of his hand while jabbing him fiercely with the point of her elbow and kicking her heel in his groin, taking advantage of his sudden pain to wiggle free, in case the gun went off.

Which it did.

Boom!

Claire backed away, panicked. "Shit. You almost killed me, Denton."

Denton lay on the wet grass and stared at the .357 in his hand, which was shaking. "Shit. Sorry. I didn't think it had bullets."

The backyard lights flicked on. "What's happening?" Marti ran from the kitchen just as John and Eric raced in from the driveway.

Seeing that Claire had almost been shot, John jumped over Denton and sheltered her protectively. "Are you all right? Are you hurt? Did he hurt you?"

Claire's entire body began to shake and John instinctively hugged her tightly to stop it. "I'm sorry," he whispered in her ear. "I'm so sorry for everything. I love you. I love you with all my heart."

"Did Eric explain?" Claire asked between chattering teeth.

"Yes, but that didn't matter. I was an ass. A complete and utter ass."

He kissed her hard and Claire wished he would never stop, until Eric said, "Excuse me, people, but I think we have a situation here."

They broke away to find everyone else had their hands up and that Denton, looking maniacal and crazed, his lips stained red, blue and orange, was waving his .357.

"Don't, Denton," Marti said. "It's not worth it."

"The hell it isn't. My freedom's worth everything."

"God, what I would give for a decent photographer right now," Eric said. "This would be a great stand alone for that hole I've got on page one."

"Shut up," Marti hissed.

"Who's he?" Denton waved the gun at Eric.

"Eric Schmaltz. He's editor of the *Citizen,*" Marti said.

"Him you can shoot," Claire added.

"Oh, so *now* she has a sense of humor." Eric took a step toward Denton, who backed off. "Don't worry. I won't try anything, bud. I'd just like you to give me the gun. In exchange, I will promise you a front page exclusive. Your side only."

It was weird the way Eric wheeled and dealed exclusives, Claire thought. He would have made a good used-car salesman. She was going to whisper that to John when she noticed that he was no longer next to her. He was carefully circling toward Denton. And, if she didn't know better, she'd say that he was working in concert with Eric.

"I don't want an exclusive. I want to go to California," Denton said.

"But Marti wouldn't hear of it. She kept saying she wanted to stay in Hunting Hills."

"You're the one who's big on Hunting Hills, Denton," Marti corrected.

"Yeah, right. Give me a break."

"We're getting off track, folks. Look, we don't have much time. You know the cops are on their way." Eric slowly lowered his right hand. "Give me the gun, Denton, and you'll have a chance. Shoot one of us and suddenly you're no longer a white collar criminal, you're a real criminal going to a real prison. Trust me, Denton, it's far worse being a real criminal."

Denton had stolen $750 million. To Claire's mind, criminality didn't get any more real than that.

"Listen to him, Daddy."

Denton's wild gaze turned toward the patio door where Lois stood, her chin lifted and her shoulders square.

"Get out of here, Lois," Marti hissed.

"Yes," agreed Denton. "Listen to your mother for once. This is adult business, Muffincakes."

Lois folded her arms. "I said, give him the gun. If you don't, I'll throw a tantrum like you wouldn't believe."

Denton looked at Marti. "I thought she quit with that when she was seven."

Marti shrugged. "Stress."

"It's all your fault. You nag her too much."

"I suppose you have a Post-it for that too."

"Please, Daddy."

"She's your daughter, Denton, listen to her." Eric was inches away. "For once, do the right thing."

"Shit." The gun lay in his hand. Eric grabbed it and John hooked Denton from behind, forcing him to his knees just as two police cars—their sirens and flashing lights off due to Hunting Hills ordinances—cruised up the driveway.

"Took them long enough," Lois said, resting her head against her quaking mother. "I called them as soon as Daddy got here."

"Smart girl." Marti looked weary.

"Well, at least it's over," Claire said. "No one got hurt and your father didn't go too far."

Lois lifted her head. "But we're broke. Mom says we don't have any money."

"I know." Claire watched as the police stuffed Denton into the cruiser. "Consider yourself extremely fortunate."

Epilogue

In typical Hunting Hills fashion, Karen did not leave her husband for his secretary. She returned home the week before Thanksgiving and everybody pretended as though nothing had happened. Birch was busted for smoking pot, which the Hunting Hills police punished by driving him to school. Chip came home from Exeter and took Lois to the Assembly Ball, though because she was under eighteen she had to leave by eight-thirty.

Their early dismissal led to them ending up in Chip's car in the Union Club parking lot doing things that girls in white dresses at coming-out balls are expected to do, though perhaps not before they, themselves, come out. There were witnesses who snitched to the Assembly Ball committee, a battalion of nine frowning matrons who started an uproar and proclaimed it a scandal—the first of many Lois would have the privilege of experiencing as a Hunting Hills native.

Marti never found out about Denton and Lisa. Nor did she ever discover that Denton had secreted away stores of cash.

Rachel did.

During spring cleaning, she came upon approximately twenty thousand dollars in Skittles bags hidden in the basement. With that windfall, Rachel gave notice and left the Amish farm in Middlefield to hop a bus for Hollywood City, California. Her dream of meeting Bob Barker would not be denied.

Roy Phelps was able to negotiate a plea bargain that put Denton behind bars for seven to ten years on several counts of securities fraud. Many of the Hunting Hills elite turned out in his support, claiming that he was a super broker who'd only been looking out for their best interests. It wasn't his fault that the market didn't go up. (One of his biggest boosters, ironically enough, turned out to be Marguerite Grayson, largely because she got her money safely out before everyone else did and also because she'd found his story of the Viagra stiffy very endearing.)

Marti immediately filed for divorce.

She could afford to do that because Herb Swan, her father, had been kind enough to grant her his inheritance early, a cool fifteen million dollars. "Die poor," was his motto, which was convenient, as "live rich" happened to be Marti's.

As for John and Claire, they were officially married the following August in the backyard of their home before a comfortable collection of family and friends. Ingrid was maid of honor. Josie was matron of honor and Waldo the Saint Bernard was best man. Claire was eight months pregnant.

It went down in Hunting Hills history as one of the bigger scandals.

About the Author

Sarah Strohmeyer is the best-selling author of the Agatha Award-winning mystery series that includes *Bubbles Unbound, Bubbles in Trouble, Bubbles Ablaze, Bubbles A Broad,* and *Bubbles Betrothed.* A former journalist whose work has appeared in the *Boston Globe,* the Cleveland *Plain Dealer,* and on Salon.com, she lives with her family outside Montpelier, Vermont. She can be contacted through *www.SarahStrohmeyer.com.*